HIPPOCRENE HANDY DICTIONARIES

Chinese

HIPPOCRENE HANDY DICTIONARIES

For the traveler of independent spirit and curious mind, this practical series will help you to communicate, not just to get by. Common phrases are conveniently listed through key words. Pronunciation follows each entry and a reference section reviews all major grammar points. *Handy Extras* are extra helpful—offering even more words and phrases for students and travelers.

ARABIC
$8.95 • 0-87052-960-9

CZECH EXTRA
$8.95 • 0-7818-0138-9

DUTCH
$8.95 • 0-87052-049-0

FRENCH
$8.95 • 0-7818-0010-2

GERMAN
$8.95 • 0-7818-0014-5

GREEK
$8.95 • 0-87052-961-7

HUNGARIAN EXTRA
$8.95 • 0-7818-0164-8

ITALIAN
$6.95 • 0-7818-0011-0

JAPANESE
$6.95 • 0-87052-962-5

KOREAN
$8.95 • 0-7818-0082-X

PORTUGUESE
$8.95 • 0-87052-053-9

RUSSIAN
$8.95 • 0-7818-0013-7

SERBO-CROATIAN
$8.95 • 0-87052-051-2

SLOVAK EXTRA
$8.95 • 0-7818-0101-X

SPANISH
$8.95 • 0-7818-0012-9

SWEDISH
$8.95 • 0-87052-054-7

THAI
$8.95 • 0-87052-963-3

TURKISH
$8.95 • 0-87052-982-X

(All prices subject to change.)

TO PURCHASE HIPPOCRENE BOOKS contact your local bookstore, or write to: HIPPOCRENE BOOKS, 171 Madison Avenue, New York, NY 10016. Please enclose check or money order, adding $4.00 shipping (UPS) for the first book and $.50 for each additional book.

HIPPOCRENE HANDY DICTIONARIES

Chinese

at your Fingertips

compiled by

LEXUS

with

Don Rimmington and Li Kaining

HIPPOCRENE BOOKS
New York

Published in the United States of America in 1991 by
HIPPOCRENE BOOKS, INC., New York,
by arrangement with Routledge, London

For information, address:
HIPPOCRENE BOOKS, INC.
171 Madison Ave.
New York, NY 10016

ISBN 0-87052- 050-4

Contents

Pronunciation Guide

Chinese in this book means Modern Standard Chinese, which used to be known as Mandarin in the West and which is now called *putonghua* or 'common speech' in China. It is spoken all over northern, central and south west China and is understood virtually everywhere in the country.

In spoken Chinese, words are made up of one or more syllables, each of these syllables being represented in the written language by a character. Chinese has also been transcribed into Western alphabetic scripts or romanizations and we are using here the standard romanization *pinyin*. We have modified the *pinyin* system slightly, adding the vowels 'ı' and 'ʊ' to distinguish them from 'i' and 'u' respectively. Syllables can be divided into initials (consonants) and finals (vowels or vowels followed by either n or ng) and we give below a full list of the initials and finals, where possible with the closest equivalent sound in English. Across the bottom of each page of the book we have also provided a key to the pronunciation of the most distinctive Chinese sounds.

INITIALS

f, l, m, n, s, w and y	similar to English
p, t and k	pronounced with a slight puff of air as in *p*op, *t*op and *c*op
h	like the Scottish lo*ch*, with a little friction in the throat
b, d and g	more abrupt than English, like p in s*p*are, t in s*t*are, and c in s*c*are
j	like j in *j*eep
q	like ch in *ch*eap
x	like sh in *sh*eep
	All these three are pronounced with the lips spread as in a smile
ch	like ch in *ch*urch
sh	like sh in *sh*irt
zh	like j in *j*udge
r	like r in *r*ung
	All these four are pronounced with the tip of the tongue curled back
c	like ts in be*ts*
z	like ds in be*ds*

FINALS

a	as in father
ai	as in aisle
an	as in ran
ang	as in rang } with the a slightly lengthened as in ah
ao	like ou in out
e	as in her, the
ei	as in eight
en	as in open
eng	like en (above) + g
er	like err, but with the tongue curled back and the sound coming from the back of the throat
i	as in magazine
ia	like ya in yard
ian	similar to yen
iang	i (above) merged with ang (above) – but without the lengthening of the a
iao	like yow in yowl
ie	like ye in yes
in	as in thin
ing	as in thing
iong	i (above) merged with ong (below)
iu	like yo in yoga
I	somewhat like i in sir, bird
o	as in more
ou	as in dough
ong	like ung in lung, but with lips rounded
u	as in rule
ua	w followed by a (above)
uai	like wi in wild
uan	w followed by an (above)
uang	w followed by ang (above)
ui	similar to way
un	like uan in truant
uo	similar to war
u or ü	like French une or German über
uan	ü (above) followed by an (above)
ue or üe	ü (above) followed by e as in let
un	like French une

In Northern Chinese the sound er is often merged with the end of syllables. This is represented in the romanization by adding r to the syllable so that dian, for example, becomes dianr.

Tones

Each syllable (or character) in Chinese has a tone and in Modern Standard Chinese there are four tones. The mark above a syllable indicates its tone: (ˉ) first tone, (ˊ) second tone, (ˇ) third tone and (ˋ) fourth tone. In many words not all syllables are pronounced with tones and in sentences quite a few syllables are without tones. In these cases no tone marks are given above the syllables.

First tone   (ˉ)   high, level pitch; constant volume; as though briefly holding a musical note

Second tone (ˊ)   rising quite quickly from middle register and increasing in volume; shorter than first tone; like a surprised 'what?'

Third tone   (ˇ)   starting low and falling lower before rising again; louder at the beginning and end than in the middle; slightly longer than first tone

Fourth tone (ˋ)   starting high, falling rapidly in pitch and decreasing in volume; short, like second tone; as 'right' might be said in agreeing to a suggestion or instruction

The tones can be described in diagram form with the vertical line representing pitch and the horizontal line the length of the sound.

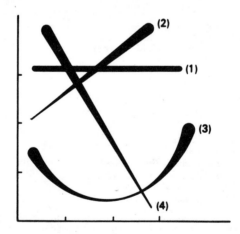

When a third tone precedes another third tone it is changed to a second tone. This adjustment has been made in marking the tones in the romanized text.

It is important to learn to pronounce the four tones and to differentiate between them. Context in Chinese normally makes the meaning clear, but ambiguities can arise if a tone is mispronounced.

English-Chinese

A

a yígè; **90 fen a bottle** jiǔmáo qián yìpíng; *see page 94*

about (*approximately*) ... zuǒyòu; **about 20** èrshí zuǒyòu; **about 6 o'clock** liùdiǎn zhōng zuǒyòu; **is the manager about?** jīnglǐ zài ma?; **I was just about to leave** wǒ gāng yào zǒu; **how about a drink?** hē diǎn shénme ba?

above zai ... shàngtou; (*with numbers*) ... yǐshàng; **above the window** zai chuānghù shàngtou; **above 50** wǔshí yǐshàng

abroad guówài

absolutely juéduì; **it's absolutely perfect** juéduì bàng; **you're absolutely right** nǐ juéduì zhèngquè; **absolutely!** juéduìde!

absorbent cotton yàomián

accelerator yóuménr

accept jiēshòu

accident shìgu; **there's been an accident** chūle ge shìgu; **sorry, it was an accident** duìbuqǐ, wǒ méi xiǎoxīn

accommodation(s): we need accommodation(s) for four wǒmen shì sìge ren, xiáng zhǎo ge zhù de dìfang; **the accommodation(s) here is/are excellent** zhèr de zhùsù tiáojiàn fēicháng hǎo

accurate zhǔnquè

ache téng; **I have an ache here** wǒ zhèr téng; **it aches** téng

acrobatics zájì

across: across the street mǎlù duìmiànr

actor yǎnyuán

actress nǚ yǎnyuán

acupuncture zhēnjiū

adapter (*electrical*) duōyòng chātóu

address dìzhǐ; **please write your address** qíng xiě yíxia nínde dìzhǐ

address book tōngxùnlù

admission rùchǎng; **how much is admission?** rùchǎngjuànr duōshao qián?

adore: I adore this country wǒ fēicháng xǐhuān zhèige guójiā; **I adore the food here** wǒ fēicháng xǐhuān chī zhèr de cài

adult dàrén

advance: in advance tíqián; **let me know in advance** qǐng tíqián gàosu wǒ

advertisement guǎnggào

advise jiànyì; **what would you advise?** nín yǒu shénme jiànyì ma?

aeroplane fēijī

affluent fēngfù de

afraid pà; **I'm afraid of heights** wǒ pà págāo; **don't be afraid** bié pà; **I'm not afraid** wǒ bú pà; **I'm afraid I can't help you** kǒngpà wǒ bāngbúshàng nǐde máng; **I'm afraid so** kǒngpà shì zhèiyàng; **are you going/coming? – I'm afraid not** nǐ qù/lái ma? – kǒngpà bú qù/lái

after yǐhòu; **after 9 o'clock** jiúdiǎn yǐhòu; **not until after 9 o'clock** jiúdiǎn yǐhòu cái xíng; **after you** nín xiān qǐng

afternoon xiàwǔ; **in the afternoon** xiàwǔ; **good afternoon!** nín hǎo!; **this afternoon** jīntian xiàwǔ

aftershave xūhòushuǐ

afterwards hòulái

again zài; **please come again** huānyíng nín zài lái

against (*wall*) kàozhe; (*as protection*) fáng; **England against China** (*sport etc*) Yīngguó duì Zhōngguó

age niánjì; **under age** wèichéngnián; **not at my age!** wǒ zhèige niánjì?; **it**

takes **ages** xūyào de shíjiān chángjíle; **I haven't been here for ages** wǒ háojiǔ méi lái zhèr le

agency dàilǐ gōngsī

ago: a year ago yìnián yǐqián; **it wasn't long ago** bùjiǔ yǐqián

agony: it's agony téngjíle

agree tóngyì; **do you agree?** nǐ tóngyì ma?; **I agree** wǒ tóngyì; **it doesn't agree with me** wǒ chībùlái

aggressive tèbié chòng

AIDS àizībìng

air kōngqì; **by air** zuò fēijī

air-bed (camping) qìchuáng

air-conditioning kōngtiáo

air hostess kōngzhōng xiáojiě

airmail: by airmail hángkōng

airmail envelope hángkōng xìnfēng

airplane fēijī

airport jīchǎng

airport bus jīchǎng bānchē

airport tax jīchǎngfèi

à la carte diǎncài

alarm jǐngbàoqì

alarm clock nàozhōng

alcohol jiǔjīng

alcoholic: is it alcoholic? zhèi hán jiǔjīng ma?

alive huózhe; **is he still alive?** tā hái huózhe ma?

all suóyǒude; **all the hotels** suóyǒude fàndiàn; **all my friends** wǒ suóyǒude péngyou; **all my money** wǒ suóyǒude qián; **all of it** quánbù; **all of them** tāmen quánbù; **all right** kéyǐ; **I'm all right** wǒ méishìr; **that's all, thank you** jiù zhèixie, xièxie; **it's all changed** dōu biàn le; **thank you – not at all** xièxie ni – búyòng xiè

allergic: I'm allergic to ... wǒ duì ... guòmǐn

allergy guòmǐn

all-inclusive price bāojià

allowed yúnxǔ; **is ... allowed?** yúnxǔ ... ma?; **I'm not allowed to eat salt** yīshēng bú ràng wǒ chī yán

all-risks (insurance) quán báoxiǎn

almost chàbuduō

alone: are you alone? nǐ yígerén ma?; **I'm alone** wǒ yíge ren; **leave me alone** bié guǎn wo

already yǐjīng

also yě

alteration biàndòng

alternative: is there an alternative? yǒu biéde bànfa ma?; **we had no alternative** wǒmen méi yǒu biéde bànfa

alternator jiāoliú fādiànjī

although suīrán

altogether yígòng; **what does that come to altogether?** yígòng duōshao qián?

always zǒng

a.m. shàngwǔ; **at 8 a.m.** shàngwǔ bādiǎn; see page 115

amazing (terrific) liǎobùqǐ; (suprising) méixiàngdào; **he is really amazing** tā zhēn liǎobùqǐ; **it's amazing it all went so smoothly** méixiàngdào néng zhème shùn

ambassador dàshǐ

ambulance jiùhùchē; **get an ambulance** jiào liàng jiùhùchē

America Měiguó

American (adjective) Měiguó; (person) Měiguoren; **the Americans** Měiguoren

among zài ... zhōng

amp ānpéi; **a 13 amp fuse** shísān ānpéi de báoxiǎnsī

an(a)esthetic mázuìjì

ancestor zǔxiān

anchor máo

ancient gǔdài

and hé

angina xīnjiǎotòng

angry shēngqì; **I'm very angry about it** nèijiàn shìr jiào wǒ shēngqì

animal dòngwu

ankle jiǎobózi

anniversary (of event) jìniànrì; **it's our (wedding) anniversary today** jīntian shì wǒmende (jiēhūn) jìniànrì

annoy tǎoyàn; **he's annoying me** tā zhēn jiào rén tǎoyàn; **it's so annoying** zhēn tǎoyàn

anorak píhóu

another: can we have another room? (different) kéyǐ huàn yíge fángjiān ma?; (extra) kéyǐ zài yào yíge fángjiān ma?; **another bottle, please** qǐng zài lái yìpíng

answer huídá; **what was his answer?**

ai	ao	c	e	ei	en	h	i	ɪ	ian	ie	iu	o
I	how	ts	her	ay	open	loch	ee	sir	yen	yeh	yoyo	or

tā shı zěnme huídáde?; **there was no answer** (*on telephone*) méi rén jiē
ant: ants máyǐ
antibiotics kàngjūnsù
anticlimax (*disappointment*) shīwàng
antifreeze fángdòngjì
antihistamine kàngzǔ'ānjì
antique gúdǒng; **is it an antique?** shı gúdǒng ma?
antique shop wénwù shāngdiàn
antisocial: he's a bit antisocial tā yóu diǎnr bù héquánr; **antisocial behavio(u)r** bù jiǎng gōnggòng dàodé de xíngwei
any: have you got any rolls/milk? yǒu miànbāojuǎn/niúnǎi ma?; **I haven't got any** wǒ méi yǒu
anybody: can anybody help? shéi lái bāngbang máng?; **there wasn't anybody there** nàr méi rén
anything: I don't want anything wǒ shénme yě bú yào; **don't you have anything else?** méi yǒu biéde ma?
apart from chúle ... yǐwài
apartment dānyuán
aperitif kāiwèijiǔ
apology dàoqiàn; **please accept my apologies** wó gěi nín dàoqiàn
appalling (*weather, film etc*) zāotòule; (*accident, injury*) yánzhòng; (*person, story*) kěpà
appear: it would appear that ... hǎoxiàng ...
appendicitis lánwěiyán
appetite wèikǒu; **I've lost my appetite** wǒ méi wèikǒu
apple píngguǒ
apple pie píngguǒpái
application form shēnqǐngbiǎo
appointment: I'd like to make an appointment wó xiǎng yuē ge shíjiān; **I have an appointment this afternoon** jītian xiàwu wǒ gēn rén yuēzhe yǒu shìr
appreciate: thank you, I appreciate it zhēn gǎnxiè nín
approve: she doesn't approve tā bù tóngyì
apricot xìngzı
April sìyuè
aqualung shuǐfèi
archaeology káogǔxué

are shì; *see page 104*
area: I don't know the area wǒ duì zhèiyídài bù shúxi
area code chángtú qūhào
arm gēbo
around *see about*
arrangement ānpái; **will you make the arrangements?** nǐ ānpai yíxia, hǎo ma?
arrest dàibǔ; **he's been arrested** tā bèi dàibǔ le
arrival dàodá
arrive dào; **when do we arrive?** wǒmen shénme shíhou dào?; **let me know as soon as they arrive** tāmen yídào, jiù gàosu wǒ; **we only arrived yesterday** wǒmen zuótiān cái dào; **has my parcel arrived yet?** wǒde bāoguǒ láile ma?
art měishù
art gallery měishùguǎn
arthritis guānjiéyán
artificial rénzàode
artist yìshùjiā
as: as fast as you can yuè kuài yuè hǎo; **do as much as you can** qǐng jìn lì ér wéi; **as you like** suí nǐde biàn; **as it's getting late** tiān bùzǎole
ashore: to go ashore shàng àn
ashtray yānhuīgāng
aside from chúle ... yǐwài
ask wèn; **can I ask you a question?** wèn yíge wèntì, xíng ma?; **that's not what I asked for** nà bú shı wǒ yào de; **could you ask him to phone me back?** qǐng tā géi wǒ huí ge diànhuà, hǎo ma?
asleep: he's still asleep tā hái zài shuìjiào
asparagus lóngxūcài
aspirin āsīpǐlín
assault: she's been assaulted tā bèi rén wūrǔle; **indecent assault** jiānwū
assistant (*helper*) zhùshǒu; (*in shop*) shòuhuòyuán
assume: I assume that ... wó xiǎng ...
asthma xiàochuǎn
astonishing jīngrén de
at: at the café zai kāfēiguǎnr; **at the hotel** zai fàndiàn; **at 8 o'clock** bādiǎn zhōng; **see you at dinner** chīfàn jiàn

ong	ou	q	u	un	ü	ʊ	ui	uo	x	yan	z	zh
ung	soul	ch	soon	open	huge	huge	way	wor	sh	yen	dz	j

atmosphere qìfen
attractive xīyǐnrén; **you're very attractive** ní hěn xīyǐnrén
aubergine qiézı
auction dàpāimài
audience *(TV)* guānzhòng; *(radio)* tīngzhòng
August bāyue
aunt: my aunt *(father's sister)* wǒ gūgu; *(mother's sister)* wǒ yímǔ
Australia Àudàlìyà
Australian *(adjective)* Àudàlìyà; *(person)* Àudàlìyaren; **the Australians** Àudàlìyaren
authorities dāngjú
automatic zìdòng
automobile qìchē
autumn qiūtian; **in the autumn** qiūtian

available: when will it be available? shénme shíhou néng yǒu?; **when will he be available?** tā shénme shíhou néng zài?
avenue dàjiē
average: the average Chinese/ American doesn't like ... Zhōngguoren/Měiguoren yìbān dōu bù xǐhuān ...; **an above average hotel** bíjiao hǎo de fàndiàn; **a below average hotel** bíjiao chà de fàndiàn; **the food was only average** zhèr de cài yìbān; **on average** píngjūn
awake: is she awake? tā xǐngle ma?
away: is it far away? yuǎn ma?; **go away!** gǔn!
awful zāotòule
axle zhóu

B

baby yīng'ér
baby-carrier *(on back)* yīng'ér bēidōu
baby-sitter línshí kān xiǎoháir de; **can you get us a baby-sitter?** nín néng bāng wǒmen zhǎo yíge línshí kān xiǎoháir de ma?
bachelor dānshēnhàn
back *(of body)* bèi; *(lower part)* yāo; **I've got a bad back** wǒde yāo bù hǎo; **at the back** zai hòumian; **in the back of the car** zai chē hòumian; **I'll be right back** wǒ jiù lái; **when do you want it back?** nǐ shénme shíhou yào wǒ huán?; **can I have my money back?** néng bǎ qián huán gei wǒ ma?; **come back!** huílai!; **I go back home tomorrow** wǒ míngtian huí jiā; **we'll be back next year** wǒmen míngnian huílai; **when is the last bus back?** zuìhòu yìbān chē shı jídiǎn?
backache: I have a backache wǒ yāoténg
back door hòuménr

backgammon shíwúzǐr qí
backpack bèibāo
back seat hòuzuò
back street xiǎohútòng
bacon xiánròu; **bacon and eggs** xiánròu jiānjīdàn
bad huài; **this meat's bad** zhèi ròu huài le; **I have a bad headache** wǒ tóu téngde lìhai; **it's not bad** búcuò; **too bad!** *(bad luck)* zhēn dǎoméi; *(nothing to be done)* méi bànfa!
badly: he's been badly injured tā shāngde hěn lìhai
bag *(suitcase)* xiāngzı; *(plastic bag)* sùliàodàir
baggage xíngli
baggage allowance xíngli zhòngliàng xiànzhì
baggage checkroom xíngli jìcúnchù
baked kǎo
bakery miànbāofáng
balcony yángtái; **a room with a balcony** dài yángtái de fángjiān; **on the balcony** zai yángtáishang

ai	ao	c	e	ei	en	h	i	ı	ian	ie	iu	o
I	how	ts	her	ay	open	loch	ee	sir	yen	yeh	yoyo	or

bald tūtóu
ball qiú
ballet bāléiwǔ
ball-point pen yuánzhūbǐ
bamboo zhúzı; (*adjective*) zhú
bamboo shoots zhúsǔn
banana xiāngjiāo
band (*music*) yuèduì
bandage bēngdài; **could you change
the bandage?** nín bāng wǒ huàn
yíxia bēngdài, hǎo ma?
bandaid xiàngpígāo
bank yínháng; **when are the banks
open?** yínháng shénme shíhou
kāiménr?
bank account yínháng zhànghù
banquet yànhuì
bar jiǔbā; **let's meet in the bar**
wǒmen zai jiǔbā pèngtóu; **a bar of
chocolate** yíkuàir qiǎokelì
barbecue yěcān kǎoròujià
barber (*shop*) lǐfàdiàn
bargain piányihuò; **a real bargain**
zhēn piányi
barmaid fúwùyuán
barman fúwùyuán; **barman!** fúwùyuán
tóngzhì!
barrette fàjiā
bartender fúwùyuán
basic: the hotel is rather basic zhèijiā
fàndiàn hěn yìbān; **will you teach
me some basic phrases?** nín néng
jiāo wǒ yìdiǎnr jīběnde cíjù ma?
basket lánzı
bath xízǎo; **can I take a bath?** wǒ
néng xǐ ge zǎo ma?; **could you give
me a bath towel?** nǐ néng gěi wo
yìtiáo yùjīn ma?
bathing yóuyǒng
bathing costume yóuyǒngyī
bathrobe yùyī
bathroom xízǎojiān; **a room with a
private bathroom** dài xízǎojiān de
fángjiān; **can I use your bathroom?**
(*toilet*) yòng yíxia nínde cèsuǒ, xíng
ma?
battery diànchí; **the battery's flat**
diànchí méi diàn le
bay hǎiwān
be: be reasonable yào jiǎng dàoli;
don't be lazy bié nàme lǎn; **where
have you been?** nǐ qù nǎr le?; **I've**

never been to ... wǒ cónglai méi
qùguo ...; *see pages 95, 104*
beach hǎitān; **on the beach** zai
hǎitānshang; **I'm going to the beach**
wǒ qù hǎibiānr
beach mat hǎitān liángxír
beach towel yùjīn
beach umbrella tàiyángsǎn
beads zhūzhu
bean curd dòufu
bean noodles fěnsī
beans dòuzı
beard húzı
beautiful (*woman*) piàoliang; (*view,
countryside*) měi; (*meal*) hǎochī; (*holiday*) yúkuài; **thank you, that's
beautiful** xièxie, ni zhēn hǎo
beauty salon měiróngtīng
because yīnwei; **because of the bad
weather** yīnwei tiānqi bù hǎo
bed chuáng; **single bed** dānren
chuáng; **double bed** shuāngren
chuáng; **you haven't made my bed**
wǒde chuáng nǐ hái méi zhénglǐ;
he's still in bed tā hái méi
qǐchuáng; **I'm going to bed** wǒ yào
shuì le
bed linen chuángdānr
bedroom wòshì
bee mìfēng
beef niúròu
beer píjiǔ; **two beers, please** qǐng lái
liǎngbēi píjiǔ
before ... ... yǐqián; **before breakfast**
zǎofàn yǐqián; **before I leave** wǒ
líkāi yǐqián; **I haven't been here
before** wó yǐqián méi láiguò zhèr
begin kāishǐ; **when does it begin?**
shénme shíhou kāishǐ?
beginner chūxuézhě; **I'm just a
beginner** wǒ gāng kāishǐ xué
beginning: at the beginning yì kāishǐ
behavio(u)r xíngwei
behind hòumian; **the driver behind
me** wǒ hòumian de sijī
beige bìjī
believe xiāngxìn; **I don't believe you**
wǒ bù xiāngxìn; **I believe you** wǒ
xiāngxìn
bell líng
belong: that belongs to me nà shı
wǒde; **who does this belong to?** zhè

shı shéide?

belongings: all my belongings wŏde quánbù jiādàng

below ... ... xià; **below zero** líng xià; **below the knee** qīgài yĭxià

belt (*clothing*) yāodài

bend (*in road*) zhuǎnwān

berth wòpù

beside zai ... pángbiān; **beside the hotel** zai fàndiàn pángbiān; **sit beside me** zuò zai wŏ pángbiān

besides chúle ... yĭwài; **besides that** chúle nà yĭwài

best zuìhǎo; **the best hotel in town** chénglĭ zuìhǎo de fàndiàn; **that's the best meal I've ever had** wŏ cónglai méi chīguo zhème hǎo de fàn

bet: I bet you 5 yuan wŏ gēn ni da wŭkuài qián de dŭ

better hǎo yìdiǎnr; **that's better!** hǎo yìdiǎnr!; **are you feeling better?** háo diǎnr le ma?; **I'm feeling a lot better** wó hǎo duō le; **I'd better be going now** wŏ háishı xiànzài zóu hǎo

between zai ... zhījiān; **between Shanghai and Beijing** zai Shànghǎi gēn Běijīng zhījiān

beyond (*past*) guòle; **beyond the mountains** guòle shān

bicycle zìxíngchē; **can we rent bicycles here?** wŏmen néng cóng zhèr zū liàng zìxíngchē ma?

big dà; **a big one** yíge dàde; **that's too big** tài dàle; **it's not big enough** búgòu dà

bigger dà yìdiǎn

bike zìxíngchē; **woman's bike** kūnchē; **bike with gears** biànsù zìxíngchē

bikini bĭjīnĭ shì yóuyŏngyī

bill zhàngdānr; **could I have the bill, please?** qĭng kāi ge zhàngdānr ba, hǎo ma?

billfold qiánjiā

billiards táiqiú

bird niǎo

biro (*tm*) yuánzhūbĭ

birthday shēngrì; **it's my birthday today** jīntian shı wŏde shēngrì; **when is your birthday?** nĭ shénme shíhou guò shēngrì?; **happy birthday!** shēngrì kuàile!

biscuit bĭnggān

bit yìdiǎnr; **just a little bit for me** wŏ jiù yào yìdiǎnr; **a big bit** yídàkuàir; **a bit of the cake** yìdiǎn dàngāo; **it's a bit too big for me** duì wŏ lái shuō, yŏu diǎnr tài dà; **it's a bit cold today** jīntian yóu diánr lěng

bite yǎo; **I've been bitten** wó gei yǎo le yíxià; **do you have something for bites?** wó gei yǎo le, yŏu shénme dōngxi kéyi cāca ma?

bitter (*taste*) kŭ

black hēi; **black and white film** hēi bái jiāojuǎnr

blackout: he's had a blackout tā yūndǎole

black tea hóngchá

bladder pángguāng

blanket tǎnzı; **I'd like another blanket** wŏ hái xiǎng zài yào yìtiáo tǎnzı

blazer shàngyī

bleach (*powder*) piǎobáifěn; (*fluid*) piǎobájì

bleed chūxuě; **he's bleeding** tā chūxuěle

bless you! *the Chinese have no word for this*

blind xiā

blinds bǎiyèchuāng

blister pào

blocked (*road, drain*) dŭzhùle

block of flats gōngyù

blond (*adjective*) jīnhuángsè

blonde jīnfà nǚláng

blood xuě; **his blood group is ...** tāde xuèxíng shı ...; **I have high blood pressure** wŏde xuěyā gāo

blouse nǚchènyī

blue lánsè

boarding pass dēngjīpáir

boat chuán

body shēntĭ

boil (*on body*) jiēzı; **boil the water** shāo kāishuĭ

boiled egg zhŭjīdàn

boiled rice mĭfàn

boiling hot (*weather*) rèjíle; (*food*) tàngjíle

bomb (*noun*) zhàdàn

bone (*in meat, body*) gútou; (*in fish*) yúcì

bonnet (*of car*) fādòngjīgàir

ai	ao	c	e	ei	en	h	i	ı	ian	ie	iu	o
I	how	ts	her	ay	open	loch	ee	sir	yen	yeh	yoyo	or

book shū; **I'd like to book a table for two** wó xiǎng dìng liǎngge ren de zuò

bookshop, bookstore shūdiàn

boot (*on foot*) xuēzı; (*of car*) xínglixiāng

booze (*noun*) jiǔ; **I had too much booze** wǒ hēduōle

border (*of country*) biānjìng

bored fán; **I'm bored** wǒ fán le

boring wúliáo

born: **I was born in ...** (*date*) wo shı ... shēng de; (*place*) wo shēng zai ...

borrow jiè; **may I borrow ...?** wǒ kéyi jiè yíxia ... ma?

boss láobǎn

both liǎ ... dōu; **we'll both come** wǒmen liǎ dōu lái; **I'll take both of them** zhèi liǎ wǒ dōu yào

bother dájiǎo; **sorry to bother you** duìbuqǐ dájiǎo nín le; **it's no bother** méi shénme; **it's such a bother** zhēn máfan

bottle píngzı; **a bottle of wine** yìpíng pútaojiu; **another bottle, please** qǐng zài lái yìpíng

bottle-opener qǐı

bottom dǐr; **the bottom of the cup/ bowl** bēidǐr/wándǐr; **the bottom of the hill/stairs** shān/lóutī dǐxia

bottom gear yídǎng

bouncer (*at club*) ménwèi

bowels chángzı

box hézı

box lunch wǔcān héfàn

box office shòupiàochù

boy nánháir

boyfriend nán péngyou; **my boyfriend** wǒde nán péngyou

bra xiōngzhào

bracelet shǒuzhuó

brake (*on car*) shāchē; (*on bike*) shǒuzhá; **there's something wrong with the brakes** shāchē yǒu máobìng; **can you check the brakes?** nín néng bāng wo jiǎncha yíxia shāchē ma?; **pedal brakes** jiǎozhá; **hub brakes** zhàngzhá; **I had to brake suddenly** wó zhǐnéng láile ge jí shāchē

brake fluid shāchē yóu

brake lining shāchēwǎ

brandy báilándì

brave yónggǎn

bread miànbāo; **could we have some bread and butter?** qǐng lái diǎnr miànbāo hé huángyóu, hǎo ma?; **some more bread, please** qǐng zài lái diǎnr miànbāo, hǎo ma?; **white bread** bái miànbāo; **brown bread** hēi miànbāo; **wholemeal bread** quánmàifěn miànbāo; **rye bread** hēimài miànbāo; **steamed bread** mántou

break dǎpò; **who broke it?** shéi dǎpò de?; **I think I've broken my arm** wǒde gēbo kěnéng duànle; **it keeps breaking** tā lǎo huà

breakdown: **I've had a breakdown** wǒde chē pāomáole; **nervous breakdown** shénjīng shuāiruò

breakfast zǎofàn; **Western-/Chinese-style breakfast** xīshì/zhōngshì zǎocān

break in: **somebody's broken in** yǒu zéi láiguo

breast qiánxiōng

breast-feed wèi múnǎi

breath hūxī; **out of breath** chuǎnbuguò qì

breathe hūxī; **I can't breathe** wó chuǎnbuguò qì lai le

breathtaking jīngrén

breeze wēifēng

breezy: **it's breezy today** jīntian guāzhe xiǎofēng

bridal suite xīnhūn tàojiān

bride xīnniáng

bridegroom xīnláng

bridge (*over river*) qiáo; (*card game*) qiáopái

brief: **I'm here on a brief visit** wǒ zai zhèr jiù zhù jǐtiān

briefcase gōngwénbāo

bright (*colour*) xiānyàn; **bright red** dà hóng

brilliant (*idea*) gāomíng; (*colour*) fēicháng xiānyàn

bring dàilai; **could you bring it tomorrow?** nǐ míngtian dàilai, hǎo ma?; **I'll bring it back** wǒ dàihuílai; **can I bring a friend too?** wǒ néng dài ge péngyou lái ma?

Britain Yīngguó

British Yīngguo; **the British**

Yīngguoren

brochure shuōmingshū; **do you have any brochures on ...?** nǐ nàr yǒu guānyu ... de shuōmingshū ma?

broke: I'm broke wǒ méi qián le

broken pòle; **... is broken ...**: pòle; **you've broken it** nǐ bǎ tā dǎ pòle; **he has a broken nose** tāde bízı pòle

brooch xiōngzhēn

brother: my brother (*elder*) wo gēge; (*younger*) wo dìdi

brother-in-law: my brother-in-law (*elder sister's husband*) wo jiěfū; (*younger sister's husband*) wo mèifū; (*wife's elder brother*) wo nèixiōng; (*wife's younger brother*) wo nèidì

brown zōngsè; **I don't go brown** wǒ shài bù hēi

browse: may I just browse around? wǒ néng zhuànzhuan kànkan ma?

bruise: I have a bruise here wǒ zhèr qīng le

brunette hēifà nǚláng

brush (*noun*) shuāzı

bubble bath pàomòyù

bucket tǒng

Buddha Fó

Buddhism Fójiào

Buddhist (*adjective*) Fójiào; (*person*) Fójiào tú

buffet: cold buffet lěngcān; **buffet meal** zìzhù cān; **buffet car** cānchē

bug (*insect*) chòuchong; **she's caught a bug** tā bìngle

building jiànzhu

bulb (*electrical*) dēngpāo; **a new bulb** xīn dēngpāo

bull gōngniú

bump pèngshāng; **I bumped my head** wǒ pèng tóu le

bumper báoxiǎngàng

bumpy (*road*) bùpíng; (*flight*) diānbō

bunch of flowers yíshù huā

bungalow píngfáng

bunion mǔnángyán

bunk beds shàngxiàchuáng

buoy fúbiāo

burglar zéi

Burma Miǎndiàn

Burmese (*adjective*) Miǎndiàn; (*person*) Miǎndiànren

burn shāoshāng; **do you have an ointment for burns?** nín yǒu zhì shāoshāng de yàogāo ma?

burnt: this meat is burnt zhèi ròu shāohúle; **my arms are so burnt** wǒde gēbo shàide hěn téng

burst: there's a burst pipe shuíguǎn liè le

bus gōnggòng qìchē; (*common abbreviation*) chē; **is this the bus for ...?** zhèi chē qù ... ma?; **when's the next bus?** xiàtang chē shı jídiǎn?

bus driver sījī

business shēngyì; **it's a pleasure to do business with you** gēn nín zuò shēngyì hěn gāoxìng; **I'm here on business** wǒ lái zhèr chūchāi

bus station gōnggòng qìchē zǒngzhàn

bus stop chēzhàn; **where is the No. 1 bus stop?** yīlù chēzhàn zài nǎr?; **will you tell me which bus stop I get off at?** nín néng gàosu wǒ zai nǎr xià ma?

bust (*of body*) qiánxiōng

bus tour chéngchē lǚyóu

busy (*restaurant*) máng; (*street*) rènao; **I'm busy this evening** wǒ jīntian wǎnshang yǒu shìr; **the line was busy** (*telephone*) zhànxiàn

but dànshı; **not ... but ...** búshı ... érshı ...

butcher ròudiàn

butter huángyóu

butterfly húdié

button niǔkòu

buy mǎi; **I'll buy it** wó mǎi; **where can I buy ...?** zai nǎr néng mǎidào ...?

by: by train/car/boat zuò huǒchē/chē/chuán; **who's it written by?** shı shéi xiěde?; **it's by Qi Baishi** shı Qí Báishí huàde; **I came by myself** wǒ shı yíge ren lái de; **a seat by the window** kào chuāng de zuòwei; **by the sea** zai hǎibiānr; **can you do it by Wednesday?** nǐ xīngqisān yǐqián néng zuòhǎo ma?

bye-bye zàijiàn

bypass (*road*) cèrào gōnglù

ai	ao	c	e	ei	en	h	i	ı	ian	ie	iu	o
I	how	ts	her	ay	open	loch	ee	sir	yen	yeh	yoyo	or

C

cab (*taxi*) chūzūchē
cabbage juǎnxīncài; **Chinese cabbage** báicài
cabin chuáncāng
cable (*electrical*) diànlǎn
cablecar lǎnchē
cadre gànbu
café kāfēiguǎnr
caffeine kāfēiyīn
cake dàngāo; **a piece of cake** yí kuàir dàngāo
calculator jìsuànqì
calendar rìlì
call: **what is this called?** zhèi jiào shénme?; **call the manager!** qǐng jiào jīnglǐ lái; **I'd like to make a call to England** wó xiǎng dǎ ge chángtú, dào Yīngguó de; **I'll call back later** (*come back*) wǒ guò yìhuǐr zài lái ba; (*phone back*) wǒ guò yìhuǐr zài dǎ ba; **I'm expecting a call from London** wǒ zai děng Lúndūn de chángtú; **would you give me a call at 7.30?** qīdiǎn bàn ní dǎ ge diànhuà jiào wo yíxia, hǎo ma?; **the meeting's been called off** huìyì qǔxiāole
call box gōngyòng diànhuà
calligraphy shūfǎ
calm (*person*) lěngjìng; (*sea*) píngjìng; **calm down!** bié zhāojí!
calories kǎ
camera zhàoxiàngjī
camp yěyíng; **is there somewhere we can camp?** yǒu kéyi yěyíng de dìfang ma?; **can we camp here?** kéyi zai zhèr yěyíng ma?
campbed xíngjūnchuáng
camping yěyíng
campsite sùyíngdì
can (*tin*) guàntou; **a can of beer** yíguàn píjiǔ
can: **can I ...?** wǒ kéyi ... ma?; **can you ...?** nǐ kéyi ... ma?; **can he ...?** tā kéyi ... ma?; **can we ...?** wǒmen kéyi ... ma?; **can they ...?** tāmen kéyi ... ma?; **can you ... for me?** qíng nǐ bāng wo ..., hǎo ma?; **can you fix it/buy it for me?** qíng nǐ bāng wo xiūxiu/mǎi, hǎo ma?; **I can't ...** wǒ bù néng ...; **he can't ...** tā bù néng ...; **can I keep it?** wǒ kéyi názhe ma?; **if I can** rúguǒ kéyi de hua; **that can't be right** búduì ba?
Canada Jiānádà
Canadian (*adjective*) Jiānádà; (*person*) Jiānádàren
cancel qǔxiāo; **I cancelled ...** wó qǔxiāo le ...; **can I cancel my reservation?** (*flight*) wǒ kéyi qǔxiāo yuánláide dìngzuò ma?; (*hotel*) wǒ kéyi qǔxiāo yuánlái dìng de fángjiān ma?; **can we cancel dinner for tonight?** wǒmen bǎ jīntian wǎnshang de fàn tuì le, xíng ma?
cancellation qǔxiāo
candies tángkuàir; **a piece of candy** yí kuàir táng
candle làzhú
canoe dúmùchuán
can-opener guàntou qǐzı
Cantonese (*adjective*) Guǎngdōng; (*person*) Guǎngdōngren; (*language*) Guǎngdonghuà
cap màozı; **bathing cap** yóuyǒngmào
capital city shǒudū
capitalism zībénzhǔyì
capitalist zībénzhǔyì
capital letters dàxiě zìmǔ
capsize: **the ship capsized** chuán fānle
captain (*of ship*) chuánzhǎng
car xiǎo qìchē
carafe bōlipíng
carat: **is it 9/14 carat gold?** zhèi shı jiǔ/shísı kǎijīn de ma?
caravan lǚxíng sùyíngchē

ong	ou	q	u	un	ü	ʊ	ui	uo	x	yan	z	zh
ung	soul	ch	soon	open	huge	huge	way	wor	sh	yen	dz	j

carbonated drink qìshuǐr

carburet(t)or qìhuàqì

card míngpiàn; **here is my card** zhèi shì wǒde míngpiàn

cardboard box yìngzhǐhé

cardigan kāijīn máoyī

cards (*poker*) púkèpái; **do you play cards?** nín píngcháng dǎ pái ma?

care: goodbye, take care zàijiàn, duōduō bǎozhòng; **will you take care of this bag for me?** nín bāng wǒ kān yíxia zhèige bāo, hǎo ma?; **care of ...** qíng zhuǎnjiāo ...

careful: be careful xiǎoxīn

careless bù xiǎoxīn; **careless driving** kāichē bù xiǎoxīn; **that was careless of you** nǐ zhèiren zhēn mǎdàhā

car ferry lúndù

car hire (*place*) chūzū qìchē gōngsī

car keys chē yàoshı

carnival kuánghuānjié

car park tíngchēchǎng

carpet dìtǎn

carrier (*on bike*) chēhòuzuò

carrot húluóbo

carry ná; **could you carry this for me?** qǐng nín bāng wǒ názhe zhèige, hǎo ma?; **I can't carry it** wǒ nábúdòng

carry-all dà lǚxíngbāo

car rental (*place*) chūzū qìchē gōngsī

car-sick: I get car-sick wǒ yūnchē

carton zhǐbāozhuāng; **a carton of orangeade** yíge zhǐbāozhuāng júzı qìshuǐr

carving diāokè

carwash xǐchē; **is there a carwash here?** zhèr yóu xǐchē de dìfang ma?

case (*suitcase*) xiāngzı; **in any case** bùguǎn zěnmeyàng; **in that case** nèiyàng de huà; **it's a special case** zhèi shı ge tèshū qíngkuàng; **in case he comes back** ruóguǒ tā huílai de huà; **I'll take an umbrella just in case** wǒ ná bá sǎn, wànyī xiàyǔ ne

cash xiànqián; **I don't have any cash** wǒ méiyǒu xiànqián; **I'll pay cash** wǒ fù xiànqián; **will you cash a cheque/check for me?** zhèizhāng zhīpiào, nín bāng wǒ duìhuàn yíxia, xíng ma?

cashdesk jiāokuǎnchù

cash dispenser zìdòng qúkuǎnjī

cash register xiànjīn chūnàjī

casino dúchǎng

cassette héshì cídài

cassette player héshì cídài fàngyīnjī

cassette recorder héshì cídài lùyīnjī

castle chéngbǎo

casual: casual clothes biànfú

cat māo

catamaran shuāngtǐchuán

catastrophe dàzāinàn

catch: where do we catch the bus? wǒmen zai nǎr shàng chē?; **he's caught some strange illness** tā déle yìzhǒng hěn qíguài de bìng

catching: is it catching? chuánrǎn ma?

cathedral dà jiàotáng

Catholic (*adjective*) tiānzhǔjiào

cauliflower càihuā

cause (*noun*) yuányīn

cave shāndòng; (*dwelling*) yáodòng

caviar yúzǐjiàng

ceiling fángdǐng

celebrations qìngzhù huódong

celery qíncài

cellophane bōlizhǐ

cemetery mùdì

center zhōngxīn; *see also* **centre**

centigrade shèshì; *see page 119*

centimetre, centimeter centimeter límǐ; *see page 117*

central zhōngxīn; **we'd prefer something more central** wǒmen xǐhuān lí shì zhōngxīn jìn yìdiǎnr

central generating station zǒng diànzhàng

central heating nuǎnqì

centre zhōngxīn; **how do we get to the centre?** dào shì zhōngxīn zěnme zǒu?; **in the centre (of town)** zai shì zhōngxīn

century shìjì; **in the 19th/20th century** zai shíjiǔ/èrshí shìjì

ceramics táoqì

certain kěndìng; **are you certain?** nǐ gǎn kěndìng ma?; **I'm absolutely certain** wó gǎn juéduì kěndìng

certainly dāngrán; **certainly not** dāngrán bù

certificate zhèngshū; **marriage certificate** jiēhūn zhèngshū; **birth**

ai	ao	c	e	ei	en	h	i	ı	ian	ie	iu	o
I	how	ts	her	ay	open	loch	ee	sir	yen	yeh	yoyo	or

certificate chūshēng zhèng
chain (for bike) liànzı; (around neck) xiàngliàn; the chain keeps coming off zhèi chē lǎo diào liànzı
chain guard (for bike) liànhé
chair yǐzı
chairman (of party) zǒng shūjì; (of state) zhǔxí
chalet (in mountains) xiǎo mùwū
chambermaid nǚ fúwùyuán
chamberpot mátǒng
champagne xiāngbīn
chance: quite by chance pèngqiǎo; no chance! bù kěnéng!
change: could you change this into Renminbi? nín bāng wo bǎ zhè huànchéng rénmínbì, hǎo ma?; I haven't got any change wǒ yìdiǎnr língqián yě méi yǒu; can you give me change for a 100 kuai note? nín bāng wo bǎ zhè yìbǎikuài qian huànchéng língde, hǎo ma?; do we have to change (trains)? wǒmen děi huàn chē ma?; for a change huànhuan yàngr; you haven't changed the sheets zhèi chuángdānr hái méi huàn; the place has changed so much zhèrde biànhua zhēn dà; do you want to change places with me? nǐ xiǎng gēn wǒ huànhuan dìfang ma?; can I change this for ...? wǒ kéyi bǎ zhèi huànchéng ... ma?
changeable (weather) biànhuà wúcháng
channel: the Taiwan Channel Táiwān hǎixiá
chaos luàn
chap xiáohuǒzı; the chap at reception zǒng fúwùtái de nèige xiáohuǒzı
charge: is there an extra charge? yào lìngwài fùqián ma?; what do you charge? yào shōu duōshao qián?; who's in charge here? zhèr shéi fùzé?
charming mírén
chart (diagram) túbiǎo; (for navigation) hǎitú
charter flight bāojī
chassis dǐpán
cheap piányi; do you have something cheaper? yǒu piányi diǎnr de ma?

cheat piàn; I've been cheated wǒ shòupiànle
check: will you check? ní jiǎnchá yíxia, hǎo ma?; will you check the steering? nǐ bāng wo jiǎnchá yíxia fāngxiàngpán, hǎo ma?; I've checked it wó jiǎnchá gùo le; will you check the bill? qíng nǐ kàn yíxia zhàngdān yǒu méi yǒu wèntí, hǎo ma?
check (for money) zhīpiào; will you take a check? zhèr shōu zhīpiào ma?
check (bill) zhàngdānr; may I have the check please? qǐng kāi ge zhàngdānr, hǎo ma?
checkbook zhīpiào bù
checked (shirt) fānggé
checkers xīyáng tiàoqí
check-in dēngjì
checkroom (for coats etc) yīmàojiān
cheek (on face) sāi; what a cheek! zhēn búyàoliǎn!
cheeky (person) hòuliǎnpí
cheerio (bye-bye) huítóu jiàn
cheers (thank you) xièxie; (toast) gānbēi
cheer up gāoxìng diǎnr
cheese nǎilào
cheesecake nǎilàogāo
chef chúshī
chemist (shop) yàofáng
cheque zhīpiào; will you take a cheque? zhèr shōu zhīpiào ma?
cheque book zhīpiào bù
cheque card zhīpiào kǎ
cherry yīngtáo
chess guójì xiàngqí; Chinese chess xiàngqí
chest (body) qiánxiōng
chewing gum kǒuxiāngtáng
chicken (animal) xiǎo jī; (meat) jīròu
chickenpox shuǐdòu
child háizi
child minder bǎomǔ
child minding service tuōyīng fúwù
children háizı
children's playground értóng lèyuán
children's pool értóng yóuyǒngchí
children's room értóng yóulèshì
chilled (wine) bīngzhèn; it's not properly chilled bīngzhèn de bú gòu
chilli sauce làjiāo jiàng

ong	ou	q	u	un	ü	ʊ	ui	uo	x	yan	z	zh
ung	soul	ch	soon	open	huge	huge	way	wor	sh	yen	dz	j

chilly yóudiǎnr lěng
chimney yāntong
chin xiàba
china cíqì
China Zhōngguó
China International Travel Service Zhōngguó Guójì Lǚxíngshè
China tea Zhōngguo chá
China Travel Service Zhōngguo Lǚxíngshè
China Youth Travel Service Zhōngguo Qīngnián Lǚxíngshè
Chinese (adjective) Zhōngguo; (person) Zhōngguoren; (language) Hànyǔ; the Chinese Zhōngguo rénmín
Chinese-style Zhōngshì
chips zhá tǔdòutiáo; potato chips zhá tǔdòupiànr
chiropodist xiūjiǎo yīsheng
chocolate qiǎokelì; a chocolate bar yìtiáo qiǎokelì; a box of chocolates yìhé qiǎokelì
choke (on car) qìménr
choose xuǎn; it's hard to choose hěn nán xuǎn; you choose for us nǐ bāng wǒmen xuǎn ba
chop: a pork/lamb chop zhūpái/yángpái
chop (seal) túzhāng; can you have a chop made for me? qíng nǐ bāng wo kè ge túzhāng, hǎo ma?
chopping board càibǎn
chopsticks kuàizi
Christian name (first name) míngzi
Christmas shèngdànjié; merry Christmas shèngdànjié kuàilè
chrysanthemum júhuā
church jiàotáng; is there a Protestant/Catholic Church here? zhèr yǒu jīdūjiào/tiānzhǔjiào jiàotáng ma?
cider píngguojiǔ
cigar xuějiā
cigarette yānjuǎnr; tipped/plain cigarettes dài guòlǜzuǐr/bú dài guòlǜzuǐr de yānjuǎnr
cine-camera diànyǐng shèyǐngjī
cinema diànyǐngyuàn
circle (theatre) lóutīng
citizen gōngmín; I'm a British/American citizen wǒ shì Yīngguó/Měiguó gōngmín

city chéngshì
city centre, city center shì zhōngzīn
claim (noun: insurance) suǒpéi
claim form suǒpéi shénqíngbiǎo
clarify chéngqīng
classical gúdiǎn
clean (adjective) gānjìng; it's not clean bù gānjìng; may I have some clean sheets? géi wo diǎnr gānjìng de chuángdānr, hǎo ma?; our room hasn't been cleaned today wǒmende fángjiān jīntian hái méi shōushi ne; can you clean my shoes/the bath for me? nǐ bāng wo bǎ xié/zǎopénr cāca, hǎo ma?
cleaning solution (for contact lenses) qīngjié yè
cleansing cream (cosmetic) xièzhuāngyóu
cleanser qùwūfěn
clear: it's not very clear bú tài qīngchu; OK, that's clear hǎole, zhèi jiù qīngchu le
clever cōngming
cliff xuányá
climate qìhou
climb pá; it's a long climb to the top yào pá dào dǐng hái hén yuǎn; we're going to climb ... wǒmen qù pá ...
climber dēngshān yùndòngyuán
climbing boots dēngshānxié
clinic zhěnsuǒ
cloakroom (for coats) yīmàojiān; (WC) xíshǒujiān
clock zhōng
close jìn; it it close? lí zhèr jìn ma?; it's close to the hotel lí fàndiàn hěn jìn; close by ... zài ... fùjìn
close (shut) guān; close the door/window guān ménr/chuāng; when do you close? nǐmen shénme shíhou guānménr?
closed: the shop/bank is closed shāngdiàn/yínháng guānménr le
closet (cupboard) guìzi
cloth (material) bùliào; (rag) mābù
clothes yīfu
clothes line shàiyīshéng
clothes peg, clothespin yīfu jiāzi
clouds yúncai; its clouding over tiān yīnxiàlaile

ai	ao	c	e	ei	en	h	i	ɪ	ian	ie	iu	o
I	how	ts	her	ay	open	loch	ee	sir	yen	yeh	yoyo	or

cloudy yīntiān
club jùlèbù
clumsy bènshǒu bènjiǎo
clutch (car) líhéqì; **the clutch is slipping** líhéqì dáchǐ
coach (long distance bus) chángtú qìchē
coach party zuò chángtú qìchē de lǚxíngtuán
coach trip zuò chángtú qìchē lǚxíng
coast hǎibiānr; **at the coast** zai hǎibiānr
coastguard hǎishang biānfáng bùduì
coat (overcoat etc) dàyī; (jacket) shàngyī
coathanger yījià
cobbled street shízǐlù
cobbler xiūxiéjiàng
cockroach zhānglàng
cocktail jīwéijiǔ
cocktail bar jiǔbā
cocoa kěkě
coconut yēzi
code: what's the (dialling) code for ...? ... de chángtú qūhào shı duōshao?
coffee kāfēi; **a white coffee, a coffee with milk** jiā niúnǎi de kāfēi; **a black coffee** bù jiā niúnǎi de kāfēi; **two coffees, please** qǐng lái liǎngbēi kāfēi
coin yìngbì
Coke (tm) Kěkǒukělè
cold (adjective) lěng; **I'm cold** wó lěngle; **I have a cold** wó gǎnmàole
coldbox (for carrying food) bǎowēnpíng
cold cream (cosmetic) lěngshuāng
collapse kuǎ; **he's collapsed** tā kuǎle
collar yīlǐng
collar bone suógǔ
colleague: my colleague wǒde tóngshì; **your colleague** nǐde tóngshì
collect: I've come to collect ... wǒ lái qǔ ...; **I collect ...** (stamps etc) wǒ shōují ...; **I want to call New York collect** wǒ yào ge Niǔyuē de guójì chángtú, shı duìfāng fùkuǎn
collect call duìfāng fùkuǎn
collective (noun) hézuòshè
college xuéyuàn
collision: we've had a collision zhuàng chē le
cologne kēlóng xiāngshuǐr

colo(u)r yánsè; **do you have any other colo(u)rs?** hái yǒu biéde yánsè ma?
colo(u)r film cǎisè jiāojuǎnr
comb (noun) shūzi
come lái; **I come from London** wǒ shı cóng Lúndūn láide; **where do you come from?** nǐ shı cóng nǎr láide?; **when are they coming?** tāmen shénme shíhou lái?; **come here** dào zhèr lái; **come with me** gēn wǒ lái; **come back!** huílai!; **I'll come back later** wo guò yìhuǐr huílai; **come in!** qǐng jìn; **he's coming on very well** (improving) tā huīfu de hén hǎo; **come on!** kuài lái!; **do you want to come out this evening?** jīntian wǎnshang chūqu wánrwanr, hǎo ma?; **these two pictures didn't come out** zhèi liǎngzhāng zhàopian méi chōng hǎo; **the money hasn't come through** yet qián hái méi dào
comfortable (hotel etc) shūfu; **it's not very comfortable** bú tài shūfu
commune gōngshè
communism gòngchánzhǔyì
communist (adjective) gòngchánzhǔyì
Communist Party gòngchándǎng
Communist Party member gòngchándǎngyuán
company (firm) gōngsī
comparison: there's no comparison méi fār bǐ
compass zhǐnánzhēn
compensation bǔcháng
compensation trade bǔcháng màoyì
complain máiyuàn; **it's no use complaining** máiyuàn méi yòng; **I want to complain about my room** wǒ duì wǒde fángjiān bù mǎnyì
complaint máiyuàn; **I have a complaint** wó yǒu yìjiàn
complete quán; **the complete set** quántào; **it's a complete disaster** quán luàntàole
completely wánquándi
complicated fùzá; **it's very complicated** fēicháng fùzá
compliment: my compliments to the chef xièxie chúshī de gāochāo shǒuyì
comprehensive (insurance) zōnghé

ong	ou	q	u	un	ü	ʊ	ui	uo	x	yan	z	zh
ung	soul	ch	soon	open	huge	huge	way	wor	sh	yen	dz	j

compulsory bìxū
computer jìsuànjī
concerned (*anxious*) guānxīn; **we are very concerned about ...** wǒmen duì ... shífēn guānxīn
concert yīnyuèhuì
concussion nǎozhèndàng
condenser (*in car*) diànróngqì
condition (*state*) qíngkuàng; (*stipulation*) tiáojiàn; **what are conditions like there?** nàr de qíngkuàng zěnmeyàng?; **I agree to your conditions** wǒ tóngyi nǐde tiáojiàn; **the car is in poor condition** zhèi chē bùxíngle; **I'm not going under any conditions** bù guan zěnme shuō, wó yě bú qù; **I will come on condition that I pay** ràng wǒ fùqián wǒ cái qù
conditioner (*for hair*) hùfàsù
condom bìyùntào
conductor (*on train*) lièchēyuán
conference dàhuì
confirm: please can I confirm my plane/hotel reservation? qǐng bāng wǒ quèrèn yíxia wǒ yuánlài dìng de zuòwei/fángjiān, hǎo ma?
confuse: it's very confusing zhēn ràng rén hútu
congratulations! gōngxǐ! gōngxǐ!
conjunctivitis jiémóyán
connection: I have a flight/rail connection there for Beijing wǒ zài nàr huàn fēijī/chē qù Běijīng
connections (*social, business*) guānxi; **I've got good connections** wó yóu hěn duō guānxi; **do you have any connections there?** nǎr yǒu méi you nǐde guānxi?
connoisseur jiànshǎngjiā
conscious (*medical*) shénzhì qīngxǐng
consciousness: he's lost consciousness tā bù xǐng rénshì le
constipation dàbiàn bù tōng
consul lǐngshì
consulate lǐngshìguǎn
contact: how can I contact ...? wó zěnme gēn ... liánxì?; **I'm trying to contact ...** wó xiǎng gēn ... liánxì yíxia
contact lenses yǐnxíng yǎnjìng
contraceptive (*noun*) bìyùn yòngpǐn
convenient (*time, location*) fāngbiàn;

that's not convenient bù fāngbiàn
cook: it's not properly cooked (*is underdone*) hái bànshēng bùshú de; **it's beautifully cooked** zuòde hén hǎochī; **he's a good cook** tā hěn huì zuòfàn
cooker lúzào
cookie xiǎodiǎnxīn
cool (*day, weather*) liángkuai
corduroy dēngxīnróng
cork (*in bottle*) ruǎnmùsāi
corkscrew kāi ruǎnmùsāi de jiúqǐzi
corn (*on foot*) jīyǎnr
corner jiǎor; **in the corner** zai jiǎorli; **a corner table** kào jiǎor de zhuōzi; **on the corner** (*of street*) lùkǒur
coronary (*noun*) xīnlì shuāijié
correct (*adjective*) duì; **that's correct** duìle; **please correct me if I make a mistake** rúguo wǒ chūle cuò, qǐng bāng wó gǎi
corridor zǒuláng
corset jiànměikù
cosmetics huàzhuāngpǐn
cost: what does it cost? zhèi yào duōshao qián?
cot (*for baby*) xiǎoháirchuáng; (*camping bed*) xíngjūnchuáng
cottage xiǎofángzi
cotton miánhuā
cotton buds (*for make-up removal etc*) miánhuaqiānr
cotton padded coat mián'ǎo
cotton wool yàomián
couch chángshāfā
couchette wòpù
cough (*noun*) késou
cough medicine zhǐké yàoshuǐr
cough syrup zhǐké tángjiāng
cough tablets zhǐké yàopiànr
could: could you ... for me? qǐng nín bāng wo ... hǎo ma?; **could you fix/buy it for me?** qǐng nín bāng wo xiūxiu/mǎi, hǎo ma?; **could I have a cup of tea/a bottle of beer?** qǐng lái yìbēi chá/yìpíng píjiǔ, hǎo ma?; **I couldn't come/go** wǒ bù néng lái/qù
country (*nation*) guójiā; **in the country** (*countryside*) zai nóngcūn
countryside nòngcūn
couple (*man and woman*) fūfù; **a couple of ...** yíduìr ...

ai	ao	c	e	ei	en	h	i	ɪ	ian	ie	iu	o
I	how	ts	her	ay	open	loch	ee	sir	yen	yeh	yoyo	or

courier (*messenger*) xìnshǐ; (*tour guide*) péitóng

course: **we had a five-course/eight-course meal** wǒmen nèidùn fàn yóu wǔdào/bādào cài; **of course** dāngrán; **of course not** dāngrán bù

court (*law*) fǎtíng; (*tennis*) wǎngqiúchǎng

courtesy bus (*airport to hotel etc*) zhuānchē

cousin (*male, older than speaker*) biǎogē; (*if son of father's brother*) tángxiōng; (*male, younger than speaker*) biǎodì; (*if son of father's brother*) tángdì; (*female, older than speaker*) biáojiě; (*if daughter of father's brother*) tángjiě; (*female, younger than speaker*) biǎomèi; (*if daughter of father's brother*) tángmèi

cover charge fúwùfèi

cow nǎiniú

crab pángxiè

cracked: **it's cracked** (*plate etc*) lièle

cracker (*biscuit*) sūdá bǐnggān

craftshop gōngyìpǐn shāngdiàn

cramp (*in leg etc*) chōujīnr

crankshaft qǔzhóu

crash: **there's been a crash** zhuàng chē le

crash course (*for learning language etc*) sùchéng bān

crash helmet tóukuī

crawl (*swimming*) zìyóuyǒng

crazy shénjīngbìng

cream (*on milk, in cake*) nǎiyóu; (*for face*) cāliǎnyóu

crèche (*for babies*) tuōérsuǒ

credit card xìnyòng kǎ

crib (*baby's cot*) xiǎoháirchuáng

crisis wēijī

crisps zhá tǔdòupiànr

crockery cānjù

crook wúlài; **he's a crook** tā shì ge wúlài

crossing (*by sea*) héngdù

crossroads shízi lùkǒu

crosswalk rénxíngdào

crowd rénqún

crowded (*streets, buses*) hén jǐ

crown (*on tooth*) yáguàn

crucial guānjiàn; **it's absolutely crucial** nèi fēicháng guānjiàn

cruise (*by ship*) zuòchuán lǚxíng

crutch (*of body*) xiàshēn

crutches shuāngguǎi

cry kū; **don't cry** bié kū

cucumber huángguā

cuisine pēngtiáo; **Chinese cuisine** Zhōngguo pēngtiáo

cultural wénhuà

Cultural Revolution Wénhuà Dàgémìng

cup bēizi; **a cup of coffee** yìbēi kāfēi

cupboard guìzi

cure zhì; **have you got something to cure it?** yǒu shénme yào kéyi zhì zhèige ma?

curlers juǎnfàqì

current (*electrical*) diànliú; (*in water*) shuǐliú

curry gālí

curtains chuānglián

curve (*noun: in road*) zhuǎnwān de dìfang

cushion kàodiàn

custom fēngsú

Customs hǎiguān

cut: **I've cut my hand** wǒ gēpò shǒu le; **could you cut a little off here?** qǐng nín cóng zhè qiē yìdiǎnr, hǎo ma?; **we were cut off** (*telephone*) xiàn duàn le; **the engine keeps cutting out** fādòngjī jīngcháng zìjǐ jiu tíng le

cutlery dāochā cānjù

cutlets ròupái

cycle qí chē; **can we cycle there?** (*is it far?*) wǒmen kéyi qí chē qù ma?

cyclist qí zìxíngchē de

cylinder (*of car*) qìgāng

cylinder-head gasket qìgāng diànquānr

cynical wánshì bù gōng

cystitis pángguāngyán

D

damage: you've damaged it ní bǎ tā nònghuàile; **it's damaged** huàile; **there's no damage** méiyǒu sǔnhuài

damn! zāole!

damp (*adjective*) cháoshī

dance tiàowǔ; **do you want to dance?** kéyi qǐng ni tiàowǔ ma?; **a Chinese dance** Zhōngguo wúdǎo

dancer wúdǎojiā; **he's a good dancer** tā shı ge hén hǎo de wúdǎojiā

dancing: do you like dancing? ni xǐhuān tiàowǔ ma?; **we'd like to go dancing** wǒmen xiǎng qù cānjiā wǔhuì; **traditional dancing** chuántǒng wúdǎo

dandruff tóupí

dangerous wēixiǎn

dare: I don't dare wǒ bù gǎn

dark (*adjective*) àn; **it's dark in here** zhèr hěn àn; **when does it get dark?** tiān shénme shíhou hēi?; **after dark** tiānhēi yǐhòu; **dark blue/green** shēn lán/lǜ

darling qīn'àide

darts tóubiāo yóuxì

dashboard yíbıǎobǎn

date: what's the date? jīntiān jǐhào?; **on what date?** jǐhào?; **can we make a date?** (*romantic, to business partner*) wǒmen dìng ge xiàcı jiànmiàn de shíjiān, hǎo ma?

dates (*to eat*) zǎor

daughter nüér; **my daughter** wó nüér

daughter-in-law xífù

dawn (*noun*) límíng; **at dawn** tiān gāng liàng

day tiān; **the day after** dì èr tiān; **the day before** qián yì tiān; **every day** měitiān; **one day** yǒuyìtiān; **can we pay by the day?** wǒmen dāngtiān fù dāngtiān de fèiyòng, xíng ma?; **have a good day!** (*said to someone who is leaving*) màn zǒu!

daylight robbery (*extortionate prices*) guì de xià rén

day trip yírìyóu

dead sǐle

deaf lóng

deaf-aid zhùtīngqì

deal (*business*) mǎimài; **we've got a good deal** wǒmen zuòle ge háo mǎimài; **it's a deal** jiù zhème dìngle; **will you deal with it?** nǐ chúli yíxia, hǎo ma?

dealer (*agent*) jīngjìrén

dear (*expensive*) guì; **it's too dear** tài guì le

death sǐwáng

decadent tuífèi

December shíèryue

decent: that's very decent of you nǐ zhēn hǎo

decide juédìng; **we haven't decided yet** wǒmen hái méi juédìng; **you decide for us** nǐ bāng wǒmen dìng yíxia ba; **it's all decided** yǐjīng pāibǎnr le

decision juédìng

deck (*on ship*) jiábǎn

deckchair zhéyǐ

declare: I have nothing to declare wǒ méi yǒu xūyao bàoguān de dōngxi

decoration (*in room*) zhuāngshì

deduct chúqù

deep shēn; **is the water deep?** shuǐ shēn ma?

deep-freeze (*noun*) lěngdòngjī

definitely yídìng; **definitely not** yídìng bù

degree (*university*) xuéwèi; (*temperature*) dù

dehydrated (*person*) tuōshuǐ

de-icer chúbīngjì

delay: the flight/train was delayed fēijı/chē wándiǎnle

deliberately gùyì
delicacy: a local delicacy dìfang
fēngwèir
delicious hǎochī
deliver sòng: **will you deliver it?**
kéyi sòng ma?
**delivery: is there another mail
delivery?** hái lái yícı xìn ma?
de luxe háohuá
denim láodòngbù
denims (*jeans*) niúzǎikù
dent: there's a dent in it pèngle ge
yìnr
dental floss yáxiàn
dentist yáyī
dentures jiǎyá
deny fǒurèn; **he denies it** tā fǒurèn
nèijiàn shìr
deodorant chúchòujì
department store bǎihuò shāngdiàn
departure chūfā
departure lounge hòujīshì
depend: it depends kànkan
qíngkuàng zài shuō; **it depends on
...** nà yào kàn ...
deposit (*downpayment*) yājīn
depressed xiāochén
depth shēndù
description miáoxiě
deserted (*beach, area*) méi dà yǒu rén
dessert tiánshí
destination mùdìdì
detergent jiéjìngjì
detour ràoxíngdào
devaluation biǎnzhí
**develop: could you develop these
films?** qǐng nín bāng wǒ chōng yixia
zhèixie jiāojuǎnr, hǎo ma?
diabetic (*noun*) tángniàobìng
diagram túbiǎo
dialect fāngyán
dialling code chángtú qūhào
diamond zuànshí
diaper niàobù
diarrh(o)ea lādùzı; **do you have
something to stop diarrh(o)ea?** yǒu
zhì lādùzı de yào ma?
diary (*for personal experiences*) rìjì;
(*business etc*) gōngzuò rìjì
dictionary cídiǎn; **a Chinese-English
dictionary** Hàn-Yīng cídiǎn
didn't *see* **not** *and pages 105-106*

die sǐ; **I'm absolutely dying for a
drink** wo kěsıle
diesel (*fuel*) cháiyóu
diet: I'm on a diet wǒ zai jiéshí
difference bùtóng; **what's the difference between ... and ...?** ... hé ...
zhījiān yǒu shénme bùtóng?; **I can't
tell the difference** wǒ kàn bù chū
yǒu shénme bùtóng; **it doesn't make
any difference** méi guānxi
different bùtóng; **they are different**
tāmen bùtóng; **they are very different** tāmen hěn bùtóng; **it's different
from this one** gēn zhèige bù yíyàng;
may we have a different table?
wǒmen huàn ge zhuōzı, xíng ma?;
ah well, that's different nà shı
lìngwài yìhuíshìr
difficult kùnnan
difficulty kùnnan; **without any
difficulty** méiyǒu yìdiǎnr kùnnan;
**I'm having difficulty learning
Chinese** wǒ xué Hànyǔ yǒu kùnnan;
**I'm having difficulty finding a
room** wó zhǎobuzháo dìfang zhù
digestion xiāohuà
dinghy xiǎochuán
dining car cānchē
dining room cāntīng
dinner wǎnfàn
dinner jacket yèlǐfú
dinner party jiāyàn
dipped headlights dídēng
dipstick liángyóugǎnr
direct (*adjective*) zhíjiē; **please give me
a direct answer** qǐng zhíjiē huída
wǒ; **is it a direct flight?** zhí fēi ma?
direction fāngxiàng; **in which direction is it?** zài něige fāngxiàng?; **is it
in this direction?** shı zhèige
fāngxiàng ma?
directory: telephone directory
diànhuàbù
directory enquiries cháhàotái
dirty zāng
disabled cánfèi
disagree: it disagrees with me (*food*)
nèige wǒ bù néng chī
disappear bújiànle; **my camera has
disappeared** wǒde zhàoxiàngji
bújiànle
disappointed: I was disappointed wó

ong	ou	q	u	un	ü	ʊ	ui	uo	x	yan	z	zh
ung	soul	ch	soon	open	huge	huge	way	wor	sh	yen	dz	j

hěn shīwàng

disappointing bù zěnmeyàng; **the film/visit was disappointing** diànyǐng/cānguǎn bù zěnmeyàng

disaster zāinàn

discharge (*pus*) chūnóng

disco dísīkè

disco dancing dísīkè

discount (*noun*) zhékòu

disease jíbìng

disgusting (*taste, food etc*) ěxīn

dish (*meal*) cài; (*plate*) pánzı

dishcloth xíwǎnbù

dishwashing liquid jiéjìngjì

disinfectant (*noun*) xiāodújì

dislocated shoulder jiānbǎng tuōjiù

dispensing chemist youquán kāi chùfāng de yàofāng

disposable nappies (*yícìxìng yòng*) niàobù

distance: what's the distance from ... to ...? cóng ... dào ... yǒu duōyuǎn?; **in the distance** zai yuǎnchù

distilled water zhēngliúshuǐ

distributor (*in car*) pèidiànqì

disturb dárǎo; **please do not disturb me** qǐng bié dárǎo wo; **the loudspeaker is disturbing us** lǎba bá wǒmen cháosīle

diversion (*traffic*) ràoxíngdào

diving board tiàobǎn

divorced líhūn

dizzy tóuyūn; **I feel dizzy** wǒ tóuyūn

dizzy spells: I suffer from dizzy spells wǒ jīngcháng tóuyūn

do zuò; **will you do it for me?** máfan nǐ bāng wo zuò yixia, hǎo ma?; **how do you do it?** gāi zěnme zuò?; **what are they doing?** tāmen zai zuò shénme?; **what do you do?** nǐ shı zuò shénme gōngzuò de?; **what am I to do?** wǒ gāi zěnme bàn?; **what shall we do tonight?** wǒmen jīntian wǎnshang gàn shénme?; **who did it?** shéi gàn de?; **well done!** gàn de hǎo!; **the meat is not done** ròu méi shú; **do you have ...?** ní yǒu ... ma?

docks mǎtou

doctor yīsheng; **he needs a doctor** tā xūyào qǐng yíwei yīsheng; **can you call a doctor?** nín kéyi qǐng yíwei yīsheng lái ma?; **I'm going to the doctor** wǒ qù kànbìng

document wénjiàn

dog gǒu

doll yángwáwa

dollar měiyuán

donkey lǘ

don't! bié!; *see* **not** *and pages 105, 114*

door mén

doorman bǎménrde

dosage jìliàng

double: double room shuāngrenjiān; **double bed** shuāngrenchuáng; **double brandy** shuāngfènr báilándì; **double 'r'** (*in spelling name*) liǎngge 'r'; **it's all double Dutch to me** zhèi gēn kàn tiānshū shìde

doubt: I doubt it wǒ yóudiǎnr huáiyí

down xià; **get down!** xiàlai!; **he's not down yet** (*is in room, bed*) tā hái méi xiàlai; **further down the road** zhèitiáo lù zài wǎn qián; **I paid 20% down** wǒ xiān fù le bǎifēnzhı èrshí

downmarket (*restaurant, hotel*) chājìn

downstairs lóuxià

dozen yìdá; **half a dozen** bàndá

dragon lóng

drain (*in sink, street*) xiàshuǐdào

draughts (*game*) xīyáng tiàoqí

draughty: it's rather draughty yǒu chuāntáng fēng

drawing pin túdīng

dreadful zāotòule

dream (*noun*) mèng; **it's like a bad dream** (*this trip etc*) xiàng zuòle chǎng èmèng; **sweet dreams!** zuò ge hǎo mèng!

dress (*woman's*) liányīqún; **I'll just get dressed** wǒ qù chuānshang yīfu

dressing (*for wound*) fūliào; (*for salad*) shālāyóu

dressing gown chényī

drink (*verb*) hē; **can I get you a drink?** hē diǎnr shénme ba?; **I don't drink** (*alcohol*) wǒ bú huì hē jiǔ; **I must have something to drink** (*alcoholic and non-alcoholic*) wó děi hē diǎnr shénme; **drink up!** kuài hē!; **I had too much to drink** wǒ hē duōle; **may I have a drink of water?** qǐng lái dianr shuǐ, hǎo ma?; **a long cool drink** yìdàbēi léngyǐn

drinkable: is the water drinkable?

ai	ao	c	e	ei	en	h	i	ɪ	ian	ie	iu	o
I	how	ts	her	ay	open	loch	ee	sir	yen	yeh	yoyo	or

zhèi shuǐ kéyi hē ma?
drive: we drove here wǒmen kāichē
lái de; **I'll drive you home** wǒ
kāichē sòng nǐ huíjiā; **is it a very
long drive?** chē yào kāi hén jiǔ ma?;
let's go for a drive wǒmen kāichē
dōudōufēng qù
driver (*of car, bus*) sījī
driver's license jiàshǐzhízhào
drive shaft zhǔdòngzhóu
driving licence jiàshǐzhízhào
drizzle: it's drizzling zai xià xiǎo
máomaoyǔ
drop: just a drop (*of drink*)
yìdīngdiǎnr; **I dropped the cup/my
watch** wó bǎ bēizı/biǎo shuāi le;
drop in some time yǒu kòng lái
wánr
drown: they drowned tāmen yānsıle
drug (*medical*) yào; (*narcotic*) dúpǐn
drugstore jiān shòu záhuò de
yàofáng
drunk (*adjective*) hēzuìle

drunken driving jiǔ hòu kāichē
dry (*adjective*) gān
**dry-clean: can I get these dry-
cleaned?** zhèi kéyi gānxǐ ma?
dry-cleaner gānxǐdiàn
duck yā
due: when is the bus due? chē gāi
jídiǎn lái?
dumb (*can't speak*) yǎbā; (*stupid*) bèn
dummy (*for baby*) xiàngpí náizuǐr
durex (*tm*) bìyùntào
**during ... ... de shíhou; during the
meal/meeting/trip** chīfàn/kāihuì/
lǚxíng de shíhou
dust huī
dustbin lājīxiāng
duty-free (*goods*) miǎnshuì
dynamo fādiànjī; (*for bike*) módiànlún
dynasty cháo: **the Ming Dynasty/
Qing (Ch'ing) Dynasty** Míngcháo/
Qīngcháo
dysentery lìji

E

each měi; **each of them** měi yígè; **one
for each of us** wǒmen yìrén yígè;
how much are they each? yígè yào
duōshao qián?; **each time** měi yícì;
we know each other wǒmen rènshı
ear ěrduo
earache: I have earache wó ěrduo
téng
early zǎo; **early in the morning**
yìzǎo; **it's too early** tài zǎo le; **a day
earlier** yìtiān yǐqián; **half an hour
earlier** bàn xiǎoshı yǐqián; **I need an
early night** wó dei zǎo shuì le
early riser: I'm an early riser wó
qǐde hén zǎo
earring ěrhuán
earth (*soil*) túrǎng
earthenware táoqì
east dōng; **to the east of ...** zai ...
yǐdōng

Easter fùhuójié
easy róngyì; **easy with the cream!**
mànzhe diǎnr dào!
eat chī; (*have a meal*) chīfàn; **I'd like
something to eat** wó xiǎng chī diǎnr
shénme; **we've already eaten** wǒmen
yǐjing chīle
eau-de-Cologne kēlóng xiāngshuǐ
eccentric gǔguài
edible kéyǐ chī de
EEC Ōuzhōu gòngtóngtǐ
efficient (*hotel, organization*) yǒu xiàolü
egg jīdàn
eggplant qiézı
Eire Àiěrlán
either: either ... or ... bú shı ... jiùshı
...; **I don't like either of them**
liǎngge wǒ dōu bù xǐhuān
elastic (*noun*) sōngjǐndàir
elastic band xiàngpíjīnr

Elastoplast (*tm*) zhíxuě gāobù
elbow gēbozhŏu
electric diàn
electric blanket (*under the sheet*) diàn rùzı
electric cooker diàn lúzào
electric fire diàn lúzı
electrician diàngōng
electricity diàn
electric outlet diànyuán chāzuò
elegant (*people*) wényǎ; (*thing*) yǎzhì
elevator diàntī
else: something else biéde dōngxi; **someone else** biéren; **somewhere else** biéde dìfang; **let's go somewhere else** wŏmen qù biéde dìfang ba; **what else?** hái yào shénme ma?; **nothing else, thanks** bú yào le, xièxie
embarrassed: he's embarrassed tā bù hǎoyìsı le
embarrassing shǐ rén bù hǎoyìsı
embassy dàshíguǎn
emergency jǐnjí qíngkuàng; **this is an emergency** zhèi shı ge jǐnjí qíngkuàng
emery board zhǐjiacuò
emotional (*person*) róngyì dòng gǎnqíng de
emperor huángdì
empty kōng
end (*noun*) jìntóu; **at the end of the road** zai mǎlù jìntóu; **when does it end?** shénme shíhou jiéshù?
energetic (*person*) yŏu jīngshen
energy (*of person*) jīnglì
engaged (*to be married*) dìnghūn; (*toilet*) yŏurén
engagement ring dìnghūn jièzhı
engine fādòngjī
engine trouble fādòngjī de máobìng
England Yīngguó
English (*spoken*) Yīngyǔ; (*written*) Yīngwén; **the English** Yīngguoren; **I'm English** wŏ shı Yīngguoren; **do you speak English?** ní jiǎng Yīngyǔ ma?
Englishman Yīngguoren
Englishwoman Yīngguoren
enjoy: I enjoyed the meal very much wŏ chīde hén hǎo; **we enjoyed the day very much** wŏmen wánrde hén hǎo; **we enjoyed today's visit very much** wŏmen jīntian de cānguān hén hǎo; **we enjoyed the film very much** zhèige diànyǐng hén hǎo
enjoyable yúkuàide
enlargement (*of photo*) fàngdà
enormous dàjíle
enough gòu; **there's not enough** bú gòu; **it's not big enough** bú gòu dà; **thank you, that's enough** gòu le, xièxie
entertainment yúlè
enthusiastic yŏu rèqíng
entrance (*noun*) rùkŏu
envelope xìnfēng
epilepsy yángjiǎofēng
equipment (*in apartment*) shèbei; (*for climbing etc*) qìxie
eraser xiàngpí
erotic sèqíngde
error cuòwù
escalator zìdòng diàntī
especially tèbié
essential: it is essential that ... ... shı juéduì bìyào de
estate agent fángdìchǎn jīngjìrén
ethnic (*restaurant*) yŏu mínzú tèsè de
Europe Ōuzhōu
European Ōuzhou de; (*person*) Ōuzhouren
even: even the English/Americans can use chopsticks lián Yīngguoren/Měiguoren dōu huì yòng kuàizı; **even I/they like it** lián wŏ/tāmen dōu xǐhuan; **even if ...** jiùshı ... yě; **I'm going even if it rains/snows** jiùshı xià yǔ/xià xuě, wó yě qù
evening wǎnshang; **good evening** ní hǎo; **this evening** jīntian wǎnshang; **in the evening** wǎnshang; **evening meal** wǎnfàn
evening dress (*for man and woman*) yè lǐfú
eventually zuìhòu
ever: have you ever been to ...? nǐ qùguo ... ma?; **if you ever come to Britain ...** rúguo nǐ jiānglái yŏu jīhuì lái Yīngguo de huà ...
every měi; **every day** měitiān
everyone měige ren
everything: everything is ready shénme dōu hǎole; **I like everything**

wǒ shénme dōu xǐhuan; **that's everything thanks** hǎole, jiù zhèixie; **is that everything you have?** hái yǒu biéde ma?

everywhere měige dìfang

exactly! duìjíle!

exam kǎoshì

example lìzi; **for example** lìrú

excellent *(food, hotel)* hǎojíle; **excellent!** hǎojíle!

except ... chúle ... yǐwài; **except Sunday** chúle xīngqitiān yǐwài

exception lìwài; **as an exception** zuòwei yíge lìwài

excess baggage chāozhòng xíngli

excessive guòfèn; **that's a bit excessive** yóu diǎnr guòfèn

exchange *(verb: money)* duìhuàn; **in exchange** zuòwei jiāohuàn

exchange rate: what's the exchange rate? duìhuànlǜ shi duōshao?

exciting *(day, holiday, film)* zhēn láijìn

exclusive *(club, hotel)* gāojí

excursion yóulǎn; **is there an excursion to ...?** dào ... yǒu yóulǎn chē ma?

excuse me *(apology, to get past)* duìbuqǐ; *(to get attention)* máfan nín, qǐng wèn ...; *(pardon?)* qǐng zài shuō yíbian, hǎo ma?; *(informal: pardon?)* shénme?; *(annoyed)* duì bù qǐ!

exhaust *(on car)* páiqìguǎn

exhausted *(tired)* lèisǐle

exhibition zhánlǎnhuì

exist cúnzài

exit chūkǒu

expect: I expect so wó xiǎng kěnéng shi zhèiyang: **she's expecting** tā huáiyùn le

expensive guì

experience jīngyàn; **an absolutely unforgettable experience** juéduì nánwàng de yícì jīnglì

experienced yǒu jīngyàn

expert zhuānjiā

expire: it's expired *(passport etc)* guòqīle

explain jiěshì; **would you explain that to me?** nín néng bāng wo jiěshì yíxia ma?

explore tànxiǎn; **I just want to go and explore** wǒ jiùshi xiǎng zìji qù kànkan

export *(verb)* chūkǒu

exposure meter bàoguāngbiǎo

express *(mail)* kuàidì; *(train)* kuàichē

extra é wài; **can we have an extra chair/room?** zài yào yìbá yǐzi/yíge fángjiān, xíng ma?; **is that extra?** *(in cost)* hái yào zài shōufèi ma?

extraordinarily fēicháng

extraordinary *(very strange)* zhēn qíguài

extremely fēicháng

extrovert wàixiàng de

eye yǎnjīng; **will you keep an eye on my bags for me?** máfan nín bāng wǒ kān yíxia bāo, hǎo ma?

eyebrow méimao

eyebrow pencil miáoméibǐ

eye drops yǎnyàoshuǐr

eyeliner yǎnxiàn

eye shadow yányǐng

eye witness jiànzhèngrén

F

fabulous tài bàngle

face liǎn

face cloth *(flannel)* xíliǎn máojīn

face mask *(for diving)* qiánshuǐ miànjù

facing: facing the sea/hotel duìzhe dàhǎi/fàndiàn

fact shìshí

factory gōngchǎng

Fahrenheit huáshì; *see page 119*

faint yūn; **she's fainted** tā yūndǎole; **I'm going to faint** wǒ kuài yūn le

fair *(fun-fair)* yóuyìchǎng; *(commercial)*

ong	ou	q	u	un	ü	ʊ	ui	uo	x	yan	z	zh
ung	soul	ch	soon	open	huge	huge	way	wor	sh	yen	dz	j

jiāoyìhuì; **it's not fair** bù gōngpíng;
OK, fair enough xíng
fake màopáirhuò
fall: he's had a fall tā shuāile yìjiāo;
he fell off his bike tā cóng
zìxíngchēshang shuāile xiàlai; **in the
fall** (*autumn*) qiūtian
false jiǎ
false teeth jiǎyá
family jiātíng
family name xìng
famished: I'm famished wǒ èsıle
famous yǒumíng
fan (*mechanical*) fēngshàn; (*hand held*)
shànzı; (*football etc*) qiúmí
fan belt fēngshàn pídài
fancy: he fancies you tā duì nǐ tè
gǎn xìngqu
fancy dress party huàzhuāng wǔhuì
fantastic tài hǎole
far yuǎn; **is it far?** yuǎn ma?; **how far
is it to ...?** dào ... yǒu duō yuǎn?; **as
far as I'm concerned** duì wǒ lái
shuō
fare chēqian; **what's the fare to ...?**
dào ... duōshao qián?
farewell party gàobié yànhuì
farm nóngchǎng
farther háiyao yuǎn; **farther than ...**
bǐ ... háiyao yuǎn
fashion (*in clothes etc*) shízhuāng
fashionable shímáo
fast kuài; **not so fast** (*as something else*)
méi zhème kuài; (*slow down a bit*)
màn yidiǎnr
fastener (*on clothes*) yīkòu
fat (*person*) pàng; (*on meat*) féi
father: my father wǒ fùqin
father-in-law yuèfù
fathom yīngxún
fattening: it's fattening zhèi dōngxi
chīle fāpàng
faucet shuǐlóngtóu
fault cuò; **it was my fault** shı wǒde
cuò; **it's not my fault** bú shı wǒde
cuò
faulty (*equipment*) yǒu máobìng
favo(u)rite zuì xǐhuan de; **that's my
favo(u)rite** nà shı wǒ zuì xǐhuan de
fawn (*colour*) qiǎn huánghèsè
February èryue
fed up: I'm fed up wǒ zhēn nıle; **I'm**

fed up with ... wǒ duì ... zhēn nıle
feeding bottle nǎipíng
feel: I feel hot/cold wǒ rè/lěng le; I
feel like a drink** wó xiǎng hē diǎnr
shénme; **I don't feel like it** wǒ bú
da xiǎng; **how are you feeling
today?** nǐ jīntian juéde zěnmeyàng?;
I'm feeling a lot better wǒ juéde
hǎo duōle
felt-tip pen ruǎntóubǐ
fen (*currency*) fēn
fence zhàlán
fender (*bumper*) báoxiǎngàng
ferry bǎidù; **what time's the last
ferry?** zuìhou yìbān bǎidù shı jídiǎn?
festival jiérì
fetch qǔ; **I'll go and fetch it** wǒ qù
ná; **will you come and fetch me?** nǐ
néng lái jiē wǒ ma?
fever fāshāo
feverish: I'm feeling feverish wǒ yǒu
diǎnr fāshāo
few: only a few jiù jǐge; **a few
minutes** jǐfēn zhōng; **he's had a
good few (to drink)** tā hēde bùshǎo
fiancé: my fiancé wǒde wèihūnfū
fiancée: my fiancée wǒde wèihūnqī
fiasco: what a fiasco! zhēn luàntàole!
field tiándì
fifty-fifty yíbànr yíbànr
fight (*noun*) dǎzhàng
figs wúhuāguǒ
figure (*of person*) tǐxíng; (*number*)
shùzı; **I have to watch my figure** wó
děi zhùyì tǐxíng le
fill zhuāngmǎn; **fill her up please**
qíng bǎ yóu jiāmǎn; **will you help
me fill out this form?** nǐ néng bāng
wǒ tiántian zhèizhāng biǎo ma?
fillet (*pork*) lǐjī; (*fish*) yúpiànr
filling: this tooth needs a filling zhèi
yá yào bǔ; **it's very filling** (*food*) zhèi
dōngxi yì chī jiù bǎo
filling station jiāyóuzhàn
film (*in cinema*) diànyǐng; (*for camera*)
jiāojuǎnr; **do you have this type of
film?** nǐ yǒu zhèizhǒng jiāojuǎnr
ma?; **16mm film** shíliù háomǐ
jiāojuǎnr; **35mm film** sānshıwǔ
háomǐ jiāojuǎnr
filter (*for camera*) lùsèjìng; (*for coffee*)
kāfēi guòlùzhǐ

ai	ao	c	e	ei	en	h	i	ı	ian	ie	iu	o
I	how	ts	her	ay	open	loch	ee	sir	yen	yeh	**yo**yo	or

filter-tipped dài guòlǜzuǐr de
filthy (*room etc*) zāng
find zhǎodào; **I can't find it** wó zhǎobúdào; **if you find it ...** rúguǒ ni zhǎodào de huà ...; **I've found a ...** wǒ fāxiànle yíge ...
fine: it's fine weather tiānr zhēn hǎo; **a 300 yuan fine** fákuǎn sānbǎi yuán; **how are you? – fine thanks** ní hǎo? – hǎo, xièxie
finger zhítou
fingernail zhǐjia
finish: I haven't finished wǒ hái méi gànwán; **I haven't finished eating** wǒ hái méi chīwán; **when I've finished** wǒ gànwán yǐhòu; **when I've finished eating** wǒ chīwán yǐhòu; **when does it finish?** shénme shíhou néng wán?; **finish off your drink** bá nǐde hēwán
fire: fire! (*something's on fire*) huǒ!; **may we light a fire here?** wǒmen néng zai zhèr diánhuǒ ma?; **it's on fire** zháohuǒle; **it's not firing properly** (*car*) zhèi chē lǎo bù háohǎo dáhuǒ
fire alarm huójǐng
fire brigade, fire department xiāofángduì
fire engine jiùhuǒchē
fire escape tàipíngtī
fire extinguisher mièhuǒqì
firm (*company*) gōngsī
first dìyī; **I was first** wǒ dìyī; **at first** shǒuxiān; **this is the first time** zhè shı̀ dìyīcì
first aid jíjiù
first aid kit jíjiùxiāng
first class (*travel etc*) yīdéng
first name míngzı
fish (*noun*) yú
fisherman yúfū
fishing diàoyú
fishing boat yúchuán
fishing net yúwǎng
fishing rod yúgānr
fishing tackle diàojù
fishing village yúcūn
fit (*healthy*) jiànkāng; **I'm not very fit** wǒ shēnti bù zěnme xíng; **he's a keep fit fanatic** tā duànlian zháolemí; **it doesn't fit** bù héshì

fix: can you fix it? (*repair*) nǐ néng xiūxiu ma?; (*arrange*) nǐ néng ānpai yíxia ma?; **let's fix a time** wǒmen dìng ge shíjiān ba; **it's all fixed up** dōu ānpaihǎole; **I'm in a bit of a fix** wǒ yóudiǎnr máfanshìr
fizzy yǒuqìde
fizzy drink qìshuǐr
flag qí
flannel xíliǎn máojīn
flash (*for camera*) shǎnguāngdēng
flashlight shǒudiàntǒng
flashy (*clothes etc*) huāshaode
flat (*adjective*) píng; **this beer is flat** zhèi píjiǔ zǒuqìle; **I've got a flat tyre/tire** wǒde chētāi biěle; (*apartment*) dānyuán
flatterer mǎpìjīng
flatware cānjù
flavo(u)r wèidao
flea tiàozao
flea bite tiàozao yǎo de gēda
flea powder tiàozào fěn
flexible (*material*) yǒu rènxing; (*arrangements*) línghuó
flies (*on trousers*) qiándāng
flight hángbān
flirt tiǎodòu
float piāo
flood hóngshuǐ
floor (*of room*) dìbǎn; **on the floor** zai dìshang; **on the second floor** (*UK*) zai sānlóu; (*USA*) zai èrlóu
floorshow yèzǒnghuì jiémù biǎoyǎn
flop (*failure*) záguōle
florist màihuārde
flour miànfěn
flower huā
flu liúgǎn
fluent: he speaks fluent Chinese tā Hànyǔ jiǎngde hěn liúlì
fly (*verb*) fēi; **can we fly there?** dào nàr yǒu fēijī ma?
fly (*insect*) cāngying
fly spray mièyíngjì
fly swat cāngyingpāir
foggy: it's foggy yǒu wù
fog lights wùdēng
folk dancing mínjiān wúdǎo
folk music mínjiān yīnyuè
follow: follow me qǐng gēn wǒ lái
fond: I'm quite fond of ... wǒ hén

xǐhuān ...

food: have you got any food? yǒu chǐde ma?; **I like Chinese food** wó xǐhuān Zhōngguo fàn; **the food here is excellent** zhèr de fàn zuòde hén hǎo

food poisoning shíwù zhòngdú

food store shípǐn diàn

fool shǎguā

foolish shǎ

foot jiǎo; **on foot** bùxíng; *see page 117*

football (*ball*) zúqiú; (*game*) zúqiusài

for: is that for me/her? nà shı géi wǒ/tā de ma?; **what's this for?** zhè shı gàn shénme de?; **for two days** liǎngtiān; **I've been here for a week** wǒ zai zhèr yǐjīng yíge xīngqi le; **a bus for ...** dào ... de gōnggòng qìchē

forbidden jìnzhǐ

Forbidden City Zíjǐnchéng

forehead nǎoménr

foreign wàiguó

foreigner wàiguoren

foreign exchange (*money*) wàihuì

foreign exchange certificate wàihuìjuànr

forest sēnlín

forget wàngjì; **I forget, I've forgotten** wǒ wàngle; **don't forget** bié wàngle

fork (*for eating*) chāzı; (*in road*) chàlù

form (*in hotel, to fill out*) biǎo

formal (*person*) zhèngjǐng; (*language*) zhèngshì; **formal dress** lǐfú

fortnight liǎngge xīngqi

fortunately xìngkuī

fortune-teller suànmìng xiānsheng

forward: could you forward my mail? nín néng bāng wǒ zhuǎn yíxia xìn ma?

forwarding address zhuǎnxìn dìzhǐ

foundation cream féndǐshuāng

fountain (*ornamental*) pēnquán; (*for drinking*) yínshuǐ lóngtóu

foyer (*of hotel, theatre*) qiántīng

fracture (*noun*) lièfèng

fractured skull: he has a fractured skull tāde tóugǔ you lièfèng

fragile hěn róngyi suì

frame (*for picture*) jìngkuàngr; (*of bike*) chējià

France Fǎguó

fraud (*crime*) zhàpiàn; (*goods*) màopáirhuò; (*person*) piànzı

free (*at liberty*) zìyóu; (*costing nothing*) miǎnfèi; **admission free** miǎnfèi rùchǎng

freezer lěngdòngjī

freezing cold lěngjíle

French Fǎguó; (*language*) Fáyǔ; **a French person** Fǎguoren

French fries zhá tǔdoutiáor

frequent jīngcháng

fresh (*weather, breeze*) qīngxīn; (*fruit etc*) xīnxian; (*cheeky*) táoqì; **don't get fresh with me** zhùyì diǎnr!

fresh orange juice xiān júzhī

friction tape (*insulating*) juéyuán jiāobù

Friday xīngqiwǔ

fridge bīngxiāng

fried egg jiānjīdàn

fried noodles chǎomiàn

fried rice chǎofàn

friend péngyou

friendly yóuhǎo

friendship store yǒuyí shāngdiàn

frog qīngwā

from cóng; **from here to the sea** cóng zhèr dào hǎibiānr; **the next boat from ...** cóng ... lái de xiàyibān chuán; **as from Tuesday** cóng xīngqièr kāishǐ; **I'm from London** wǒ shı Lúndūnren

front qián; **in front** zai qiábianr; **in front of us** zai wǒmen qiánbianr; **at the front** zai qiánbianr

front fork (*of bike*) qiánchā

frozen bīngdòngde

frozen food bīngdòng shípǐn

fruit shuíguǒ

fruit juice guǒzhī

fruit salad shuíguǒ shālā

frustrating: it's very frustrating zhēn jiào ren shēnqì

fry zhá; **nothing fried, please** búyào zhá de dōngxi

frying pan chǎocàiguō

full mǎn; **my case is full** wǒde xiāngzı mǎnle; **it's full** (*hotel*) quán zhùmǎnle, (*restaurant*) quán zuòmǎnle; **I'm full** wó bǎole

full-bodied (*wine*) nóng

fun: it's fun hén hǎowánr; **it was great fun** zhēn hǎowánr; **just for**

ai	ao	c	e	ei	en	h	i	ı	ian	ie	iu	o
I	how	ts	her	ay	open	loch	ee	sir	yen	yeh	yoyo	or

fun jiùshı còu ge rènao; **let's go out and have some fun** wǒmen chūqu wánrwanr ba
funeral zànglǐ
funny (*strange*) qíguài; (*amusing*) yǒu yìsı
furniture jiājù
further: 2 **kilametres/kilometers**

further hái you liǎng gōngli; **go further down the road** shùnzhe zhèitiáo lù zài wǎng qián zǒu
fuse (*noun*) báoxiǎnsī; **the lights have fused** báoxiǎnsī duànle
fuse wire báoxiǎnsī
future jiānglái; **in future** jiānglái

G

gale dàfēng
gallon jiālún; *see page 119*
gallstones dǎnjiēshí
gamble dǔqián; **I don't gamble** wǒ bù dǔqián
game yóuxì; (*match*) bǐsài
games room yóuyìshì
gammon làròu
garage (*for petrol*) jiāyóuzhàn; (*for repairs*) xiūchēchǎng; (*for parking*) tíngchēchǎng
garbage lājī
garden huāyuán
garlic dàsuàn
gas méiqì; (*gasoline*) qìyóu
gas cylinder (*for Calor gas etc*) méiqìpíng
gasket diànquānr
gas pedal yóumenr
gas permeable lenses kě tòuqì de yǐnxíng yǎnjìng
gas station jiāyóuzhàn
gas tank yóuxiāng
gastroenteritis chángwèiyán
gate dàménr; (*at airport*) dēngjīkǒu
gauge (*specification*) guīgé; (*railway*) guǐjù
gay (*homosexual*) gǎo tóngxìngliàn de
gear chǐlún; **the gears keep sticking** chǐlún láo gei yǎozhù; **a bike with gears** biànsù zìxíngchē
gearbox biànsùxiāng; **I have gearbox trouble** wǒde biànsùxiāng chū máobìng le
gear lever, gear shift biànsùgǎnr

general delivery liújú dàilǐng yóujiàn
generous: that's very generous of you nǐ zhēnshı tài hǎole; **he is very generous** tā zhèi ren hěn dàfang
gentleman (*man*) xiānsheng; **that gentleman over there** nèibiānr de nèiwei xiāngsheng; **he's such a gentleman** tā zhēn yǒu shēnshı fēngdu
gents (*toilet*) nán cèsuǒ
genuine zhēnzhèng
German Déguó; (*person*) Déguoren; (*language*) Déyǔ
German measles fēngzhěn
Germany Déguó
get: have you got ...? nǐ yǒu ... ma?; **how do I get to ...?** dao ... zěnme qù hǎo?; **where do I get ... from?** nár yǒu ...?; **can I get you a drink?** hē diǎnr shénme ba?; **will you get it for me?** máfan nǐ bāng wo nálai, hǎo ma?; **when do we get there?** wǒmen shénme shíhou dào?; **I've got to ...** wó děi ...; **I've got to go** wó déi zǒule; **where do I get off?** wǒ zai nǎr xià chē; **it's difficult to get to** nàr hěn nán qù; **when I get up** (*in morning*) wó zǎoshang qǐchuang de shíhou
ghastly kěpà
ghost guǐ
giant panda dà xióngmāo
giddy: ... makes me giddy ... jiào wǒ tóuyūn
gift lǐwù

gigantic jùdà
gin dùsōngzı jīnjiǔ; **a gin and tonic**
jīn tuōníkè
girl nǚháir
girlfriend nǚpéngyou
give gěi; **will you give me ...?** nǐ
néng géi wǒ ... ma?; **I'll give you
100 kuai** wǒ géi ni yìbǎi kuài; **I gave
the ticket to him** wó bǎ piào gěi tā
le; **will you give it back?** nǐ néng
huánhuilai ma?; **would you give
this to ...?** ní bǎ zhè gěi ... hǎo ma?
glad gāoxìng
glamorous (*woman*) yǒu mèilì
gland xiàn
glandular fever líbāxiàn rè
glass (*material*) bōli; (*drinking*) bōlibēi;
a glass of water yìbēi liángkāishuǐ
glasses (*spectacles*) yǎnjìng
glazed tile (*on pagoda*) liúliwǎ
gloves shǒutào
glue (*noun*) jiāoshuǐr
gnat wénzı
go qù; **we want to go to ...** wǒmen
xiǎng qù ...; **I'm going there
tomorrow** wǒ míngtian qù nàr;
when does it go? (*bus etc*) chē
shénme shíhou kāi?; **where are you
going?** nǐ qù nǎr?; **let's go** wǒmen
zǒu ba; **he's gone** tā zǒule; **it's all
gone** dōu méile; **I went there
yesterday** wǒ zuótian qùde nàr; **a
dumpling to go** yíge bāozı,
dàizǒude; **go away!** gǔn!; **it's gone
off** (*milk etc*) zhèi biànzhìle; **we're
going out tonight** wǒmen jīntian
wǎnshang chūgu; **do you want to go
out tonight?** nǐ jīntian wǎnshang
xiǎng chūqu ma?; **has the price
gone up?** zhǎngjiàle ma?
goal (*sport*) défēn
goat shānyáng
goat's cheese yángnǎi nǎilào
Gobi Desert Gēbìtān
god shén
God shàngdì
goddess nǚshén
gold jīnzı
golf gāoěrfūqiú
golf clubs gāoěrfūqiú gùn
golf course gāoěrfū qiúchǎng
gong luó

good hǎo; **good!** hǎo!; **that's no good**
nèi bù hǎo; (*no use*) nèi méiyòng;
good heavens! tiān na!
goodbye zàijiàn
good-looking hǎokàn
gooey (*food etc*) tiánnì; (*sticky*)
niánhuhu de
goose é
gorgeous (*meal*) hǎochījíle; (*woman*)
měijíle
gourmet shíwù pǐnchángjiā
gourmet food gòng pǐncháng de
shípǐn
government zhèngfǔ
gradually zhújiàn de
grammar yúfǎ
gram(me) kè; *see page 117*
granddaughter sūnnǚ
grandfather zǔfù
grandmother zúmǔ
grandson sūnzı
grapefruit yòuzı
grapes pútao
grass cǎo; (*lawn*) cǎodì
grateful gǎnji; **I'm very grateful to
you** wǒ fēichang gǎnji nǐ
gravy ròuzhī
gray huīsè
grease (*for car*) dàhuángyóu; (*on food*)
yóuzhī
greasy (*food*) yóunì
great wěidà; **that's great!** hǎojíle!
Great Britain Dà Búlièdiān
Great Leap Forward Dàyuèjìn
greedy (*for money, possessions etc*) tān;
(*for food*) chán
green lǜsè
greengrocer càidiàn
green tea lǜchá
grey huīsè
grilled kǎo
gristle (*on meat*) ruángǔ
grocer záhuòdiàn
ground dì; **on the ground** zai
dìshang; **on the ground floor** zai
yīlóu
ground beef niúròu mò
group (*travel, visiting etc*) tuán; (*study,
work etc*) xiáozǔ
group insurance tuánti báoxiǎn
group leader xiǎozúzhǎng; (*of tourist
group*) tuánzhǎng

ai	ao	c	e	ei	en	h	i	ı	ian	ie	iu	o
I	how	ts	her	ay	open	loch	ee	sir	yen	yeh	**yo**yo	or

guarantee (*noun*) bǎoxiū; **is it guaranteed?** bǎo bù bǎoxiū?
guardian (*of child*) jiānhùren
guest kèren
guesthouse bīnguǎn
guide (*noun*) xiángdǎo; (*tourist*) dǎoyóu
guidebook dǎoyóu shǒucè

guilty yǒuzuì
guitar jíta
gum (*in mouth*) chǐyín; (*chewing gum*) kǒuxiāngtáng
gun qiāng
gymnasium tǐyùguǎn
gyn(a)ecologist fùkē yīsheng

H

hair tóufa
hairbrush fàshuā
haircut lǐfà; **just an ordinary haircut please** jiù jiǎndan de lǐge fà
hairdresser lǐfàshī
hairdryer diànchuīfēng
hair foam péngfàyè
hair grip fàqiǎ
hair lacquer dìngfǎyè
half yíbànr; **half an hour** bàn xiǎoshī; **a half portion** bàn fènr; **half a litre/liter** bàn shēng; **half as much** zhèige de yíbànr; **half as much again** duō yíbànr
halfway: we are halfway to Beijing wǒmen dào Běijīng, yǐjing zǒule yíbànr lù le
ham huótuǐ
hamburger hànbǎobāo
hammer (*noun*) chuízɪ
hand shǒu; **will you give me a hand?** nǐ néng bāng wǒ yíxia ma?
handbag nǚyòng shǒutíbāo
hand baggage shǒutí xíngli
handbrake shǒuzhá
handkerchief shǒujuànr
handle (*noun*) fúshǒu; **will you handle it?** zhèishìr nǐ bàn yíxia, hǎ ma?
handlebars chēbǎ
hand luggage shǒutí xíngli
handmade shǒugōng de
handsome piàoliang
hanger (*for clothes*) yījià
hangover: I've got a terrible hangover wǒ zuótian hē duōle, jīntian hái

nánshòu
happen fāshēng; **how did it happen?** shɪ zěnme huí shìr?; **what's happening?** zěnme le?; **it won't happen again** bú huì zài yǒu zhèizhǒng shìr le
happy kuàile; **we're not happy with the room** wǒmen búda xǐhuān zhèige fángjiān
harbo(u)r gángkǒu
hard yìng; (*difficult*) nán
hard-boiled egg: can I have a hard-boiled egg please? yíge jīdàn, qíng zhǔde lǎo yìdiǎnr
hard lenses yìngpian yǐnxíng yǎnjìng
hardly: hardly ever hén shǎo
hardware store wǔjīn shāngdiàn
harm (*noun*) hàichu
hassle: it's too much hassle tài máfanle; **we had a hassle-free trip** wǒmen zhèicɪ lǚxíng hěn shùnli
hat màozɪ
hate: I hate ... wǒ hèn ...
have yǒu; **do you have ...?** ní yǒu ... ma?; **can I have ...?** qíng géi wǒ ... hǎo ma?; (*ordering food*) qíng lái ..., hǎo ma?; (*in a shop*) wó xiǎng mǎi ...; **can I have some water?** qíng géi wo diǎnr liángkāishuǐ, hǎo ma?; **I have ...** wó yǒu ...; **I don't have ...** wǒ méi yǒu ...; **can we have breakfast in our room?** wǒmen kéyǐ zai fángjiānli chī zǎofàn ma?; **have another** zài lái yíge; **I have to leave early** wó děi záodiǎnr zǒu; **do I**

have to ...? wǒ yídìng děi ... ma?; **do we have to ...?** wǒmen yídìng děi ... ma?; *see page 105, 111*

hay fever huāfēnrè

he tā; **is he here?** tā zài ma?; **where does he live?** tā zhù nǎr?; *see page 97*

head tóu; **we're heading for Fuzhou** wǒmen xiànzai de fāngxiàng shì qù Fúzhōu

headache tóuténg

headlights chētóudēng

headphones ěrjī

head waiter fúwù zúzhǎng

head wind nìfēng

health jiànkāng; **your health!** zhù nǐ jiànkāng!

healthy (*person*) jiànkāng; **this food is very healthy** zhèige chīle duì shēnti hǎo

hear: can you hear me? nǐ néng tīngjiàn ma?; **I can't hear you** wǒ tīngbújiàn; **I've heard about it** wǒ tīngshuōguo

hearing aid zhùtīngqì

heart xīnzàng

heart attack xīnjī géngsǐ

heat rè; **not in this heat!** zhèi dà rè tiānr?

heated rollers jiārè juǎnfàqì

heater (*in car*) sànrèqì

heating nuǎnqì

heat rash fèizi

heat stroke zhòngshǔ

heatwave rèlàng

heavy zhòng

hectic mánglùàn

heel (*of foot, of shoe*) gēnr; **could you put new heels on these?** qǐng nín bāng wo huànhuan xiéhòugēnr, hǎo ma?

heelbar xiūxiépù

height (*of person*) shēngāo; (*of mountain*) gāodù

helicopter zhíshēng fēijī

hell: oh hell! zāole!; **go to hell!** géi wo gǔn!

hello éi; (*in surprise*) èi!; (*on phone*) wéi

helmet (*for motocycle*) tóukuī

help (*verb*) bāngzhù; **can you help me?** nǐ néng bāng wǒ ge máng ma?;

thanks for your help xièxie nǐde bāngzhù; **help!** jiùmìng a!

helpful: he was very helpful tā bāngle dà máng; **that's helpful** hén yǒuyòng

helping (*of food*) fènr

hepatitis gānyán

her tā; **I don't know her** wǒ bú rènshi tā; **will you send it to her?** nǐ jì gěi tā, hǎo ma?; **it's her** shì tā; **with her** gēn tā yìqǐ; **this is for her** zhèi shì gěi tā de; **I'll do it for her** wǒ bāng tā zuò; **that's her suitcase** nà shì tāde xiāngzi; *see pages 97-98*

herbs (*medicinal*) cǎoyào; (*for food*) zuóliào

here zhèr; **here you are** (*giving something*) géi nǐ; **here he comes** tā láile

hers tāde; **that's hers** nà shì tāde; *see page 98*

hey! hèi!

hi! èi!

hiccups dǎgé

hide cáng

hideous (*appearance*) chǒu; (*taste, food*) nánchī; (*conditions*) zāotòule

high gāo

high beam gāodēng

highchair yīng'ér gāojiáoyǐ

highway gōnglù

hiking túbù lǚxíng

hill shān

hillside shānyāo

hilly yǒu shàngxiàpō de

him tā; **I don't know him** wǒ bú rènshi tā; **will you send it to him?** nǐ jì gěi tā, hǎo ma?; **it's him** shì tā; **with him** gēn tā yìqǐ; **this is for him** zhèi shì gěi tā de; **I'll do it for him** wǒ bāng tā zuò; *see pages 97-98*

hip túnbù

hire zū; **can I hire a bike here?** zhèr kéyi zū zìxíngchē ma?; **do you hire them out?** zhè kéyi chūzū ma?

his: it's his room shì tāde fángjiān; **it's his** shì tāde; *see page 98*

historical relics wénwù

history lìshǐ; **the history of China** Zhōngguo lìshǐ

hit dǎ; **he hit me** tā dǎle wǒ; **I hit my head** wǒde tóu gěi pèngle yíxia

hitch: is there a hitch? yǒu wèntí

ai	ao	c	e	ei	en	h	i	ɪ	ian	ie	iu	o
I	how	ts	her	ay	open	loch	ee	sir	yen	yeh	yoyo	or

ma?
hitch-hike dābiànchē
hitch-hiker dābiànchē de ren
hit record chàngxiāo chàngpiān
hole kŏng
holiday jiàrı; **I'm on holiday** wŏ zai dùjià
home jiā; **at home** (*in my house etc*) zai jiā; (*in my country*) zai wŏmen guójiā; **I go home tomorrow** wŏ míngtian huí jiā; **home sweet home** háishı jiāli hăo
home address jiātíng zhùzhı
homemade zìji jiālı̆ zuò de
homesick: I'm homesick wó xiăngjiāle
honest chéngshí
honestly? zhēnde ma?
honey fēngmì
honeymoon mìyuè; **it's our honeymoon** wŏmen zai dù mìyuè
honeymoon suite xīnhūn fūfù tàojiān
Hong Kong Xiānggǎng
hono(u)r: it's an hono(u)r to ...... hěn róngxìng
hood (*of car*) fādòngjīgàir
hoover (*tm*) xīchénqì
hope xīwàng; **I hope so** dànyuàn shı zhèiyang; **I hope not** dànyuàn búshı zhèiyang
horn (*of car*) lăba
horrible zāotòule
hors d'oeuvre lěngpánr
horse mǎ
horse riding qí mǎ
hose (*for car radiator*) shuĭxiāng shéguǎnr
hospital yīyuàn
hospitality hàokè; **thank you for your hospitality** xièxie nínde hàokè
host zhŭren
hostel zhāodàisuŏ
hot rè; (*curry etc*) là; **I'm hot** wŏ rèle;

I'd like something hot wó xiǎng chī diǎnr rède; **it's so hot today** jīntian zhēn rè
hotdog règǒu
hotel (*superior, where foreigners usually stay*) fàndiàn; (*small*) lǚguǎn; **at my hotel** zai wŏ zhùde fàndiàn
hotel clerk (*receptionist*) dàtīng fúwùyuán
hotplate (*on cooker*) kǎopán; (*for keeping food warm*) bǎowēnpán
hot-water bottle rèshuĭdài
hour xiǎoshí; **one hour** yì xiǎoshı; **half an hour** bàn xiǎoshı; **two hours** liáng xiǎoshı; **a quarter of an hour** yíkè zhōng
house fángzı
housewife jiātíng fùnǚ
hovercraft qìdiànchuán
how zěnme; **how do I get there?** wo zěnme qù hǎo?; **how did it happen?** shı zěnme huí shìr?; **how many?** duōshao?; **how much?** duōshao qián?; **how often?** duōchang shíjian yícì?; **how are you?** ní hǎo!; **how do you do?** ní hǎo!; **how about a beer?** hē diǎnr píjiǔ ba?; **how nice!** zhēn hǎo!; **would you show me how to?** qǐng géi wŏ shìfàn yíxia, hǎo ma?
humid cháoshī
humidity shīdù
humo(u)r: where's your sense of humo(u)r? nǐde yōumògǎn nǎr qù le?
hundredweight yīngdàn; *see page 118*
hungry: I'm hungry wŏ èle; **I'm not hungry** wŏ bú è
hurry: I'm in a hurry wŏ yóu diǎnr jíshır; **hurry up!** kuài diǎnr!; **there's no hurry** bù jí
hurt: it hurts zhēn téng; **my back hurts** wŏde yāo téng
husband: my husband wŏ zhàngfu
hydrofoil shuĭyìchuán

ong	ou	q	u	un	ü	ʊ	ui	uo	x	yan	z	zh
ung	s**ou**l	ch	s**oo**n	**open**	h**uge**	h**uge**	**way**	w**or**	sh	y**en**	dz	j

I

I wǒ; **I am English** wǒ shì Yīngguoren; **I live in Manchester** wǒ zhù zai Mànchèsītè
ice bīng; **with ice** jiā bīngkuàir; **with ice and lemon** jia bīngkuàir níngméng
ice cream bīngjílíng
ice-cream cone dànjuǎnr bīngjílíng
iced coffee bīngzhèn kāfēi
ice lolly bīnggùnr
idea zhúyì; **good idea!** hǎo zhúyì!
ideal (*solution, time*) líxiǎng
identity papers shēnfènzhèng
ideogram, ideograph fāngkuàirzì
idiot shǎguā
idyllic tiányuánshī bān de
if rúguǒ; **if you could** rúguǒ kéyi de huà; **if not** rúguǒ bùxíng de huà
ignition diánhuǒ
ill yǒu bìng; **I feel ill** wǒ bù shūfu
illegal bù héfǎ
illegible zìjì bù qīng
illness jíbìng
imitation (*leather etc*) fǎng
immediately mǎshang
immigration yíjū
import (*verb*) jìnkǒu
important zhòngyào; **it's very important** hěn zhòngyào; **it's not important** bú zhòngyào
impossible bù kěnéng
impressive (*building*) xióngwěi; (*person*) kuíwǔ
improve: it's improving yóu gǎijìn; **I want to improve my Chinese** wó xiǎng jìnyíbù tígāo zìjide Hànyǔ shuǐpíng
improvement gǎijìn
in: in my room zai wǒ fángjiānli; **in the town centre** zai shì zhōngxīn; **in London** zai Lúndūn; **in one hour's time** guò yì xiǎoshì; **in August** zai bāyuè; **in English** yòng Yīngyu; **in**

Chinese yòng Hànyǔ; **is he in?** tā zài ma?
inch yīngcùn; *see page 117*
include bāokuò; **is ... included in the price?** ... bāokuò zai jiàgé zhīnèi ma?
incompetent wúnéng
inconvenient bù fāngbiàn
increase (*noun*) zēngjiā
incredible (*very good*) liǎobuqǐ; (*amazing*) ràng ren bù xiāngxìn de
indecent xiàliú
independent (*adjective*) dúlì
India Yìndù
Indian (*adjective*) Yìndu; (*person*) Yìnduren
indicator (*on car*) zhīshìdēng
indigestion xiāohuà bù liáng
indoor pool shìnèi yóuyǒngchí
indoors shìnèi
industry gōngyè
inefficient méiyǒu xiàolü
infection gánrǎn
infectious chuánrǎn
inflammation fāyán
inflation tōnghuò péngzhàng
informal (*clothes*) suíbiàn; (*occasion, meeting*) fēi zhèngshì; **informal dinner** biànyàn
information qíngbào
information desk wènxùnchù
information office chuándáshì
injection zhùshè
injured shòushāng; **she's been injured** tā shòushāngle
injury shāng
inland telegram guónèi diànbào
in-law: my in-laws wǒde qìngjia
inner tube nèidài
innocent (*not guilty*) wúgū; (*naive*) yòuzhì
inquisitive hàoqí
insect kūnchóng

insect bite chóngzı yǎo de
insecticide shāchóngjì
insect repellent qūchóngjì
inside zai ... li; **inside the room** zai fángjiānli; **let's sit inside** wǒmen jìnqu zuò ba
insincere bù chéngkěn
insist: I insist wǒ jiānchí dàodǐ
insomnia shīmián
instant coffee sùróng kāfēi
instead dàitı; **I'll have that one instead** wǒ jiù yào nèige ba; **instead of ...** dàitı ...
insulating tape juéyuán jiāobù
insulin yídǎosù
insult (noun) wūrǔ
insurance báoxiǎn
insurance policy báoxiǎndānr
intellectual (noun) zhīshıfènzı
intelligent cōngming
intentional: it wasn't intentional nà bú shı gùyì de
interest: places of interest míngshèng
interested: I'm very interested in ... wǒ duì ... hén gǎn xìngqu
interesting yǒu yìsı; **that's very interesting** hén yǒu yìsı
international guójì; **international football team** guójiā zúqiúduì
international telegram guójì diànbào
interpret fānyì; **would you interpret?** nǐ fānyì yíxia, hǎo ma?
interpreter fānyì
intersection (crossroads) shízı lùkǒu
interval (during play etc) mùjiān xiūxi
into: I'm not into that (don't like) wǒ

bù xǐhuān nèige
introduce: may I introduce ...? wǒ lái jièshào yíxia, zhèiwei shı ...
introvert nèixiàng de
invalid (noun) bù néng zìlǐ de bìngren
invalid chair bìngren zhuānyòngyǐ
invitation yāoqǐng; **thank you for the invitation** xièxie nínde yāoqǐng
invite yāoqǐng; **can I invite you out for a meal?** wo qǐng nín chūqu chīfàn, hǎo ma?
involved: I don't want to get involved in it zhèishìr, wǒ bù xiǎng jièrù
iodine diǎn
Ireland Àiěrlán
Irish (adjective) Àiěrlán; (people) Àiěrlánren
iron (material) tiě; (for clothes) yùndǒu; **can you iron these for me?** qíng nǐ bāng wo yùnyun zhèxie yīfu, hǎo ma?
ironmonger wǔjīn shāngdiàn
is shì; see pages 95, 104-106
island dǎo
isolated gūlì
it: is it ...? shı ... ma?; **where is it?** zai nǎr?; **it's her** shı tā; **that's just it** (just the problem) jiù shı zhèige wèntí; **that's it** (that's right) duìle; see pages 97-98
itch: it itches yǎngyang
itinerary lǚxíng rìchéng
ivory xiàngyá

J

jack (for car) qiānjīndǐng
jacket shàngyī
jade yù
jade carving yùdiāo
jam (to eat) guójiàng; **a traffic jam** jiāotōng dǔsāi; **I jammed on the brakes** wǒ láile ge jí shāchē
January yīyue
Japan Rìben
Japanese (adjective) Rìben; (person) Rìbenren; (language) Rìyǔ
jasmine tea mòlì huā chá
jaundice huángdǎn
jaw xiàé

ong	ou	q	u	un	ü	ʊ	ui	uo	x	yan	z	zh
ung	**soul**	ch	**soon**	open	**huge**	**huge**	**way**	wor	sh	yen	dz	j

jazz juéshì yīnyuè
jealous jìdù; **he's jealous** tā jìdùle
jeans niúzǎikù
jellyfish hǎizhé
jetty mǎtóu
Jew Yóutàiren
jewel(le)ry shǒushì
Jewish Yóutàiren de
jiffy: just a jiffy yìfēn zhōng!
job gōngzuò; **just the job!** (just right) zhènghǎo; **it's a good job you told me!** nǐ xìnghǎo gàosù le wǒ
jog: I'm going for a jog wǒ qù páopǎo bù
jogging pǎobù
join: I'd like to join wǒ yuànyi cānjiā; **can I join you?** (go with) wǒ kéyi gēn nǐ yìqǐ qù ma?; (sit with) wǒ kéyi gēn nǐ zuòzuo ma?; **do you want to join us?** (go with) ní xiǎng gēn wǒmen yìqǐ qù ma?; (sit with) ní xiǎng gēn wǒmen yìqǐ zuòzuo ma?
joint (in body) guānjié
joint venture hotel zhōng wài hézī de fàndiàn
joke xiàohua; **you've got to be joking!** nǐ zài kāi wánxiào ba!; **it's no**

joke zhè bú shì kāi wánxiào
jolly: it was jolly good hǎojíle; **jolly good!** hǎojíle!
journey lǚxíng; **have a good journey!** yílù shùnfēng!; **safe journey!** yílù píng'ān!
jug guànr; **a jug of water** yí guànr shuǐ
July qīyuè
jump: you made me jump nǐ xiàle wǒ yítiào; **jump in!** (to car) kuài shàng chē!
jumper tàotóu máoyī
junction (road) jiāochākǒu; (railway) jiāodàokǒu
June liùyuè
junk (rubbish) pòlànr; (boat) fānchuán
just: just one jiù yíge; **just me** jiù wǒ yíge; **just for me** jiù wǒ yào; **just a little** jiù yìdiǎnr; **just here** jiù zai zhèr; **not just now** xiànzài bùxíng; **that's just right** zhénghǎo; **it's just as good** zhèige yě yíyàng; **he was here just now** tā gāngcái hái zai zhèr; **I've only just arrived** wǒ gāng dào

K

keen: I'm not keen wǒ bù hén xiǎng
keep: can I keep it? wǒ kéyi názhe ma?; **please keep it** názhe ba; **keep the change** búyòng zhǎole; **will it keep?** (food) néng fàng ma?; **it's keeping me awake** ràng wǒ shuìbùzháo; **it keeps on breaking** lǎoshì pò; **I can't keep anything down** (food) wǒ yì chī jiù tù
kerb lùbiān jiēshí
kerosene méiyóu
ketchup fānqiéjiàng
kettle shāoshuǐhú
key yàoshi
kid: the kids xiǎoháir; **I'm not kidding** wǒ bú shì kāi wánxiào

kidneys (in body) shèn; (food) yāozi
kill shā
kilo gōngjīn; see page 118
kilometre, kilometer gōnglǐ; see page XYZ
kind: that's very kind zhēn hǎo; **this kind of ...** zhèizhǒng ...
kiosk shòuhuòtíng
kiss (noun) wěn; (verb) qīnwěn
kitchen chúfáng
kitchenette xiǎo chúfáng
Kleenex (tm) zhǐjīn
knee xīgài
kneecap hùxī
knickers sānjiǎokù
knife dāozi

ai	ao	c	e	ei	en	h	i	ɪ	ian	ie	iu	o
I	how	ts	her	ay	open	loch	ee	sir	yen	yeh	yoyo	or

knit dǎ máoxiàn
knitting needles máoyīzhēn
knock: there's a knocking noise from the engine fādòngjī de shēngyīn bú zhèngcháng; **he's had a knock on the head** tāde tóu gěi pèngle yíxia; **he's been knocked over** tā chuàngchēle
knot (*in rope*) jié
know (*person*) rènshı; (*fact*) zhīdào; **I don't know** wǒ bù zhīdào; **do you know a good restaurant?** nǐ zhīdào nǎr de fànguǎnr hǎo ma?; **who knows?** shéi zhīdào?; **I didn't know that** nà, wǒ bù zhīdào; **I don't know him** wǒ bú rènshı tā
Korea: North Korea Běi Cháoxiǎn; **South Korea** Nán Cháoxiǎn
Korean (*adjective*) Cháoxiǎn; (*person*) Cháoxiǎnren; (*language*) Cháoxianyǔ

L

label biāoqiānr
laces (*for shoes*) xiédàir
lacquer (*for hair*) dingfǎyè
ladies (room) nǚ cèsuǒ
lady nǚshı; **ladies and gentlemen!** nǚshımen, xiānshengmen!
lager píjiǔ
lake hú
lamb yángròu
lamp dēng
lamppost diànxiàngānr
lampshade dēngzhào
land (*not sea*) lùdì; **when does the plane land?** fēijī shénme shíhou dào?
landscape fēngjǐng
lane (*on motorway*) chēdào; **a country lane** xiāngjiān xiǎolù
language yǔyán
language course yǔyán kè
Lao (*adjective*) Lǎowō; (*person*) Lǎoworen
Laos Lǎowō
large dà
laryngitis hóuyán
last zuìhòu; **last year** qùnián; **last Wednesday** shàng xīngqisān; **last night** zuótian wǎnshang; **when's the last bus?** mòbān chē shı jídiǎn?; **one last drink** zuìhòu yìbēi; **when were you last in London?** nǐ shàngcì shı shénme shíhou lái Lúndūn de?; **how long does it last?** yào duōchang shíjiān?; **at last!** (*when someone finally arrives*) nǐ zǒngsuàn láile!; (*when finishing a lot of work*) kě wánle!
last name xìng
late wǎn; **sorry I'm late** duìbuqǐ, wǒ lái wǎnle; **don't be late** bié wǎnle; **the bus was late** chē lái wǎnle; **we'll be back late** wǒmen huílái de huì bíjiao wǎn; **it's getting late** bù zǎole; **is it that late!** yǐjīng zhème wǎnle!; **it's too late now** xiànzai tài wǎnle; **I'm a late riser** wǒ píngcháng qǐde bíjiao wǎn
lately zuìjìn
later hòulái; **later on** hòulái; **I'll come back later** wǒ guò yihuǐr zài lái; **see you later** huítóujiàn; **no later than Tuesday** xīngqi'èr yǐqián
latest: the latest news zuì xīn xiāoxi; **at the latest** zuìwǎn
laugh dà xiào; **don't laugh** bié xiào; **it's no laughing matter** méi shénme hǎoxiàode
launderette, laundromat zìzhù xǐyīfáng
laundry (*clothes*) yàoxǐ de yīfu; (*place*) xǐyīdiàn; **could you get the laundry done?** qǐng bāng wo bǎ zhèixie yīfu sòngqu xǐxi, hǎo ma?
lavatory cèsuǒ
law fǎlù; **against the law** wéifǎ
lawn cǎodì
lawyer lùshī

ong	ou	q	u	un	ü	ʊ	ui	uo	x	yan	z	zh
ung	soul	ch	soon	open	huge	huge	way	wor	sh	yen	dz	j

laxative xièyào

laze around: I just want to laze around wó zhǐshı xiǎng xiūxi yíxia

lazy lǎn; **don't be lazy** bié tōulǎn; **I had a nice lazy holiday** wǒ fàngjià shénme yě méi gàn, tòngtong kuàikuai xiūxile yìtiān

lead (*electrical*) diànxiàn; **where does this road lead?** zhèitiáo lù néng qù nǎr?

leader língdǎo

leaf shùyè

leaflet shuōmíngshū; **do you have any leaflets on ...?** ní yǒu guānyú ... de shuōmíngshū ma?

leak lòu; **the lavatory is leaking** mátǒng lòushuǐle

learn: I want to learn ... wó xiǎng xué ...

learner: I'm just a learner wǒ cái gānggang kāishǐ xué

lease (*verb*) chūzū

least: at least 50 zhìshǎo wǔshí

leather pígé

leave: when does the bus leave? chē shénme shíhou kāi? **I leave tomorrow** wǒ míngtian zǒu; **he left this morning** tā jīntian zǎoshang zǒule; **may I leave this here?** wǒ néng bǎ tā liú zhèr ma?; **I left my bag in the bar** wó bǎ bāo là zai jiǔbā nàr le; **she left her bag here** tā bǎ bāo là zai zhèr le; **leave the window open please** qíng bǎ chuāng kāizhe; **there's not much left** shèngde bù duō le; **I've hardly any money left** wǒ méi shèng jǐge qián le; **I'll leave it up to you** háishı nǐ lái juédìng ba

lecherous hàosè

leech mǎhuáng

left zuǒ; **on the left** zai zuǒbiānr

left-hand drive zuǒbianr kāichē

left-handed zuópiězı

left luggage office xíngli jìcúnchù

leg tuǐ

legal héfǎ

lemon níngméng

lemonade qìshuǐr

lemon tea níngméngchá

lend: would you lend me your ...? qíng jiè wǒ ... yòngyong, hǎo ma?

lens (*of camera*) jìngtóu; (*contact*) yǐnxíng yǎnjìng

lens cap jìngtóu gàir

lesbian gǎo tóngxìngliàn de nǚren

less: less than an hour búdào yì xiǎoshí; **less than that** bǐ nà sháo diǎnr; **less hot** méi nème rè

lesson kè; **do you give lessons?** nǐ jiāo kè ma?

let: would you let me use it? wǒ yòngyong, xíng ma?; **will you let me know?** nǐ dào shíhou gàosu wǒ, hǎo ma?; **I'll let you know** dào shíhou wǒ gàosu nǐ; **let me try** wǒ shìshı kàn; **let me go!** fàngshǒu!; **let's leave now** wǒmen zǒu ba; **let's not go yet** wǒmen xiān bié zǒu; **will you let me off at ...?** wǒ zai ... xià, xíng ma?; **rooms to let** fángwū chūzū

letter (*in mail*) xìn; (*of alphabet*) zìmǔ; **are there any letters for me?** yóu wǒde xìn ma?

letterbox xìnxiāng

lettuce shēngcài

level crossing píngjiāo dàokǒu

lever (*noun*) gǎnr

liable (*responsible*) yǒu yìwu

liberate jiěfàng; **a liberated woman** yíwèi sīxiang jiěfàng de fùnǚ

library túshūguǎn

licence, license zhízhào

license plate (*on car*) chēpáir

lid gàir

lie (*untruth*) huǎnghuà; **can he lie down for a while?** tā tǎng yìhuǐr, hǎo bù hǎo?; **I want to go and lie down** wó xiǎng qù tǎng huǐr

lie-in: I'm going to have a lie-in tomorrow míngtian wǒ yào shuì ge lǎnjiào

life shēnghuó; **not on your life!** dá sı wǒ, yě bú gàn!; **that's life** zhè jiùshı mìng!

lifebelt jiùshēngquān

lifeboat jiùshēngtǐng

lifeguard jiùshēngyuán

life insurance rénshòu báoxiǎn

life jacket jiùshēngyī

lift (*in hotel etc*) diàntī; **could you give me a lift?** dā ge chē, xíng ma?; **do you want a lift?** nǐ yào dā chē ma?; **thanks for the lift** xièxie nǐ; **I got a**

lift wǒ dāle ge biànchē
light (*noun*) dēng; (*on bike*) chēdēng;
 (*not heavy*) qīng; **the light was on**
 dēng liàngzhe; **do you have a light?**
 (*for cigarette*) jiè ge huǒ, xíng ma?; **a**
 light meal biànfàn; **light blue** qiǎn
 lánsè
light bulb dēngpào
lighter (*cigarette*) dáhuǒjī
lighthouse dēngtǎ
light meter bàoguāngbiǎo
lightning shǎndiàn
like: I'd like a ... wǒ yào ...; **I'd like**
 a cup of tea/coffee wǒ yào bēi chá/
 kāfēi; **would you like a ...?** nǐ yào ...
 ma?; **I'd like to ...** wó xiǎng ...; **I'd**
 like to come/go wó xiǎng lái/qù;
 would you like to ...? ní xiǎng ...
 ma?; **I like it** wó xǐhuān; **I like you**
 wó xǐhuān nǐ; **I don't like it** wǒ bù
 xǐhuān; **he doesn't like it** tā bù
 xǐhuān; **do you like ...?** ní xǐhuān ...
 ma?; **I like swimming** wó xǐhuān
 yóuyǒng; **OK, if you like** hǎo,
 zhǐyào ní xǐhuān; **what's it like?** tā
 xiàng shénme?; **do it like this** zhào
 zhèiyang zuò; **one like that** nèiyàng
 de yíge
likely hén kěnéng
line (*of people, writing*) háng; (*on paper*)
 xiàn; (*telephone*) xiàn; **please line up**
 here qǐng zai zhèr páiduì; **would**
 you give me a line? (*telephone*) qǐng
 jiē wàixiàn
linen (*for beds*) chuángdānr
linguist yǔyánxuéjiā; **I'm no linguist**
 wǒ wàiyǔ bùxíng
lining chènlǐ
lion shīzı
lip zuǐchún
lip pencil miáochúnbǐ
lip salve chúngāo
lipstick kǒuhóng
liqueur guǒzıjiǔ
liqueur glass xiáo jiǔbēi
liquid yètǐ
liquor jiǔ
liquor store jiǔdiàn
list mùlù
listen tīng; **I'd like to listen to ...** wó
 xiǎng tīng ...; **listen!** nǐ tīng!
litre, liter shēng; *see page XYZ*

litter (*rubbish*) luàndiū de fèiwù
little xiǎo; **just a little, thanks** jiù
 yìdiǎnr, xièxie; **just a very little** jiù
 yìdīngdiǎnr; **a little cream** yìdiǎnr
 nǎiyóu; **a little more** zài lái yìdiǎnr;
 a little better háo diǎnr le; **that's too**
 little (*not enough*) tài shǎole
live zhù; **I live in ...** wǒ zhù zai ...;
 where do you live? nǐ zhù zai nǎr?;
 where does he live? tā zhù zai nǎr?;
 we live together wǒmen zhù zai
 yìqǐ
lively (*person*) huópo; (*town*) rènao
liver (*in body, food*) gān
lizard xīyì
loaf dà miànbāo
lobby (*of hotel*) qiántīng
lobster lóngxiā
local: a local newspaper dāngdì de
 bàozhǐ; **a local restaurant** dāngdì de
 fàndiàn; **a local-style dish** dìfang
 fēngwèir
lock (*noun*) suǒ; (*for bike*) chēsuǒ; **it's**
 locked suǒshangle; **I locked myself**
 out of my room wó bǎ zìjǐ suǒ zai
 ménwài le
log: I slept like a log wǒ shuìde hěn
 xiāng
lollipop bàngtáng
London Lúndūn
lonely gūdān; **are you lonely?** nǐ
 juéde gūdān ma?
long cháng; **how long does it take?**
 yào duōchang shíjian?; **it is a long**
 way? hén yuǎn ma?; **a long time**
 hěn cháng shíjian; **I won't be long**
 wǒ jiù lái; **don't be long** bié tài jiǔle;
 that was long ago nà hén jiǔ le; **I'd**
 like to stay longer wǒ yuàn duō dāi
 xie rìzı; **long time no see** háo jiǔ bú
 jiàn le; **so long** zàijiàn
long distance call chángtú diànhuà
loo: where's the loo? cèsuǒ zai nǎr?;
 I want to go to the loo wó xiǎng
 fāngbian fāngbian
look: that looks good kànlai bú cuò;
 you look tired nǐ lèile ba?; **I'm just**
 looking, thanks wó zhǐshì kànkan,
 xièxie; **you don't look your age** nǐ
 kànzhe méi nènme dà; **look at him**
 kàn ta; **I'm looking for ...** wǒ zai
 zhǎo ...; **look out!** xiǎoxīn!; **can I**

have a look? wǒ néng kànkan ma?;
can I have a look around? wǒ néng
zai zhèr zhuànzhuan ma?
loose (*handle*) sōng; **my button is
loose** wǒde kòuzı kuài diàole
loose change língqián
lorry kǎchē
lorry driver kǎchē sījī
lose diūshī; **I've lost my ...** wǒde ...
diūle; **I'm lost** wǒ mílùle
lost property office, lost and found
shīwù zhāolíng chù
lot: a lot, lots hěn duō; **not a lot** bù
hěn duō; **a lot of money** hěn duō
qián; **a lot of women** hěn duō fùnǚ;
a lot cooler liángkuai duōle; **I like it
a lot** wǒ hén xǐhuān; **is it a lot
further?** hái hén yuǎn ma?; **I'll take
the (whole) lot** wǒ quán yào le
loud dàshēng de; **the music is rather
loud** zhèi yīnyuè tài chǎole
lounge (*in house*) kètīng; (*in hotel*)
xiūxishì
lousy (*meal, hotel, holiday, weather*)

chàjìn
love: I love you wǒ ài ni; **he's fallen
in love** tā àishang shénme ren le
lovely (*meal*) hǎochī; (*view, weather*)
zhēn hǎo
low (*prices, bridge*) dī
low beam dīdēng
LP mìwén chàngpiān
luck yùnqi; **hard luck!** zhēn bù
zǒuyùn; **good luck!** zhù nǐ shùnlì!;
just my luck! wǒ mìng bù hǎo!; **it
was pure luck** chúnshı gěi
pèngshang de
lucky: that's lucky! zhēn gěi
pèngshangle!
lucky charm hùfú
luggage xíngli
lumbago yāoténg
lump (*medical*) zhǒngkuàir
lunch wǔfàn
lungs fèi
luxurious (*hotel, furnishings*) háohuá
luxury (*in disapproving sense*) shēchǐ
luxury goods gāojí xiǎofèipǐn

M

mad fēng
madam nǚshì
magazine zázhì
magnificent (*view, day, meal*) hǎojíle
maid nǚ fúwùyuán
maiden name jiéhūn qián de míngzı
mail (*noun*) yóujiàn; **is there any mail
for me?** yóu wǒde xìn méiyou?;
where can I mail this? zhèige zai
nǎr jì?
mailbox xìnxiāng
main zhǔyào de; **where's the main
post office?** zǒng yóujú zai nǎr?
main road dàlù
make zuò; **do you make them
yourself?** shı nǐ zìjǐ zuò de ma?; **it's
very well made** zuòde hén hǎo;
what does that make altogether?
yígòng duōshao qián?; **I make it**

only 500 yuan wǒ suànde shı wúbǎi
kuài
make-up huàzhuāngpǐn
make-up remover qīngjiéshuāng
Malay (*adjective*) Mǎlái; (*person*)
Mǎláiren
Malaysia Mǎláixīyà
Malaysian (*adjective*) Mǎláixīyà;
(*person*) Mǎláixīyàren
male chauvinist pig dànánzı zhǔyi
man nánde
manager jīnglǐ; **may I see the
manager?** kéyi jiànjian jīnglǐ ma?
Mandarin *see* **Standard Chinese**
manicure xiū zhǐjiǎ
many hěn duō
Mao Tse Tung jacket
zhōngshānzhuāng
map: a map of ... ... de dìtú; **it's not**

on this map bú zài zhèizhāng dìtúshang
marble (noun) dàlǐshí
March sānyue
marijuana dàmá
mark: there's a mark on it zhèr yóudiǎnr máobìng; could you mark it on the map for me? qǐng nín bāng wo zai zhèizhāng dìtúshang biāo yíxia, hǎo ma?
market (noun) shìchǎng
marmalade júzıjiàng
married: are you married? nǐ jiēhūnle ma?; I'm married wǒ jiēhūnle
martial arts wǔshù
mascara jiémáogāo
mass: I'd like to go to mass wó xiǎng qù zuò mísa
mast (on ship) wéigān; (for television etc) diànshìtǎ
masterpiece jiézuò
matches huǒchái
material (cloth) bùliào
matter: it doesn't matter méi guānxi; what's the matter? zěnmele?
mattress rùzı
maximum (noun) zuìdà
May wǔyue
may: may I ...? wo kéyi ... ma?; may I have another bottle? wo kéyi zài lái yìpíng ma?
maybe yéxǔ
mayonnaise dànhuángjiàng
me wǒ; come with me gēn wǒ lái; it's for me nà shı wǒde; it's me shì wǒ; see page 97
meal fàn: let's go and have a meal wǒmen chīfàn qù ba: does that include meals? chīfàn bāokuò zai nèi ma?; that was an excellent meal wǒmen chīde hén hǎo
mean: what does this word mean? zhèige cír shı shénme yìsı?; what does he mean? tā shı shénme yìsı?
measles mázhěn; German measles fēngzhěn
measurements chǐcùn
meat ròu
mechanic: do you have a mechanic here? nǐ zhèr yóu gǎo jīxiè de ma?
medicine yào

medieval zhōngshìjì
medium (steak) gāngshóu de; he is medium height tā shı zhōngděnggèr
medium-rare bànshēngshóu de
medium-sized zhōnghào
meet: pleased to meet you xìnghuì! xìnghuì!; where shall we meet? wǒmen zai nǎr pèngtóu?; let's meet up again in/at ... wǒmen zai ... pèngtóu, zěnmeyàng?
meeting huìyi
meeting place (formal) huìjiàn dìdiǎn; (informal) pèngtóu dìdiǎn
melon (watermelon) xīguā; (honeydew melon) hāmìguā
member chéngyuán; I'd like to become a member of ... wǒ yuànyi jiārù ...
men nánde
mend: can you mend this? nín néng xiūxiu zhèige ma?
men's room nán cèsuǒ
mention: don't mention it búyòng kèqi
menu càidānr; may I have the menu please? kàn yíxia càidānr, xíng ma?
mess: it's a mess luàntàole
message: are there any messages for me? yóu wǒde xìn shénmede ma?; I'd like to leave a message for ... wǒ xiang gěi ... liúge huàr
metal (noun) jīnshǔ
metre, meter mǐ; see page 117
midday: at midday zhōngwǔ
middle: in the middle zai zhōngjiān; in the middle of the road zai lù dāngzhōng
midnight: at midnight bànyè
might: I might want to stay another 3 days wó kěnéng hái xiǎng zài zhù sāntian; you might have warned me! nǐ yīnggāi shìxiān gàosu wǒ yíxia!
migraine piāntóuténg
mild (taste) qīngdàn; (weather) nuǎnhuo
mile yīnglǐ; that's miles away! tài yuǎnle!; see page 117
military (adjective) jūnshì
milk niúnǎi
milkshake bīngnǎi
millimetre, millimeter háomǐ

ong	ou	q	u	un	ü	ʊ	ui	uo	x	yan	z	zh
ung	soul	ch	soon	open	huge	huge	way	wor	sh	yen	dz	j

minced meat ròumò

mind: I don't mind wǒ wúsuǒwèi; would you mind if I ...? wǒ kéyi ... ma?; never mind méi guānxi; I've changed my mind wó gǎibiàn zhúyì le; I've got something on my mind wó yǒu xīnshìr

mine: it's mine shi wǒde; see page 98

mineral water kuàngquánshuǐ

Ming Dynasty Míngcháo

Ming vase Qīnghuācí

minimum (adjective) zuìxiǎo

mint (sweet) bòhetáng

minus (minus sign) fù; 4 minus two sì jiǎn èr; minus 3 degrees língxià sān dù

minute fēn; in a minute yìhuǐr; just a minute jiù yìfēn zhōng

mirror jìngzi

Miss xiáojiě; Miss Wang Wáng xiáojiě

miss: I miss you wó hěn xiǎng nǐ; there's a ... missing shǎole yíge ...; we missed the bus wǒmen méi gǎnshang chē

mist wù

mistake cuòwu; I think there's a mistake here wǒ juéde zhèr yǒu ge cuòr

misunderstanding wùhuì

mixture hùnhéwù; (medicine) yàoshuǐr

mix-up: there's been some sort of mix-up with ... ... chūle diǎnr wèntí

modern xiàndài

modern art xiàndàipài yìshu

moisturizer cāliǎnyóu

moment: I won't be a moment jiù yìfēn zhōng

monastery (Buddhist) sìyuàn

Monday xīngqīyī

money qián; I don't have any money wǒ méi qián; do you take English/American money? shōu Yīngbàng/Měiyuán ma?

Mongolia Ménggǔ; Inner Mongolia Nèiměng; Outer Mongolia Wàiměng

Mongolian (adjective) Ménggǔ; (person) Ménggǔrén

month yuè

monument jìniànbēi

moon yuèliang

moorings lǎnzhù

moped jīdòng jiǎotàchē

more duō yìdiǎnr; may I have some more? zài géi wǒ yìdiǎnr, hǎo ma?; more water, please qǐng zài géi diǎnr shuǐ; no more, thanks bú yào le, xièxie; more expensive/difficult guì/nán yìdiǎnr; more than 50 wǔshi duō; more than that bǐ nèi duō diǎnr; a lot more duōde duō; I don't ... any more wǒ bú ... le; I don't stay there any more wǒ bú zhù zai nàr le

morning zǎoshang; good morning ní zǎo!; this morning jīntian zǎoshang; in the morning (before 8.00) zǎoshang; (after 8.00) shàngwu

mosquito wénzi

mosquito net wénzhàng

most: I like this one most wǒ zuì xǐhuān zhèige; most of the time dàbufen shíjian; most hotels dàbufen fàndiàn

mother: my mother wó mǔqin

motif (in pattern) jīběn huāwén

motor mǎdá

motorbike mótuōchē

motorboat qìtǐng

motorist kāichē de

motorway gāosù gōnglù

motor yacht jīfānchuán

mountain shān; up in the mountains shānli; a mountain village shāncūn

mouse láoshǔ

moustache xiǎohúzi

mouth zuǐ

move: he's moved to another hotel tā bān dao lìng yìjiā fàndiàn qu le; could you move your car? qǐng nín nuó yíxia chē, hǎo ma?

movie diànyǐng; let's go to the movies wǒmen kàn diànyǐng qu ba

movie camera diànyǐng shèyǐngjī

movie theater diànyǐngyuàn

moving: a very moving tune hěn dòngrén de qǔzi

Mr xiānsheng; Mr Wang Wáng xiānsheng

Mrs fūren; Mrs Wang Wáng fūren

Ms nǚshi; Ms Wang Wáng nǚshi

much duō; much better hǎo duōle; much cooler liángkuài duōle; not much bù duō; not so much méi nème duō

muffler (*on car*) xiāoshēngqì

mug: I've been mugged wó gěi ren qiǎngle

muggy (*weather*) mènrè

mule luózı

mumps sāixiànyán

murals bìhuà

muscle jīròu

museum bówùguǎn

mushroom mógu

music yīnyuè; **do you have the sheet music for ...?** ní yǒu ... de yuèpǔ ma?

musician yīnyuèjiā

mussels yíbèi

must: I must ... wǒ bìxū ...; **I mustn't drink ...** wǒ yídìng bùnéng hē ...; **you mustn't forget** nǐ yídìng bié wàngle

mustache xiǎohúzı

mustard jièmo

my wǒde; **my room** wǒde fángjiān; *see page 98*

myself: I'll do it myself wǒ zìjǐ lái

N

nail (*of finger*) zhǐjiǎ; (*in wood*) dīngzı

nail clippers zhǐjiǎ dāo

nailfile zhǐjiǎ cuò

nail polish zhǐjiǎ yóu

nail polish remover zhǐjiǎ chúyóuyè

nail scissors zhǐjiǎ jiǎn

naked luótǐ

name (*personal name*) míngzı; (*surname*) xìng; **what's your name?** (*personal name*) nǐ jiào shénme míngzı?; (*surname*) nín guì xìng?; **what's its name?** tā jiào shénme?; **my name is ...** (*personal name*) wǒ jiào ...; (*surname*) wǒ xìng ...

nap: he's having a nap tā zhèngzai xiūxi; **I'm going for a nap** wǒ qù dǎ ge dǔnr

napkin (*serviette*) cānjīn

nappy niàobù

narrow (*road*) zhǎi

nasty (*taste*) ràng ren ěxīn; (*person*) ràng ren tǎoyàn; **what nasty weather!** zhèi guǐ tiānqi!; **whew, what a nasty cut!** āiya, shāngde bù qīng!

national (*state*) guójiā; (*nation-wide*) quánguó; **National People's Congress** quánguó réndà

nationality guójí

natural zìrán

naturally dāngrán

nature (*trees etc*) dàzìrán

nausea ěxīn

near jìn; **is it near here?** lí zhèr jìn ma?; **near the hotel/post office** fàndiàn/yóujú fùjìn; **where is the nearest ...?** lí zhèr zuì jìn de ... zai nǎr?; **do you go near ...?** nǐ dào ... nèiyíkuàir qù ma?

nearby fùjìn

nearly chàbuduō

neat (*room etc*) zhěngjié; (*drink*) chún

necessary bìyào; **is it necessary to ...?** yǒu bìyào ... ma?; **it's not necessary** méi bìyào

neck (*of body*) bózı; (*of dress, shirt*) lǐngzı

necklace xiàngliàn

necktie lǐngdàir

need: I need a ... wǒ xūyào yíge ...; **do I need a ...?** wǒ xūyào yíge ... ma?; **it needs more salt** xūyào duō jiā diǎnr yán; **there's no need** bù xūyào; **there's no need to shout!** méi bìyào zhème dà de shēng!

needle zhēn

needlework and fancy goods cìxiù shǒugōngyi pǐn

negative (*film*) dǐpiàn

neighbo(u)r línjū

neighbo(u)rhood: in the neighbo(u)rhood of ... zai ... fùjìn

neither: neither of us wǒmen liǎngge

dōu bù; **neither one (of them)** liǎngge dōu bù; **neither ... nor ... ...** hé ... dōu bù ...; **he doesn't like it and neither do I** tā bù xǐhuān, wó yě bù xǐhuān; **I'm not going and neither is he** wǒ bú qù, tā yě bú qù

Nepal Níbóěr

Nepalese (*adjective*) Níbóěr; (*person*) Níbóěren; (*language*) Níbóeryǔ

nephew: my nephew (*brother's son*) wǒ zhízi; (*sister's son*) wǒ wàisheng

nervous jǐnzhāng

net (*fishing, tennis*) wǎng

nettle xúnmá

nettle rash xúnmá zhěn

neurotic shénjīng guòmǐn

neutral (*uncommitted*) zhōnglì; (*neither good or bad*) zhōngxìng; (*gear*) kōngdǎng

never (*referring to the past or present*) cónglái bù; (*referring to the future*) jué bú huì

new xīn

news (*media*) xīnwén; (*information*) xiāoxi; **is there any news?** yǒu shénme xiāoxi ma?

newspaper bàozhǐ; **do you have any English newspapers?** yǒu Yīngwén bàozhǐ ma?

newsstand bàotān

New Year xīnnián; **Happy New Year** xīnnián hǎo; **Chinese New Year** Chūnjié

New Year's Eve xīnnián qiánxī; **Chinese New Year's Eve** Chúxī

New York Niǔyuē

New Zealand Xīnxīlán

New Zealander Xīnxīlánren

next xià yíge; **it's at the next corner** zai xià yíge lùkǒu; **next week/ Monday** xià xīngqī/xīngqíyī; **next to the post office** zai yóujú pángbiān; **the one next to that** pángbiān de nèige

nextdoor (*adverb, adjective*) gébì

next of kin jìnqīn

nice (*person, town, day*) hén hǎo; (*meal*) hǎochī; **that's very nice of you** ni tài hǎole; **I'd like a nice cold drink** wǒ hén xiǎng hē bēi léngyǐn

nickname wàihào

niece: my niece (*brother's daughter*)

wǒ zhínǚ; (*sister's daughter*) wǒ wàishengnǚ

night yèli; **at night** yèli; **I'm staying for two/three nights** wǒ zhù liǎngge/sānge wǎnshang; **good night** wǎn ān

nightcap (*drink*) línshuì qián hē de jiǔ

nightclub yèzǒnghuì

nightdress shuìqún

night flight yèjiān hángbān

nightie shuìqún

nightlife yè shēnghuó

nightmare èmèng

night porter yèjiān zhíbānyuán

night train yèchē

nits (*bugs, in hair etc*) jīzi

no bù; **no more than ...** bù néng chāoguò ...; **I've no money** wǒ méi qián; **there's no more** méiyǒule; **oh no!** (*upset*) tiān na!; *see pages 105, 113*

nobody méirén

noise zàoyīn

noisy cháo; **it's too noisy** tài chǎole

non-alcoholic (*drink*) bù hán jiǔjīng de

none shénme yě méiyǒu; **none of them** méi yíge

nonsense húshuō

non-smoking (*compartment, section of plane*) fēi xīyān qū

non-stop (*travel*) zhídá

noodles miàntiáo

no-one méirén

nor: he doesn't like it and nor do I tā bù xǐhuan, wó yě bù xǐhuan; **I can't use chopsticks, nor can he** wǒ bú huì yòng kuàizi, tā yě bú huì

normal zhèngcháng

north běi; **to the north of ...** zai ... yíběi

northeast dōngběi; **to the northeast of ...** zai ... de dōngběibù

Northern Ireland Běi Ái'ěrlán

northwest xīběi; **to the northwest of ...** zai ... de xīběibù

nose bízi; **my nose is bleeding** wǒ bízi chūxuěle

not bù; **I'm not coming/going** wǒ bù lái/qù; **it's not cheap/expensive** bù piányi/guì; **I don't smoke** wǒ bú huì xīyān; **not for me** wǒ bú yào; **it**

wasn't hot yesterday zuótian bú rè; **they didn't come/go** tāmen méi lái/qù; **he didn't say anything** tā shénme yě méi shuō; **it's not important** méi shénme; **not that one** bú shì nèige; *see page 105-106, 114*

note (*bank note*) chāopiào; (*written message etc*) biàntiáo

notebook bǐjìběn

nothing: nothing for me thanks wǒ shénme dou bú yào; **I've bought nothing** wǒ shénme dou méi mǎi; **it's nothing** méi shénme; **nothing else thanks** bú yào le, xièxie

November shíyīyue

now xiànzai; **I'm not coming now** xiànzai wǒ bù lái; **I'm not hungry now** wǒ xiànzai bú è

nowhere: nowhere in China is ... zhōngguo shénme dìfang dou bù ...;

I have nowhere to stay wǒ shénme dìfang yě méi dìr zhù; **we are going nowhere tomorrow** wǒmen míngtian nár yě bú qù

nuisance: he's being a nuisance (*pestering woman etc*) tā zhèi ren hén tǎoyàn

numb (*limb etc*) mámù

number (*figure*) shùzì; **what number?** jǐ hào?; **what's your telephone number?** nǐde diànhuà shì duōshao?

number plates chēpáir

nurse hùshì

nursery (*pre-school*) tuōérsuǒ

nut (*chestnut*) lìzi; (*hazelnut*) zhēnzi; (*walnut*) hétao; (*for bolt*) luósī; **please tighten this nut** qǐng shàngshangjǐn zhèige luósī

nutter: he's a nutter (*is crazy*) tā yǒu shénjīngbìng

O

oar shuāngjiǎng

obligatory yǒu yìwù de

oblige: much obliged duōxiè

obnoxious (*person*) tǎoyàn

obvious: that's obvious hěn míngxiǎn

occasionally óu'ěr

o'clock *see page 115*

October shíyue

octopus zhāngyú

odd (*strange*) qíguài; (*number*) dān

odometer lìchéngbiǎo

of de; **the manager of the hotel/bank** fàndiàn/yínháng de jīnglǐ; **try one of mine** (*cigarettes etc*) lái, shìshì wǒde

off: 20% off jiǎnjià bǎifēn zhī èrshí; **the lights were off** dēng mièle; **just off the main road** jiù zai dàmǎlù pángbiānr

offend: don't be offended bié shēngqì

office (*place of work*) bàngōngshì

officer (*said to policeman*) tóngzhì

official (*noun*) guānyuán; **is that offi-**

cial? shì guānfāng de ma?

off-season dànjì

often jīngcháng; **not often** bù jīngcháng

oil (*for car, for salad*) yóu; **it's losing oil** lòu yóu le; **will you change the oil?** zhèr kéyi huàn yóu ma?; **we'll soon be out of oil** kuài méi yóu le

oil painting yóuhuà

oil pressure yóuyā

ointment yàogāo

OK hǎo; **are you OK?** hai hǎo ma?; **that's OK thanks** xíngle, xièxie; **that's OK by me** wǒ méi wènti

old lǎo; **how old are you?** (*to children*) nǐ duō dà le?; (*to adults*) nǐ duō dà niánling?; (*to old people*) nín duō dà niánjì le?

old-age pensioner lǐng yánglǎojīn de ren

old-fashioned guòshí

old town (*old part of town*) jiùchéng

olive gánlǎn

ong	ou	q	u	un	ü	ʋ	ui	uo	x	yan	z	zh
ung	soul	ch	soon	op**en**	huge	huge	way	wor	sh	yen	dz	j

olive oil gánlǎn yóu

omelet(t)e chǎojīdàn

on zai ... shang; **on the roof** zai fángdǐngshang; **on the beach** zai hǎitānshang; **on Friday** xīngqiwǔ; **on television** zai diànshìshang; **I don't have it on me** wo shēnshang méiyǒu; **this drink's on me** wǒ lái mǎi; **a book on Beijing** guānyú Běijīng de shū; **the warning light comes on** hóngdēng liàngle; **the light was on** dēng liàngzhe; **what's on in town?** chéngli yǎn shénme?; **it's just not on!** (not acceptable) méiménr!

once (one time) yícì; (formerly) cóngqián; **at once** (immediately) mǎshàng

one yī; **that one** nèige; **the green one** lǜ de nèige; **the one with the black skirt on** chuān hēi qúnzi de nèiwei; **the one in the blue shirt** chuān lán chènyī de nèiwei

onion yángcōng

only zhǐ; **only one** zhí yǒu yíge; **only once** zhí yǒu yícì; **it's only 9 o'clock** cái jiúdiǎn; **I've only just arrived** wǒ gānggang dào

open (adjective) kāi; **it won't open** kāi bù kāi; **when do you open?** nimen shénme shíhou kāimen?; **in the open** (in open air) lùtiān

opening times yíngyè shíjiān

open top (car) chǎngpéng

opera gējù; **Peking Opera** jīngjù

operation (medical) shǒushù

operator (telephone) diànhuàyuán

opportunity jīhui

opposite: opposite the hotel fàndiàn duìmiàn; **it's directly opposite** zhèng duìzhe

oppressive (heat) mènjíle

optician yǎnjìngdiàn

optimistic lèguān

optional kéyi xuǎnzé de

or (in statement) huòzhě; (in question) háishì; **do you want this or that?** nǐ yào zhèige háishì nèige?

orange (fruit) gānzi; (colour) júhuángsè

orange juice (fresh) xiānjúzhī; (fizzy) qìshuǐr; (diluted) júzishuǐr

orchestra guǎnxián yuèduì

order: could we order now? (in restaurant) wǒmen xiànzai diǎncài, xíng ma?; **I've already ordered** wó yǐjīng diǎnle cài le; **I didn't order that** wǒ méi diǎn nèige cài; **it's out of order** (lift etc) tā huàile

ordinary pǔtōng

organization (company) dānwèi

organize zǔzhī; **could you organize it?** nǐ néng ānpái yíxia ma?

original yuánláide; **is it an original?** shì yuánzuò ma?

ornament zhuāngshìpǐn

ostentatious (clothes, colour etc) xiānyàn de

other biéde; **other places/banks/hotels** biéde dìfang/yínháng/fàndiàn; **other people** biéren; **do you have any others?** hái yǒu biéyàng de ma?; **the other one** lìng yíge; **the other waiter** lìng yíwei fúwùyuán; **some other time, thanks** zài shuō ba

otherwise yàobùrán

ouch! āi yao!

ought: he ought to be here soon tā zhè jiù gāi lái le

ounce àngsī; see page 118

our: our hotel wǒmen zhù de lǚguǎn; **our suitcases** wǒmende xiāngzi; see page 98

ours wǒmende; **that's ours** nà shì wǒmende; see page 98

out: he's out tā chūqule; **get out!** gǔnchūqù!; **I'm out of money** wǒ méi qián le; **it's a few kilometres out of town** chūle chéng méiyǒu jǐ gōnglǐ jiù dàole

outboard (motor) xiánwài mǎdá

outdoors lùtiān

outlet (electrical) diànyuán chāzuò

outside wàimian; **can we sit outside?** wǒmen kéyi dào wàimian qu zuò ma?

outskirts: on the outskirts of ... zai ... jiāoqu

oven kǎoxiāng

over: over here zai zhèr; **over there** zai nàr; **over 100** yìbǎi duō; **I'm burnt all over** wó gěi shàitòule; **the holiday's over** jiàqī guòle

overcharge: you've overcharged me nǐ duō shōule wǒde qián

ai	ao	c	e	ei	en	h	i	ɪ	ian	ie	iu	o
I	how	ts	her	ay	open	loch	ee	sir	yen	yeh	yoyo	or

overcoat dàyī
overcooked shāolǎole
overexposed (*photograph*) bàoguāng
    shíjian tài cháng
overheat: it's overheating (*car*)
    fādòngjī tài rè le
overlook: overlooking the sea
    tiàowàng dàhǎi
overnight (*travel*) guòyè
oversleep: I overslept wǒ
    shuìguòtóule

overtake chāoguò
overweight (*person*) tài pàngle
owe: how much do I owe you?
    yígòng duōshao qián?
own: my own ... wǒ zìjide ...; **are you
    on your own?** jiù nǐ yīge rén ma?;
    I'm on my own jiù wǒ yíge rén
owner wùzhǔ
oyster mǔli
oyster sauce háoyóu

P

pack: a pack of cigarettes yìbāo yān;
    I'll go and pack wǒ qu shōushi
    xíngli
package (*at post office etc*) bāoguǒ
packaged noodles guàmiàn
package holiday/tour zōnghé fúwù
packed lunch héfàn
**packed out: the place was packed
    out** zhèige dìfang rén zhēn duō
packet xiǎobāo; **a packet of cigarettes**
    yìbāo yān
paddle (*noun*) dānjiǎng
paddy field dàotián
padlock (*noun*) guàsuǒ
page (*of book*) yè; **could you page Mr
    ...?** nǐ néng jiào yíxia ... xiānsheng
    ma?
pagoda tǎ
pain téng; **I have a pain here** wǒ
    zhèr téng
painful téng
painkillers zhǐténgyào
paint (*noun*) (*decorator's*) yóuqī; (*artist's*)
    yóucǎi; **I'm going to do some
    painting** (*artist*) wǒ qu huà diǎnr huà
paintbrush (*artist's*) huàbǐ
painting huàr; **Chinese painting**
    guóhuà; **oil painting** yóuhuà
pair: a pair of ... yíduìr ...
pajamas shuìyī
Pakistan Bājīsītǎn
Pakistani (*adjective*) Bājīsītǎn; (*person*)

Bājīsītanren
pal huǒbànr
palace gōngdiàn
pale cāngbái; **pale blue** dàn lánsè
palm tree zōnglǘshù
palpitations (*of heart*) xīnjì
pancake làobǐng
panda xióngmāo
panic: don't panic bié huāng
panties xiǎo sānjiǎokù
pants (*trousers*) kùzi; (*underpants*)
    kùchǎ
panty girdle jiànměikù
pantyhose liánkùwà
paper zhǐ; (*newspaper*) bàozhǐ; **a piece
    of paper** yìzhāng zhǐ
paper handkerchiefs zhǐjīn
paraffin méiyóu
parallel: parallel to ... yǔ ...
    píngxíng
parasol yángsǎn
parcel bāoguǒ
pardon (me)? (*didn't understand*)
    duìbuqǐ, wǒ méi tīngqīng
parents: my parents wǒ fùmǔ
parents-in-law (*husband's*) yuèfù
    yuèmǔ; (*wife's*) gōnggong pópo
park (*noun*) gōngyuán; **where can I
    park?** zai nǎr kéyi tíngchē?; **there's
    nowhere to park** méi dìr tíngchē
parka fēngxuě dàyī
parking lights tíngchēdēng

ong	ou	q	u	un	ü	ʊ	ui	uo	x	yan	z	zh
ung	soul	ch	soon	open	huge	huge	way	wor	sh	yen	dz	j

parking lot tíngchēchǎng
parking place: there's a parking place! nàr yǒu ge tíngchē de kòngr!
part (*noun*) yíbùfen
partner (*boyfriend, girlfriend etc*) bànr; (*in business*) màoyi huǒbànr
party (*group*) tuántǐ; (*political*) dǎng; **let's have a party** zánmen yíkuàir jùju, zěnmeyàng?
pass (*in mountains*) guānkǒu; (*overtake*) chāoguò; **he passed out** tā yūndǎole; **he made a pass at me** tā gēn wǒ tiáoqíng
passable (*road*) kéyi tōngxíng
passenger lǚkè
passport hùzhào
past: in the past guòqu; **it's just past the bank/hotel** guòle yínháng/fàndiàn jiùshì
pastry (*dough*) miàntuánr; (*small cake*) gāodiǎn
patch: could you put a patch on this? nín bāng wǒ zai zhèr dǎ ge bǔdīng, hǎo ma?
path xiǎolù
patient: be patient! nàixīn diǎnr!
patio yuànzi
pattern tú'àn; **a dress pattern** fúzhuāng zhǐyàng
paunch dàdùpí
pavement (*sidewalk*) rénxíngdào
pavilion tíngzi
pay (*verb*) fùqián; **it's already paid for** zhèige yǐjīng fùqián le; **can I pay, please?** suànzhàng ba?; **I'll pay for this** wǒ lái mǎi
pay phone tóubìshì gōngyòng diànhuà
peace and quiet ānjìng
peach táozi
peanuts huāshēng
pear lí
pearl zhēnzhū
peas wāndòu
peculiar (*taste, custom*) guài
pedal (*noun*) jiǎodēng
pedalo jiǎotāchuán
pedestrian xíngren
pedestrian crossing rénxíng héngdào
pee: I need to go for a pee wǒ yào qu xiǎo ge biàn

peeping Tom: he's a peeping Tom tā shì xiǎoliúmáng, zhuān'ài tōukàn nǚde huàn yīfu shénmede
peg (*for washing*) yīfu jiāzi; (*for tent*) mùzhuāng
Peking Běijīng
Peking duck Běijīng kǎoyā
pen gāngbǐ; **do you have a pen?** ní yóu bǐ ma?
pencil qiānbǐ
penfriend bíyǒu; **shall we be penfriends?** wǒmen xiānghù tōngxìn, jiāo ge péngyou, hǎo ma?
penicillin pánnǐxilín
penis yījīng
penknife qiānbǐdāo
pen pal bíyǒu
pensioner lǐng yánglǎojīn de ren
people rén; **a lot of people** hěn duō ren; **the Chinese people** Zhōngguo rénmín
People's Republic of China Zhōnghuá Rénmín Gònghéguó
pepper (*spice*) hújiāo; **green pepper** qīngjiāo; **red pepper** hóng shìzijiāo
peppermint (*sweet*) bòhetáng
per: per night méiwǎn; **how much per hour?** yì xiǎoshi duōshao qián?
per cent: ... per cent bǎifēn zhī ...
perfect hǎojíle
perfume xiāngshuǐr
perhaps yéxǔ
period (*of time*) shíqī; (*menstruation*) yuèjīng
perm diàntàng
permit (*noun*) xúkězhèng
person rén
personal effects zìyòng wùpǐn
pessimistic bēiguān
petrol qìyóu
petrol can yóutǒng
petrol station jiāyóuzhàn
petrol tank (*in car*) yóuxiāng
pharmacy yàofáng
phone *see* **telephone**
photogenic shàngxiàng
photograph zhàopiàn; **would you take a photograph of us?** qǐng nín bāng wǒmen zhàoge xiàng, hǎo ma?
photographer shèyǐngshī
photo studio zhàoxiàngguǎn
phrase: a useful phrase yíge yǒuyòng

de cír
phrasebook xiǎocídiǎn
pianist gāngqínjiā
piano gāngqín
pickpocket páshǒu
pick up: when can I pick them up?
(clothes from laundry etc) shénme
shíhou néng qǔ?; **will you come and
pick me up?** nǐ lái jiē wǒ, hǎo ma?
picnic (noun) yěcān
picture huàr
pie (meat) xiànrbǐng; **apple pie**
píngguopái
piece kuàir; **a piece of ...** yíkuàir ...
pig zhū
pigeon gēzı
piles (medical) zhìchuāng
pile-up (crash) jiāotōng dà shìgu
pill yàowánr; (contraceptive) bìyùnyào;
I'm on the pill wǒ chī bìyùnyào
pillarbox xìntǒng
pillow zhěntou
pillow case zhěntào
pin (noun) biézhēn
pineapple bōluó
pineapple juice bōluózhī
pink fěnhóng
pint pǐntuō; see page 117
pipe (for smoking) yāndǒu; (for water)
shuǐguǎnr
pipe cleaner yāndǒu tōngtiáo
pipe tobacco yānsī
pity: it's a pity zhēn kěxī
pizza yìdàlìshì xiànrbǐng
place (noun) dìfang; **is this place
taken?** zhèr yǒu rén ma?; **would
you keep my place for me?** máfan
nín bāng wo liúzhe zhèige zuòr, hǎo
ma?; **at my place** zai wǒ nàr
place mat pánzı diànr
plain (food) dàn; (not patterned) sùshǎir
de
plane fēijī
plant zhíwù
plaster cast shígāo bēngdài
plastic sùliào
plastic bag sùliàodàir
plate pánzı
platform zhàntái; **which platform,
please?** qǐngwèn, zai jǐhào zhàntái?
play (verb) wánr; (noun: in theatre)
huàjù

playboy huāhuā gōngzǐ
playground (park) értóng lèyuán;
(school) cāochǎng
pleasant yúkuài
please qǐng; **yes please** hǎo, xièxie;
could you please ...? qǐng nín ...,
hǎo ma?
plenty: plenty of ... hěn duō ...;
that's plenty, thanks gòule, xièxie
pleurisy xiōngmóyán
pliers qiánzı
plonk (cheap wine) piányi de pútaojiǔ
plug (electrical) chātóu; (for car)
huǒhuāsāi; (in sink) sāizı
plughole shuǐchíkǒu
plum lǐzı
plumber guǎnzıgōng
plum blossom méihuā
plus (plus sign) zhèng; **four plus two**
sì jiā èr
p.m. (1.00–6.00) xiàwu; (6.00–12.00)
wǎnshang; **at 2 p.m.** xiàwu
liángdiǎn; **at 10 p.m.** wǎnshang
shídiǎn; see page 115
pneumonia fèiyán
poached egg hébāodàn
pocket kǒudàir; **in my pocket** zai wó
kǒudàirli
pocketbook (woman's handbag) nǚyòng
shǒutíbāo
pocketknife zhédiédāo
podiatrist xiūjiǎo yīsheng
point: could you point to it? qǐng nín
zhǐgei wo kàn, hǎo ma?; **four point
six** sì diǎnr liù; **there's no point** bù
zhíde
points (in car) báijīn
poisonous yǒu dú
police jǐngchá; **call the police!** kuài
jiào jǐngcha qu!
policeman jǐngchá
police station pàichūsuǒ
polish (for shoes) xiéyóu; (for floor)
dìbǎnlà; (for furniture) dǎguānglà;
will you polish my shoes? qǐng
bāng wǒ cāca xié, hǎo ma?
polite yóu lǐmào
politician (positive term) zhèngzhìjiā;
(negative term) zhèngkè; (neutral term)
zhèngjiè rénwù
politics zhèngzhì
polluted wūrǎnle de

ong	ou	q	u	un	ü	ʋ	ui	uo	x	yan	z	zh
ung	soul	ch	soon	open	huge	huge	way	wor	sh	yen	dz	j

pond chítáng
pony xiáomǎ
pool *(for swimming)* yóuyǒngchí; *(game)* dànzıqiú
pool table qiútái
poor *(not rich)* qióng; *(quality)* lièzhì; poor old chap! kělián de lǎo jiāhuo!
Pope jiàohuáng
pop music liúxíng yīnyuè
popsicle *(tm)* bīnggùnr
pop singer liúxíng gēshǒu
popular shòu huānyíng
population rénkǒu
pork zhūròu
port *(for boats)* gángkǒu
porter *(in hotel)* fúwùyuán; *(at station etc)* bānyùngōng
portrait huàxiàng
Portugal Pútáoyá
Portuguese *(adjective)* Pútáoyá; *(person)* Pútáoyáren; *(language)* Pútáoyáyǔ
poser *(phoney person)* wěijūnzǐ
posh *(restaurant)* háohuá; *(person)* shàngliú shèhui de
possibility kěnéngxìng
possible kěnéng; is it possible to ...? yóu kěnéng ...?; as ... as possible jìn kěnéng ...
post *(noun: mail)* xìn; could you post this for me? qǐng bāng wo bǎ zhèige jìzǒu, hǎo ma?
postbox xìnxiāng
postcard míngxìnpiàn
poster zhāotiēhuà
poste restante liújú dàilǐng yóujiàn
post office yóujú
pot hú; a pot of tea for two yìhú chá, liǎngge ren hē; pots and pans chuījù
potato tǔdòu
potato chips zhá tǔdòupiànr
potato salad tǔdòu shālà
pottery *(objects)* táoqì; *(workshop)* táoqìchǎng
pound *(money)* yīngbàng; *(weight)* bàng; *see page XYZ*
pour: it's pouring down xià dàyǔ le
powder *(for face)* huàzhuāngfěn
powdered milk náifěn
power cut tíngdiàn
power point diànyuán chāzuò

power station fādiànzhàn
practise, practice: I need to practise wǒ xūyào liànlian
pram yīng'ér shǒutuīchē
prawn cocktail xiārén pīnpánr
prawns duìxiā
prefer: I prefer jasmine tea wǒ háishı xǐhuan hē mòli huāchá
preferably: preferably tomorrow háishı míngtian hǎo
pregnant huáiyùn
Premier zónglǐ
prescription *(for chemist)* chǔfāng
present *(gift)* lǐwù; here's a present for you zhèshı géi nǐ de lǐwù; at present xiànzai
president *(of company)* zǒngcái; *(of country)* zóngtǒng
press: could you press these? qǐng bāng wo yùnyun zhèxie yīfu, hǎo ma?
pretty piàoliang; it's pretty expensive tài guìle
price jiàgé
prickly heat fèizı
priest shénfù
prime minister shǒuxiàng
print *(picture)* bǎnhuá
printed matter yìnshuāpǐn
priority *(in driving)* yōuxiān
prison jiānyù
private sīren; private bath dài xízǎojiān de
prize jiángpǐn
probably kěnéng
problem wèntì; I have a problem wó yǒu ge wèntì; no problem! méi wèntì!
program(me) *(theatre)* jiémùdānr; *(schedule)* rìchéng
promise: I promise wó bǎozhèng; is that a promise? yì yán wéi dìng?
pronounce: how do you pronounce this? zhèi zěnme niàn?
properly: it's not repaired properly xiūde bù hǎo
prostitute jìnǚ
protect bǎohù
protection factor *(of suntan lotion)* bǎohù zuòyong
Protestant jīdūjiàotú
proud jiāo'ào

ai	ao	c	e	ei	en	h	i	ı	ian	ie	iu	o
I	how	ts	her	ay	open	loch	ee	sir	yen	yeh	yoyo	or

prunes huàméi
public (*adjective*) gōnggòng
public convenience gōnggòng cèsuǒ
public holiday gōngjià
pudding bùdīng
pull lā; **he pulled out without indicating** tā méi dǎ zhǐshìdēng jiù chāochē
pullover máobèixīn
pump (*noun*) bèng; (*for bike*) dǎqìtǒng
punctual zhǔnshí
puncture (*noun*) chuānkǒng; **this tyre/tire is punctured** zhèi dài sāqì
pure (*gold etc*) chún; **pure silk** zhēnsī
purple zǐsè

purse (*for money*) qiánbāo; (*handbag*) nǚyòng shǒutíbāo
push tuī; **don't push in!** bié jiā sānr!
push-chair értóng shǒutuīchē
put fàng; **where did you put ...?** ní bǎ ... fàng zai nǎr le?; **where can I put ...?** wó bǎ ... fàng zai nǎr?; **could you put the lights on?**qíng dǎkāi dēng, hǎo ma?; **will you put the light out?** qíng guānshang dēng, hǎo ma?; **you've put the price up** nǐ tíjià le; **could you put us up for the night?** wǒmen kéyi zai zhèr guò yíyè ma?
pyjamas shuìyī

Q

quality zhìliàng; **poor quality** lièzhì; **good quality** yōuzhì
quarantine jiǎnyì
quart *see page 117*
quarter sìfēn zhī yī; **quarter of an hour** yíkè zhōng; *see page 115*
quay mǎtou
quayside: on the quayside zai mǎtoushang
question wèntí; **that's out of the question** méiyou kěnéng
queue (*verb*) páiduì; **there was a big**

queue páiduì de ren hěn duō
quick kuài; **that was quick** zhēn kuài; **which is the quickest way?** (*to get somewhere*) nǎ tiáo lù zuì kuài?
quickly kuài diǎnr
quiet (*place, hotel*) ānjìng; **be quiet!** ānjìng diǎnr!
quinine kuíníngshuǐ
quite: quite a lot xiāngdāng duō; **it's quite different** hěn bù yíyàng; **I'm not quite sure** wǒ bú tài qīngchu

R

rabbit tùzi
rabies kuángquǎnbìng
race (*for horses, cars*) bǐsài; **I'll race you there** wǒmen bǐbi kàn shéi xiān dào
racket (*sport*) qiúpāi
radiator (*of car*) shuǐxiāng; (*in room*)

nuǎnqì
radio shōuyīnjī; **I heard it on the radio** wǒ cóng shōuyīnjīli tīngdào de
rag (*for cleaning*) mābù
rail: by rail zuò huǒchē
railroad, railway tiělù
railroad crossing píngjiāo dàokǒu

ong	ou	q	u	un	ü	ʊ	ui	uo	x	yan	z	zh
ung	soul	ch	soon	open	huge	huge	way	wor	sh	yen	dz	j

rain (*noun*) yǔ; **in the rain** zai yǔli; **it's raining** xiàyǔ le
rain boots yǔxié
raincoat yǔyī
rape (*noun*) qiángjiān
rare (*object etc*) xīyǒu; (*steak*) nèn diǎnr
rash (*on skin*) pízhěn
rat láoshǔ
rate (*for changing money*) duìhuànlǜ; **what's the rate for the pound?** yīngbàng de duìhuànlǜ shı duōshao?; **what are your rates?** (*at car hire etc*) zūjīn shı duōshao?
rather: it's rather late tài wǎnle; **I'd rather ...** wǒ háishı xiǎng ...; **I'd rather have boiled rice** wǒ háishı xiǎng chī mǐfàn
raw (*meat*) shēng
razor (*dry*) tìhúdāo; (*electric*) diàntìdāo
razor blades dāopiànr
reach: within easy reach hěn jìn
read (*book*) kànshū; (*newspaper*) kànbào; **I can't read it** wǒ kàn bù qīng; **could you read it out?** qíng nǐ niàn yíxia, hǎo ma?
ready zhǔnbèi hǎo de; **when will it be ready?** shénme shíhòu néng hǎo?; **I'll go and get ready** wǒ qù zhǔnbèi yíxia; **I'm not ready yet** wǒ hái méi hǎo ne
real zhēn de
really zhēn de; **I really must go** wǒ zhēn déi zǒu le; **is it really necessary?** zhēn yǒu bìyào ma?
realtor fángdìchǎn jīngjìrén
rear: at the rear zai hòutou
rear light wěidēng
rearview mirror hòushìjìng
rear wheels hòulún
reasonable (*prices etc*) hélǐ; **be reasonable** yīnggāi jiǎng dàoli
receipt shōujù
recently zuìjìn
reception (*in hotel*) zǒng fúwùtái; (*for guests*) zhāodàihuì
reception desk zǒng fúwùtái
receptionist dàtīng fúwùyuán
recipes hípǔ; **can you give me the recipe for this?** qíng nín gàosu wǒ zhèige cài shı zěnme zuòde, hǎo ma?
recognize rènshı; **I didn't recognize it** wǒ méi rènchūlai

recommend: could you recommend ...? qíng nín tuījiàn ..., hǎo ma?
record (*music*) chàngpiān
record player diànchàngjī
red hóngsè
red wine hóng pútaojiǔ
reduction (*in price*) jiǎnjià
refreshing tíshén
refreshment chádiǎn
refrigerator bīngxiāng
refund tuìkuǎn; **do I get a refund?** kéyi tuìqián ma?
region dìqū
registered guàhào; **a registered letter** guàhàoxìn
registration number (*of car*) chēhào
relative: my relatives wǒde qīnqi
relaxing: it's very relaxing zhēn shūfu
reliable (*person, car*) kěkào
religion zōngjiào
remains (*of old city etc*) yízhǐ
remember: I don't remember wǒ jìbude le; **I remember** wǒ jìde; **do you remember?** nǐ jìde ma?
remote (*village etc*) piānpì
rent (*noun: for apartment etc*) fángzū; (*verb: car etc*) chūzū; **I'd like to rent a bike** wǒ xiǎng zū liàng zìxíngchē
rented bike gòng chūzū de zìxíngchē
repair (*verb*) xiūlǐ; **can you repair it?** nǐ kéyi xiūxiu ma?
repeat chóngfù; **could you repeat that?** qíng nǐ zài shuō yíbiàn, hǎo ma?
representative (*noun: of company*) dàibiǎo
request (*noun*) qǐngqiú
rescue (*verb*) jiù
reservation yùdìng; **I have a reservation** wó jǐjing yùdìng le
reserve yùdìng; **I reserved a room in the name of ...** wó yǐ ... de míngzı dìngle ge fángjiān; **can I reserve a table for tonight?** wǒ kéyi dìng ge jīntian wǎshang de zuò ma?
rest (*repose*) xiūxi: (*remainder*) shèngxia de; **I need a rest** wǒ xūyào xiūxi yíxia; **the rest of the group** tāmen biéde ren
restaurant (*small*) fànguǎnr; (*large*)

fàndiàn

rest room cèsuǒ

retired: I'm retired wǒ tuìxiūle

return: a return ticket to London qù Lúndūn de láihuípiào; **I'll return it tomorrow** wǒ míngtian huán

returnable (*deposit*) yājīn

reverse charge call duìfāng fùkuǎn

reverse gear dàochē dǎng

revolting ràng ren ěxīn

rheumatism fēngshībìng

rib lèigǔ; **I have a broken rib** wǒde lèigǔ duànle yìgen

ribbon (*for hair*) fàdài

rice (*uncooked*) dàmǐ; (*cooked*) mǐfàn

rice bowl fànwǎn

rice field dàotián

rich (*person*) yǒuqián; (*food*) yóunì; **it's too rich** tài nìle

ride: can you give me a ride into town? wǒ dāge chē jìnchéng, xíng ma?; **thanks for the ride** xièxie nín

ridiculous: that's ridiculous tài kěxiàole

right (*correct*) duì; (*not left*) yòu; **you're right** duì; **you were right** nǐ duìle; **that's right** duì; **that can't be right** yídìng bú duì; **right!** duì!; **is this the right road for ...?** qù ..., zhème zǒu duì ma?; **on the right** zai yòubianr; **turn right** wǎng yòu guǎi; **not right now** xiànzai bù xíng

right-hand drive yòubianr kāichē

ring (*on finger*) jièzhı; **I'll ring you** wo géi ni dǎ diànhuà

ring road huánchénglù

ripe (*fruit*) shú

rip-off: it's a rip-off zhè shı qiāo zhúgàng; **rip-off prices** qiāo zhúgàng de jiàr

risky màoxiǎn; **it's too risky** tài màoxiǎnle

river hé; **by the river** zai hébiānr

road lù; **is this the road to ...?** qù ..., shı zhèitiáo lù ma?; **further down the road** zhèitiáo lù zài wǎng qián

road accident jiāotōng shìgù

road hog kāichē búgù biéren de ren

road map dàolùtú

roadside: by the roadside kào lùbiānr

roadsign lùbiāo

roadwork(s) xiūlù

roast beef kǎo niúròu

roast pork kǎo zhūròu

rob: I've been robbed wǒ ràng ren géi qiǎngle

robe (*housecoat*) zhàopáo

rock (*stone*) yánshí; **on the rocks** (*with ice*) jiā bīngkuàir

rocky (*coast etc*) yǒu xuányá qiàobì de

roll (*bread*) miànbāo juǎnr

Roman Catholic Tiānzhǔjiào

romance làngmàn

Rome: when in Rome ... rù jìng suí sú

roof fángdǐng; **on the roof** fángdǐngshang

roof rack chēdǐng xínglijià

room fángjiān; **do you have a room?** yǒu fángjiān ma?; **a room for two people** yíge shuānrenjiān; **a room for three nights** yìjiān fáng, zhù sānge wǎngshang; **a room with a bathroom** dài xízǎojiān de fángjiān; **in my room** zai wǒ fángjiānli; **there's no room** méi dìfang le

room service fángjiān fúwù

rope shéngzı

rose méiguì

rotary (*for traffic*) huánxíng jiāochā

rough (*sea, crossing*) fēnglàng hěn dà; **the engine sounds a bit rough** fādòngjī de shēngyīn yóu diǎnr bú duì; **I've been sleeping rough** (*in open air*) wǒ zai lùtiān shuì de

roughly (*approximately*) dàyuē

roulette lúnpándǔ

round (*adjective*) yuán; **it's my round** gāi wǒ mǎi le

roundabout (*for traffic*) huánxíng jiāchā

round-trip: a round-trip ticket to ... qù ... de láihuípiào

route lùxiàn; **what's the best route?** něitiáo lùxiàn zuì hǎo?

rowboat, rowing boat huázı

rubber (*material*) xiàngjiāo; (*eraser*) xiàngpí

rubber band xiàngpíjīnr

rubbish (*waste*) lājī; (*poor quality goods*) lièzhìpǐn; **that's rubbish!** húshuō!

rucksack bēibāo

rude cūlǔ; **he was very rude** tā zhèi

ren hěn bú kèqi
rug xiǎo dìtǎn
ruins fèixū
rum lánmújiǔ
rum and coke kékoukělè jiā lánmújiǔ
run (*person*) pǎo; **I go running** wǒ
jīngcháng pǎobù; **quick, run!** kuài
pǎo!; **how often do the buses run?**

gōnggòng qìchē duóchang shíjian
yítàng?; **he's been run over** tā
zhuàng chē le; **I've run out of gas/
petrol** wǒde qìyóu yòngwánle
rupture (*medical*) shànqì
Russia Éguó
Russian (*adjective*) Éguó; (*person*)
Éguoren; (*language*) Éyǔ

S

saccharine tángjīng
sad nánguò
saddle (*for bike*) chēzuò; (*for horse*)
mǎānzi
safe ānquán; **will it be safe here/
there?** zhèr/nàr ānquán ma?; **is it
safe to drink/eat?**zhèi kéyi hē/chī
ma?; **is it safe to swim here?** zhèr
kéyi yóuyǒng ma?; **could you put
this in your safe?** qǐng nín bāng wo
bǎ zhè fàng zai báoxiǎnxiāngli, hǎo
ma?
safety pin biézhēn
sail (*noun*) fān; **can we go sailing?**
zhèr kéyi wánr fānchuán ma?
sailor shuíshǒu; (*naval*) shuǐbīng
salad shālà
salad cream shālà yóu
salad dressing shālà yóu
sale: is it for sale? shɪ màide ma?;
it's not for sale bú shɪ màide
sales clerk shòuhuòyuán
salmon dà mǎhāyú
salt yán
salty: it's too salty tài xiánle
same yíyàng; **I want one the same as
this** yào yíge gēn zhèi yíyàng de; **the
same size** yíyàng dà de; **the same
again, please** zài lái yíge; **it's all the
same to me** wǒ wú suǒwèi; **thanks
all the same** búguò háishi yào xièxie
nǐ
sampan shānbǎn
sand shāzɪ
sandals liángxié; **a pair of sandals**

yìshuāng liángxié
sandwich sānmíngzhì; **a chicken/ham
sandwich** jīròu/huótuǐ sānmíngzhì
sandy yǒu shā de; (*colour*) shātānsè; **a
sandy beach** shātān
sanitary belt yuèjīngdài
sarcastic fěngcì
sardines shādīngyú
satisfactory jiào ren mǎnyì de; **this is
not satisfactory** zhè bú jiào ren
mǎnyì
Saturday xīngqiliù
sauce zhī
saucepan píngdǐguō
saucer diézɪ
sauna zhēngqìyù
sausage xiāngcháng
sauté potatoes jiān tǔdòu
save (*life*) jiù
savo(u)ry (*tasty*) hǎochī; (*salty*) xián
say shuō; **how do you say ... in
Chinese?** ... Zhōngwén zěnme
shuō?; **what did you/he say?** nǐ/tā
shuō shénme?; **I/he said ...**wǒ/tā
shuō ...; **I wouldn't say no** (*yes
please*) wǒ dāngrán bú huì shuō bù!
scald: he's scalded himself tā
tàngzhele
scarf (*for neck*) wéijīn; (*for head*) tóujīn
scarlet dàhóng
scenery fēngjǐng
scent (*perfume*) xiāngwèir
schedule rìchéng
scheduled flight bānjī
school xuéxiào; (*university*) dàxué; **I'm

ai	ao	c	e	ei	en	h	i	ɪ	ian	ie	iu	o
I	how	ts	her	ay	open	loch	ee	sir	yen	yeh	yoyo	or

still at school wǒ hái zai shàngxưé
science kēxưé
scissors: a pair of scissors yìbá jiǎnzı
scooter (*motor scooter*) qīngqí
scorching: it's really scorching (*weather*) tiānr rèsıle
score: what's the score? (*in game*) bǐfēn shı duōshao?
scotch (*whisky*) wēishìjì
Scotch tape (*tm*) tòumíng jiāozhǐ
Scotland Sūgélán; **I'm Scottish** wǒ shı Sūgélánren
scrambled eggs chǎojīdàn
scratch: I've/he's scratched my/ himself wǒ/tā huále yíxia; **it's only a scratch** jiùshı huále yíxia
scream (*verb*) jiānjiào
screw (*noun*) luósīdīng
screwdriver luósīdāo
scroll huàzhóu
scrubbing brush (*for floors*) yìngmáoshuā
scruffy (*appearance, person*) lāta; (*hotel*) yòu zāng yòu luàn
sea hǎi; **by the sea** zai hǎibiānr
sea air: we are going to get some sea air wǒmen qù hǎibiānr hūxī yíxia xīnxian kōngqı
seafood hǎiwèir
seafood restaurant hǎiwèir fàndiàn
seafront qiánhǎiyánr; **on the seafront** zai qiánhǎiyánr
seagull hǎi'ōu
seal (*for name etc*) túzhāng; (*animal*) hǎibào
search (*verb*) zhǎo; **I searched everywhere** wǒ dàochù dōu zhǎobiànle
search party sōusuǒduì
seashell bèikér
seasick: I feel seasick wǒ yūnchuánle; **I get seasick** wǒ yūnchuán
seaside: by the seaside zai hǎibiānr; **let's go to the seaside** wǒmen qù hǎibiānr ba?
season jìjié; **in the high season** wàngjì; **in the low season** dànjì
seasoning zuóliao
seat zuòwei; **is this anyone's seat?** zhèige zuòwei yǒu rén ma?
seat belt ānquándài; **do you have to wear a seat belt?** yào bu yào jì

ānquándài?
sea urchin háidǎn
seaweed hǎicǎo; (*edible*) zǐcài
secluded pìjìng
second (*adjective*) dì'èr; (*of time*) yìmiǎo zhōng; **just a second!** zhè jiù dé!; **can I have a second helping?** zài lái yìfènr, xíng ma?
second class (*travel*) èrděng
second-hand jiù; **second-hand shop** jiùhuòdiàn; **second-hand bookshop** jiùshūdiàn
secret (*noun*) mìmì
security check ānquán jiǎnchá
sedative zhìténgyào
see kànjian; **I didn't see it** wǒ méi kànjian; **have you seen my husband/wife?** nǐ kànjian wǒ zhàngfu/fūren le ma?; **I saw him/ her this morning** wǒ jīntian zǎoshang kànjian tā/tā le; **can I see the manager?** wǒ néng jiànjian jīnglǐ ma?; **see you tonight!** wǎnshang jiàn!; **can I see?** wǒ kéyi kànkan ma?; **oh, I see** (*I understand*) ò, wǒ míngbaile; **will you see to it?** (*arrange it*) nǐ ānpái yíxia, hǎo ma?
seldom hén shǎo
self-service zìzhù
sell mài; **do you sell ...?** nǐ mài bu mài ...?; **will you sell it to me?** nèige kéyi mài gei wǒ ma?
sellotape (*tm*) tòumíng jiāodài
send (*mail*) jì; (*person*) pài; **I want to send this to England** zhèige jì dao Yīngguó qù; **I'll have to send this food back** zhèi cài wó děi sònghuíqu
senior: Mr Wang senior Lǎo Wáng
senior citizen lǎoniánren
sensational (*tremendous*) tè láijìn
sense: I have no sense of direction wǒ zhèi ren lǎo diàoxiàng; **it doesn't make sense** méi dàoli
sensible (*person*) jiǎng dàoli; (*idea*) yǒu dàoli
sensitive (*person, skin*) míngǎn
sentimental (*person*) hěn dòng gǎnqíng de; (*film, novel etc*) ràng ren dòng gǎnqíng de
separate fēnkai; **can we have separate bills?** wǒmen fēnkai suànzhàng, xíng ma?

ong	ou	q	u	un	ü	ʊ	ui	uo	x	yan	z	zh
ung	soul	ch	soon	open	huge	huge	way	wor	sh	yen	dz	j

separated: we're separated wǒmen fēnjūle

separately (*pay, travel*) fēnkai

September jiǔyʋe

septic huànóng

serious (*person*) yánsù; (*situation, problem, illness*) yánzhòng; **it's a serious problem** wèntí hěn yánzhòng; **I'm serious** wǒ shuō de shɪ shíhuà; **he looks very serious** tā kànshangqʋ hěn yánsù; **you can't be serious!** nǐ zai kāi wánxiào ba; **is it serious, doctor?** yīsheng, yán bu yánzhòng?

seriously: seriously ill bìngzhòng

service: the service there was excellent nàr de fúwù zhēn bàng; **could we have some service, please?** kéyi zhàogu wǒmen yíxia ma?; **church service** lǐbài; **the car needs a service** zhèi chē yào jiǎnxiū yíxia le

service charge (*in restaurant*) xiǎofèi

service station jiāyóuzhàn

serviette cānjīn

set: it's time we were setting off wǒmen gāi zǒu le

set menu fènrfàn

settle up: can we settle up now? (*pay*) wǒmen xiànzài fùqián, xíng ma?

several jǐge

sew féng; **could you sew this back on?** qǐng nín bāng wó bǎ zhèi féngshangqʋ, hǎo ma?

sexist (*noun: male*) dà nánzɪzhǔyi; (*female*) dà nǚzɪzhǔyi

sexy xìnggǎn

shade: in the shade zai yīnliángr dìr

shadow yǐngzɪ

shake: let's shake hands wǒmen wòwo shǒu ba

shallow (*water*) qiǎn

shame: what a shame! zhēn kěxī!

shampoo (*noun*) xǐfàjīng; **can I have a shampoo and set?** qǐng bāng wo xǐxi tóu, zài zuòzuo tóufa, hǎo ma?

share: we are sharing a room wǒmen hézhù yìjiān fáng; **we don't mind sharing a table** wǒmen héyòng yìzhāng zhuōzɪ yě xíng; **let's share the cost** zhèi qián wǒmen yìqǐ píngtān, hǎo ma?

shark shāyú

shark's fin soup yúchì tāng

sharp (*knife*) kuài; (*taste*) kǔ; (*pain*) lìhai

shattered: I'm shattered (*very tired*) wǒ lèisɪle

shave: I need a shave wǒ yào guāgua liǎn; **can you give me a shave?** qǐng bāng wǒ guāgua liǎn, hǎo ma?

shaver diàntìdāo

shaving brush tìhú máoshuā

shaving foam tìhú pàomò

shaving point diàntìdāo chāxiāo

shaving soap tìhú yòng zào

shawl pēijiān

she tā; **is she here?** tā zài ma?; **is she a friend of yours?** tā shɪ nǐde péngyou ma?; **she's not English** tā bú shɪ Yīngguoren; *see page 97*

sheep yáng

sheet chuángdānr

shelf jiàzɪ

shell kér

sherry xʋělìjiǔ

ship chuán; **by ship** zuò chuán

shirt chènyī

shit! zāole!

shock (*surprise*) chījīng; **I got an electric shock from the ...** wó gěi ... guòle yíxia

shock-absorber jiǎnzhènqì

shocking ràng ren chījīng de

shoe xié; **my shoes** wǒde xié; **a pair of shoes** yìshuāng xié

shoelaces xiédàir

shoe polish xiéyóu

shoe repairer xiūxiéjiàng

shop shāngdiàn

shopping: I'm going shopping wǒ qù mǎi dōngxi

shop window chúchuāng

shore (*of sea, lake*) àn

short (*person*) ǎi; (*thing*) duǎn; **the short man over there** nèibiānr nèige ǎigèr; **these trousers are too short** zhèitiáo kùzɪ tài duǎnle; **I'd like my hair cut short** tóufa qíng jiǎnde duǎndiǎnr; **it's only a short distance from here** lí zhèr bù yuǎn

short-change: you've short-changed me ni shǎo zhǎo wo qián le

short circuit duǎnlù

shortcut jiéjìng
shorts duǎnkù; (*underpants*) nèikù
should: what should I do? wǒ gāi zěnme bàn?; **he shouldn't be long** tā bú huì qù duō jiǔ; **you should have told me** ní běnlái gāi gàosu wǒ
shoulder jiānbǎng
shoulder blade jiānjiágǔ
shout (*verb*) hǎn
show: could you show me it? qíng nǐ ná gei wǒ kànkan, hǎo ma?; **could you show me how to do it?** qíng nǐ zuò gei wǒ kànkan, hǎo ma?; **does it show?** néng kànchulai ma?; **we'd like to go to a show** wǒmen xiǎng kàn ge jiémù shénmede
shower (*in bathroom*) línyù; **with shower** dài línyù
showercap línyùmào
show-off: don't be a show-off bié chuī
shrimps xiā
shrine shénkān
shrink: it's shrunk (*clothing*) suōshuǐle
shut (*verb*) guānshang; **when do you/ they shut?** nǐmen/tāmen jídiǎn guānménr?; **I've shut myself out** wó bǎ zìjǐ guān zai wàitou le; **shut up!** zhù zuǐ!
shutter (*on camera*) kuàiménr; (*on window*) bǎiyèchuāng
shutter release kuàiménr kāiguān
shy hàixiū
Siberia Xībólìyà
Siberian Xībólìyà
sick (*ill*) bìngle; **I think I'm going to be sick** (*vomit*) wó xiǎng tù
side biānr; (*in game*) duì; **at the side of the road** zai lùbiānr; **the other side of town** chéng nèitóu
side lights cèdēng
side street hútòng
sidewalk rénxíngdào
siesta wǔshuì
sight: the sights of ... ... de míngshèng
sightseeing: sightseeing tour yóulǎn; **we're going sightseeing** wǒmen qù yóulǎn shìróng
sign páir; (*roadsign*) lùbiāo; (*Chinese character*) Hànzì; **what's written on that sign?** hèige páirshang xiěde

shénme?; **where do I sign?** wǒ zài nǎr qiānzì
signal: he didn't give a signal (*driver, cyclist*) tā méi dǎ xìnhào
signature qiānzì
signpost lùbiāo
silence chénmò
silencer xiāoyīnqì
silk sīchóu
Silk Road sīchòu zhī lù
silly (*person, thing to do etc*) chǔn; **that's silly!** zhēn chǔn!
silver (*noun, adjective*) yín
silver foil yín bó
similar chàbuduō
simple (*easy*) jiǎndān
since: since yesterday cóng zuótian qǐ; **since we got here** cóng wǒmen lái zhèr qǐ
sincere qīnqiè
sing chànggē
Singapore Xīnjiāpō
singer gēchàngjiā
single: a single room yíge dānrenjiān; **a single to ...** ... de dānchéngpiào; **I'm single** wǒ shì dānshēn
sink (*in kitchen*) shuǐchí; **the ship sank** chuán chénle
sir xiānsheng; **excuse me, sir** xiānsheng, máfán nin
sister: my sister (*older*) wó jiějie; (*younger*) wǒ mèimei
sister-in-law: my sister-in-law (*wife of older brother*) wǒ sǎosao; (*wife of younger brother*) wǒ dìxí
sit: may I sit here? wǒ kéyi zuò zhèr ma?; **is anyone sitting here?** yǒu rén zuò zhèr ma?
sitting: the second sitting for lunch dì'èr bōr chī wǔfàn de
situation qíngkuàng
size chǐcùn; **do you have any other sizes?** yǒu biéde chǐcùn méi yǒu?
sketch (*noun*) sùxiě
ski (*noun*) xuěqiāo; (*verb*) huáxuě; **a pair of skis** yìfù xuěqiāo
ski boots huáxuě xié
skid: I/the car skidded wó/chē dǎle ge huá
skiing huáxuě; **we're going skiing** wǒmen huáxuě qù

ski instructor huáxuě jiàoliàn
ski-lift shàngshān diàoyǐ
skin pífu
skin-diving qiánshuǐ; **I'm going skin-diving** wǒ qiánshuǐ qù
skinny tài shòu
ski-pants huáxuě kù
ski pole huáxuě zhàng
skirt qúnzı
ski run huáxuě dào
ski slope huáxuě pō
skull nǎoké
sky tiān
sleep shuìjiào; **I can't sleep** wǒ shuìbuzháo jiào; **did you sleep well?** shuìde hǎo ma?; **I need a good sleep** wǒ xūyào hǎohao shuì yíjiào
sleeper (rail) wòpù
sleeping bag shuìdài
sleeping car (rail) wòpù chēxiāng
sleeping pill ānmiányào
sleepy (person) kùn; (town) ānjìng; **I'm feeling sleepy** wǒ kùnle
sleeve xiùzı
slice (noun) piànr
slide (photography) huàndēngpiànr
slim (adjective) miáotiao; **I'm slimming** wǒ zai jiéshí
slip (under dress) chènqún; **I slipped** (on pavement etc) wǒ huále yíxia
slippery huá; **it's slippery here** zhèr huá
slow màn; **slow down!** (driving, speaking) màn diǎnr!
slowly màn; **could you say it slowly?** qǐng nín jiǎngde màn diǎnr, hǎo ma?; **very slowly** hěn màn
small xiǎo
small change língqián
smallpox tiānhuā
smart (clothes) shuài
smashing: we had a smashing time/meal wǒmen wánrde/chīde tè tòngkuai
smell: there's a funny smell yǒu ge guài wèir; **it smells** (smells bad) yǒu wèir le; **what's the smell?** shénme wèir?; **what a lovely smell!** zhēn xiāng!
smile (verb) xiào
smoke (noun) yān; **do you smoke?** nǐ chōu yān ma?; **do you mind if I**

smoke? wǒ kéyi zai zhèr chōu yān ma?; **I don't smoke** wǒ bú huì chōu yān
smooth (surface) huáliu
smoothy: he's a real smoothy tā zhèi ren tè yuánhuá
snack: I'd just like a snack wǒ jiùshı suíbiàn chī diǎnr
snackbar kuàicānguǎnr
snake shé
sneakers lǚyóuxié
snob shìliyǎnr
snorkel huànqìguǎnr
snow (noun) xuě
so: not so fast bié zhème kuài; **who said so?** shéi zhème shuō?; **it's so hot/beautiful!** zhēn rè/měi!; **I'm a lawyer – so am I** wǒ shı lǜshı – wó yě shı; **I'm hungry – so am I** wǒ èle – wó yě èle; **we are going tomorrow – so are we** wǒmen míngtian zǒu – wǒmen yě míngtian zǒu; **I like tea – so do I** wó xǐhuan chá – wó yé xǐhuan; **thank you so much** fēicháng gǎnxiè; **it wasn't – it was so!** bú shı – shì!; **how was it? – so-so** zěnmeyàng? – mǎmahūhu
soaked: I'm soaked wǒ shītòule
soap féizào
soap-powder xǐyīfěn
sober: I'm sober (I haven't had a drink) wǒ méi hē jiǔ; (I'm not drunk) wǒ méi zuì
soccer zúqiú
socialism shèhuìzhǔyì
socialist (adjective) shèhuìzhǔyì; (person) shèhuìzhǔyìzhě
sock wàzı
socket (electrical) chāzuò
soda (water) sūdá
sofa shāfā
soft (material etc) ruǎn
soft drink ruǎn yǐnliào
soft lenses ruǎnpiànr wúxíng yǎnjìng
soldier zhànshı
sole (of shoe) xiédǐ; (of foot) jiáodǐ; **could you put new soles on these?** qǐng nín huàn shuāng xīn xiédǐ, hǎo ma?
solid (strong) jiēshı; (not liquid or gas) gùtǐ
some: may I have some water/tea?

qǐng lái diǎnr shuǐ/chá, hǎo ma?; **do you have some matches/paper?** ní yóu huǒchái/zhǐ ma?; **some are cheap/expensive** yǒude guì/piányi; **some of them/us** tāmen/wǒmen yǒuderen; **can I have some?** wǒ lái diǎnr, xíng ma?; **that's some drink!** (strong) zhèi jiǔ zhēn lìhai!; (excellent) zhèi jiǔ zhēn bàng!

somebody, someone: someone is looking/waiting for you yǒu rén zhǎo/děng ni; **I am looking/waiting for someone** wǒ zai zhǎo/děng rén

something: there's something I want to tell you wǒ yào gàosu nǐ jiàn shìr; **something's gone wrong** chū shìrle; **I've got something to give you** wǒ xiǎng sòng ni diǎnr dōngxi; **I'm going to buy something** wǒ qù mǎi dōngxi; **I've got something in my eye** wó yǎnjīngli jìnqule diǎnr dōngxi; **I want to have something to drink/eat** wó xiǎng hē/chī diǎnr shénme

sometime: sometime tomorrow/next year míngtian/mínnian shénme shíhou

sometimes yǒude shíhou

somewhere: I am looking for somewhere to stay/eat wó xiǎng zhǎo ge dìfang zhù/chīfàn

son: my son wǒ érzi

song gēr

son-in-law: my son-in-law wó nǚxù

soon yìhuǐr; **he/I'll be back soon** tā/wǒ yìhuǐr jiu huílai; **as soon as you can** yuè kuài yuè hǎo

sore: it's sore here zhèr téng

sore throat: I have a sore throat wó sǎngzi téng

sorry: (I'm) sorry duìbuqǐ; **sorry?** (didn't understand) nín gāngcái shuō shénme?

sort: what sort of ...? shénme yàng de ...?; **a different sort of ...** bù yíyàng de ...; **will you sort it out?** zhèi shìr zhèn nín jiějué yíxia, hǎo ma?

soup tāng

sour (taste) suān

south nán; **to the south of ...** zai ... yǐnán

South Africa Nánfēi

South African (adjective) Nánfēi; (person) Nánfēiren

southeast dōngnán; **to the southeast of ...** zai ... dōngnánbù

southwest xīnán; **to the southwest of ...** zai ... xīnánbù

souvenir jìniànpǐn

Soviet Union Sūlián

soy sauce jiàngyóu

spa (hot springs) wēnquán liáoyǎng shèngdì

space heater qúnuǎnqì

spade tiěqiāo

Spain Xībānyá

spanner huó bānshǒu

spare part língbùjiàn

spare tyre/tire bèiyòng lúntāi

spark(ing) plug huǒhuā sāi

speak: do you speak English? ní jiǎng Yīngyǔ ma?; **I don't speak ...** wǒ bù jiǎng ...; **can I speak to ...?** (on telephone) máfan nín zhǎo yíxia ..., hǎo ma?; **speaking** (on telephone) wǒ jiù shì

special tèbié; **nothing special** méi shénme tèbié de

specialist zhuānjiā

special(i)ty (field of study) zhuānyè; **the special(i)ty of the house** (restaurant) zhèr de náshǒucài

spectacles yǎnjìng

speed (noun) sùdu; **he was speeding** tā chāosùle

speedboat kuàitǐng

speed limit sùdu xiànzhì

speedometer chēsù lǐchéng biǎo

spell: how do you spell it? zěnme pīn?

spend huā: **I've spent all my money** wǒde qián dōu huāle

spice zuóliào

spicy: it's very spicy (hot) zhēn là

spider zhīzhū

spin-dryer shuǎigānjī

splendid (very good) hǎojíle

splint (for broken limb) jiábǎn

splinter (in finger) cìr

splitting: I've got a splitting headache wǒ tóuténgde lìhài

spoke (in wheel) fútiáo; **this spoke is broken** zhèi fútiáo duànle

sponge hǎimián

ong	ou	q	u	un	ü	ʊ	ui	uo	x	yan	z	zh
ung	soul	ch	soon	open	huge	huge	way	wor	sh	yen	dz	j

spoon xiǎosháor
sport yùndòng
sport(s) jacket shàngyī
spot (*on face etc*) fěncì; **will they repair it on the spot?** tāmen dāngshí néng xiū ma?
sprain: I've sprained my ... wǒde ... wǎile
spray (*for hair*) dìngfǎyè
spring (*season*) chūntian; (*of car, seat*) tánhuáng
square (*in town*) guángchǎng; **ten square metres** shí píngfāngmǐ
squash (*sport*) bìqiú
stain: I've got a stain on my trousers/skirt wǒ kùzi/qúnzi zhèr nòngzāngle
stairs lóutī
stale (*bread, taste*) bù xīnxian
stall: the engine keeps stalling fādòngjī lǎo xīhuǒ
stalls (*in theatre*) zhèngtīng qiánzuò
stamp (*noun*) yóupiào; **a stamp for England, please** mǎi yìzhāng dào Yīngguó de yóupiào
stand: I can't stand ... (*can't tolerate*) wǒ shòubuliǎo ...
standard (*adjective*) biāozhǔn
Standard Chinese Pǔtōnghuà
standby (*reserve*) bèiyòng
star xīngxing
start (*noun*) kāishǐ; **when does the film start?** diànyǐng shénme shíhou kāishǐ?; **the car won't start** chē fādòng bùqǐlái
starter (*of car*) diánhuǒ kāiguān; (*hors d'oeuvres – cold dishes*) lěngpánr
starving: I'm starving wǒ èsǐle
state (*in country*) zhōu; **the States** (*USA*) Měiguó
station zhàn
statue sùxiàng
stay: where are you staying? nǐmen zhù zai nǎr?; **I'm staying at ...** wǒ zhù zai ...; **I'd like to stay another week** wó xiǎng zài zhù yíge xīngqi; **I'm staying in tonight** jīntian wǎnshang wǒ bù chūqu; **we enjoyed our stay** wǒmen guòde hěn yúkuài
steak niúpái
steal tōu; **my bag has been stolen** wǒde bāo gěi tōule

steamed roll huājuǎnr
steep (*hill*) dǒu
steering wheel fāngxiàngpán; **there's something wrong with the steering** fāngxiàngpán yǒu máobing
step (*in front of house etc*) táijiē
stereo lìtǐshēng
sterling yīngbàng
stew dùn
steward (*on plane*) chéngwùyuán
stewardess (*on plane*) kōngzhōng xiáojiě
sticking plaster zhíxué gāobù
sticky: it's sticky niánhūhude
sticky tape jiāodài
still: I'm still waiting wǒ hái zai děng; **will you still be open at six?** liùdiǎn hái kāiménr ba?; **it's still not right** hái bú duì; **that's still better** zhèiyang gèng hǎo; **keep still!** bié dòng!
sting: a bee sting mìfeng zhēde gēda; **I've been stung** wó gěi zhē yíxià
stink (*noun*) chòuwèir; **it stinks** (*smells*) yǒu chòuwèir; (*is awful*) zhēn chàjìn
stockings chángtǒngwà
stolen: my wallet/watch has been stolen wǒde qiánbāo/biǎo gěi tōule
stomach wèi; **do you have something for an upset stomach?** yǒu shénme zhì fǎnwèi de yào ma?
stomach-ache wèiténg
stone (*rock*) shítou; *see page 118*
stop (*bus stop*) chēzhàn; **which is the stop for ...?** dào ... qù de chēzhàn zai nǎr?; **please, stop here** (*to taxi driver etc*) qǐng zai zhèr tíng; **do you stop near ...?** zai ... fùjìn tíng ma?; **stop doing that!** bié nèiyang!
stopover: we have a stopover at ... wǒmen zai ... tíng yíxià
store (*shop*) shāngdiàn
stor(e)y (*of buildings*) céng
storm bàofēngyǔ
story (*tale*) gùshı
stove lúzı
straight (*road etc*) zhí; **it's straight ahead** yīzhí wǎng qián zǒu; **straight away** mǎshang; **a straight whisky, please** yìbēi wēishìjì, shénme yě bù jiā

straighten: can you straighten things out? (*sort things out*) nǐ néng qù chúlǐ yíxia ma?

strange (*odd*) qíguài; (*unknown*) mòshēng

stranger shēngren; **I'm a stranger here** wǒ dìyīcì lái zhèr

strap (*on watch, on dress, on suitcase*) dàir

strawberry cǎoméi

stream xiǎoxī

street jiē; **on the street** zai jiēshang

street café jiētóu kāfēiguǎnr

streetcar yóuguǐ diànchē

streetmap jiēqūtú

strep throat sǎngzǐténg

strike: they're on strike tāmen zai bàgōng

string shéngr; **have you got some string?** yóu diǎnr shéngr ma?

striped dàitiáotiao de

stroke: he's had a stroke tā zhòngfēngle

stroll: let's go for a stroll wǒmen liūdaliuda qù, zěnmeyàng?

stroller (*for babies*) értóng shǒutuīchē

strong (*person*) zhuàng; (*taste*) nóng

stroppy (*official, waiter*) bù hézuò

stuck: the key's stuck yàoshi nábuchūlái le; **the drawer's stuck** chōuti lābuchūlái le

student xuésheng

stupid bèn; **that's stupid** zhēn bèn

sty(e) (*in eye*) jiǎnxiànyán

subtitles zìmù

suburb jiāoqū

subway (*underground*) dìtiě

successful: were you successful? chénggōngle ma?

suddenly tūrán

sue: I intend to sue wǒ yào qù kònggào

suede fānpí

sugar táng

suggest: what do you suggest? ní yǒu shénme jiànyì?

suit (*noun*) tàozhuāng; **two suits** liǎngtào yīfu; **it doesn't suit me** (*clothes*) wǒ chuān bù héshì; **it suits you** (*clothes*) nǐ chuān héshì; **that suits me fine** duì wǒ hen fāngbiàn

suitable (*time, place*) héshì

suitcase shǒutíxiāng

sulk: he's sulking tā zai shēng mènqì

sultry (*weather, climate*) mènrè

summer xiàtian; **in the summer** xiàtian

sun tàiyang; **in the sun** zai tàiyang dǐxia; **out of the sun** bié zai tàiyang dǐxia; **I've had too much sun** wǒ shàide tài lìhai le

sunbathe shài tàiyang

sunburn: I've got sunburn wǒ shàibàopíle

Sunday xīngqitiān

sunglasses tàiyangjìng

sun lounger (*chair for lying on*) tàiyangyǐ

sunny: if it's sunny rúguǒ chū tàiyang de huà; **a sunny day** dàqíngtiānr

sunrise rìchū

sun roof (*in car*) tiānchuāng

sunset rìluò

sunshade tàiyangsǎn

sunshine yángguāng

sunstroke zhòngshǔ

suntan: I want to get a good suntan wó xiǎng shàihēi diǎnr

suntan lotion fángshàijì

suntan oil fángshàiyóu

sun worshipper xǐhuān shài tàiyang de

super (*time, holiday, person*) hǎojíle; **super!** hǎojíle!

superb bàngjíle

supermarket chāojí shìchǎng

supper wǎnfàn

supplement (*extra charge*) fùjiāfèi

suppose: I suppose so wó xiǎng shì zhèiyang

suppository shuānjì

sure: I'm sure zhēn de; **are you sure?** zhēn de ma?; **sure!** dāngrán!

surf lànghuā; **let's go surfing** wǒmen qù wánr chōnglàng, zěnmeyàng?

surfboard chōnglàngbǎn

surname xìng

suprise: to my great suprise ... wǒ méi xiǎngdào ...; **that was a nice suprise** tài hǎole, zhēn méi xiǎngdào

suprising: that's not suprising nà bù qíguài

suspension (*of car*) chēqiáo

swallow (*verb*) yàn
swearword zāngzìr
sweat (*verb*) chūhàn; (*noun*) hàn;
covered in sweat quánshēn shı̄ hàn
sweater máoyī
sweatshirt chángxiù hànshānr
Sweden Ruìdiǎn
sweet (*taste*) tián; (*noun: dessert*) tiánshí
sweet and sour tángcù
sweets tángkuàir
swelling zhǒngkuàir
sweltering: it's sweltering zhèi tiānr rèsı̄le
swerve: I had to swerve (*when driving*) wǒ zhíhǎo láile ge jízhuǎnwānr
swim (*verb*) yóuyǒng; **I'm going for a swim** wǒ qù yóuyǒng; **do you want to go for a swim?** ní xiǎng qù yóuyǒng ma?; **I can't swim** wǒ bú huì yóuyǒng
swimming yóuyǒng; **I like swimming** wó xǐhuān yóuyǒng
swimming costume yóuyǒngyī
swimming pool yóuyǒngchí
swimming trunks yóuyǒngkù
switch (*noun*) kāiguān; **could you switch it on/off?** qǐng nín kāikai/guānshang, hǎo ma?
switchboard zǒngjī
Switzerland Ruìshì
swollen zhǒng
swollen glands línbajiē zhǒngdà
sympathy tóngqíng
synthetic rénzào de

T

table zhuōzı̄; **a table for two** liǎngge rén; **at our usual table** lǎo dìfang
tablecloth zhuōbù
table tennis pīngpāngqiú
tactful (*person*) lǎoliàn
tailor cáifeng
Taiwan Táiwān
Taiwanese (*adjective*) Táiwān; (*person*) Táiwānren
take ná; **can I take one?** kéyi ná ma?; **someone's taken my suitcase** yǒu rén bá wǒde xiāngzı̄ názoule; **will you take this to room 12?** qíng bǎ zhèi sòng dao shíèrhào fángjiān, hǎo ma?; **will you take me to the airport?** qǐng sòng wǒ qù jīchǎng, hǎo ma?; **do you take credit cards?** zhèr kéyi yòng xìnyòng kǎ ma?; **OK, I'll take it** hǎo, wǒ yàole; **how long does it take?** yào duō cháng shíjian?; **it'll take 2 hours** yào liǎngge xiǎoshı̄; **is this seat taken?** zhèr yǒu rén ma?; **I can't take too much sun** wǒ bú da néng shài tàiyang; **to take away** (*food*) dàizǒu de; **will you take this back, it's broken** zhèige huàile,

kéyi tuì ma?; **could you take it in a bit here please?** (*dress, jacket*) qǐng nín bǎ zhèr zài shōu yìdiǎnr, hǎo ma?; **when does the plane take off?** fēijī shénme shíhou qǐfēi?; **can you take a little off the top?** (*to hairdresser*) qǐng nín bá dǐngshang zài jiǎn yìdiǎnr, hǎo ma?
talcum powder shuǎngshēnfěn
talk (*verb*) shuōhuà
tall gāo
tampax wèishēngshuān
tampons wèishēngshuān
tan: I want to get a good tan wó xiǎng shàhēi diǎnr
tank (*of car*) yóuxiāng
Taoism Dàojiào
Taoist (*adjective*) Dàojiào; (*person*) Dàojiàotú
tap shuǐlóngtou
tape (*for cassette*) cídài; (*sticky*) jiāodài
tape measure juánchǐ
tape recorder lùyīnjī
taste (*noun*) wèir; **it has a peculiar taste** yóu diǎnr guài wèir; **it tastes very nice/revolting** zhèi wèir zhēn

ai	ao	c	e	ei	en	h	i	ı	ian	ie	iu	o
I	how	ts	her	ay	open	loch	ee	sir	yen	yeh	yoyo	or

hǎo/ěxīn; **can I taste it?** kéyi chángchang ma?
taxi chūzūchē; **will you get me a taxi?** qǐng nín bāng wǒ jiào liàng chūzūchē, hǎo ma?
taxi-driver chūzūchē sījī
taxi rank, taxi stand chūzūchē diǎnr
tea chá; (*green tea*) lǜchá; (*black tea*) hóngchá; **tea for two please** qǐng lái liǎngge rén de chá; **could I have a cup of tea?** qǐng lái bēi chá, hǎo ma?
teabag chádàir
teach: could you teach me? nín kéyi jiāojiao wǒ ma?; **could you teach me Chinese?** nín kéyi jiāojiao wǒ Hànyǔ ma?
teacher lǎoshī
teacup chábēi; (*with lid*) gàibēi
teahouse cháguǎnr
team duì
teapot cháhú
tea towel cāwǎnbù
teenager qīngshàonián (*approx 9–25 in China*)
teetotal: he's teetotal tā bù hē jiǔ
telegram diànbào; **I want to send a telegram** wǒ yào dǎ ge diànbào
telephone diànhuà; **can I make a telephone call?** wǒ kéyi dǎ ge diànhuà ma?; **could you talk to him for me on the telephone?** nǐ bāng wo gěi tā dǎ ge diànhuà, hǎo ma?
telephone box/booth diànhuàtíng
telephone directory diànhuàbù
telephone number diànhuà hàomǎ; **what's your telephone number?** nǐde diànhuà hàomǎ shì duōshao?
telephoto lens shèyuǎn jìngtóu
television diànshì; **I'd like to watch television** wó xiǎng kàn diànshì; **is the match on television?** zhèige bǐsài diànshìshang bō ma?
tell: could you tell him ...? qǐng nín gàosu ta ..., hǎo ma?
temperature (*weather*) qìwēn; (*fever*) fāshāo; **he has a temperature** tā fāshāole
temple miào
temporary línshí
tenant (*of apartment*) fángkè
tennis wǎngqiú

tennis ball wǎngqiú
tennis court wǎngqiúchǎng; **can we use the tennis court?** zhèige wǎngqiúchǎng wǒmen kéyi lái ma?
tennis racket wǎngqiúpāir
tent zhàngpeng
term (*at university, school*) xuéqī
terminus (*rail*) zhōngdiǎnzhàn
terrace píngtái; **on the terrace** zai píngtáishang
Terra Cotta Army Bīngmáyǒng
terrible zhēn zāogāo
terrific bàngjíle
testicle gāowán
Thai (*adjective*) Tàiguó; (*person*) Tàiguoren
Thailand Tàiguó
than bǐ; **smaller/bigger than** bǐ ... xiǎo/dà
thanks, thank you xièxie; **thank you very much** fēicháng gǎnxiè; **thank you for everything** xièxie nǐ zuò de yíqiè; **no thanks** bú yào, xièxie
that: that woman/man nèige nǚde/ nánde; **that one** nèige; **is that ...?** nà shì ... ma?; **I hope/think that ...** wǒ xīwàng/xiǎng ...; **that's perfect** hǎojíle; **that's strange** qíguài; **that's it** (*that's right*) duìle; **is it that expensive?** nàme guì?; *see pages 98-100*
theatre, theater jùyuàn
their tāmende; **their house** tāmende fángzı; *see page 98*
theirs tāmende; *see page 98*
them tāmen; **it's for them** zhèi shì gěi tāmen de; **I'll do it for them** wǒ bāng tāmen zuò; **with them** gēn tāmen yìqǐ; **I gave it to them** wó gěi tāmen le; **who? – them** shéi? – tāmen; **I don't want/like them** wǒ bú yào/xǐhuān; *see page 97*
then (*afterwards*) ránhòu; (*at that time*) nà shíhou
there nàr; **over there** zai nàr; **up there** nàr shàngtou; **is/are there ...?** yǒu ... ma?; **there is/are ...** yǒu ...; **there you are** (*giving something*) géi
thermal spring wēnquán
thermometer wēndùjì; (*clinical*) tǐwēnbiǎo
thermos flask rèshuǐpíng

ong	ou	q	u	un	ü		ʊ	ui	uo	x	yan	z	zh
ung	soul	ch	soon	open	huge		huge	way	wor	sh	yen	dz	j

thermostat (*in car*) héngwēnqì

these (*adjective*) zhèixie; **can I have these?** wǒ yào zhèixie, xíng ma?; *see page 103*

they tāmen; **are they Chinese/ Japanese?** (*people*) tāmen shɪ Zhōngguoren/Rɪbenren ma?; (*objects*) shɪ Zhōngguo/Rɪben de ma?; **are they coming/going?** tāmen lái/qù ma?; **they are too expensive** tài guì le; *see page 97*

thick hòu; (*stupid*) bèn

thief zéi

thigh dàtuǐ

thin báo

thing (*object*) dōngxi; (*matter*) shɪr; **have you seen my things?** nǐ kànjian wǒde dōngxi le ma?; **I've got a lot of things to do** wó yóu hěn duō shɪr yào zuò; **first thing in the morning** (*very early*) yìzǎo

think xiǎng; **what do you think?** ní zěnme xiǎng?; **I think so** wó xiǎng shɪ zhèiyang; **I don't think so** wǒ bú zhèiyang xiǎng; **I'll think about it** wó kǎolǜ yíxia

third class sānděng

third party insurance dìsān báoxiǎn

thirsty: I'm thirsty wó kěle

this: this hotel zhèige fàndiàn; **this street** zhèitiáo jiē; **this one** zhèige; **this is my friend** zhè shɪ wǒ péngyou; **this is my favo(u)rite restaurant** zhè shɪ wǒ zuì xǐhuān de fàndiàn; **is this yours?** zhè shɪ nǐde ma?; *see pages 99-100*

those (*adjective*) nèixie; **not these, those** bù shɪ zhèixie, shɪ nèixie; *see page 103*

thread (*noun*) xiàn

throat sǎngzɪ

throat lozenges rùnhóutáng

throttle (*on motorbike*) yóuménr

through jīngguò; **does it go through Beijing/Shangai?** jīngguò Běijīng/ Shànghǎi ma?; **Monday through Friday** cóng xīngqiyī dào xīngqiwǔ; **straight through the city centre/ center** yìzhí chuānguò shɪ zhōngxīn

through train zhídáchē

throw (*verb*) rēng; **don't throw it away** bié bǎ tā rēngle; **I'm going to throw up** wó yóu diǎnr ěxīn

thumb dàmúzhǐ

thumbtack túdīng

thunder (*noun*) léi

thunderstorm léiyǔ

Thursday xīngqisì

Tibet Xīzàng

Tibetan (*adjective*) Xīzàng; (*person*) Xīzàngren

ticket piào

ticket office (*bus, rail*) shòupiàochù

tie (*necktie*) lǐngdàir

tight (*clothes etc*) jǐn; **the waist is too tight** yāo zhèr tài jǐnle

tights liánkùwà

time shíjiān; **I've got no time** wǒ méi shíjiān; **there's not much time** shíjiān bù duōle; **what's the time?** jídiǎn le?; **at what time do you close?** nǐmen shénme shíhou guānménr?; **for the time being** zànshí; **from time to time** yǒushíhou; **right on time** zhǔnshí; **this time** zhèicì; **last time** shàngyicì; **next time** xiàcì; **four times** sìcì; **did you have a good time?** wánrde hǎo ma?; *see page 115*

timetable shíkèbiǎo; (*school*) kèchéngbiǎo

tin (*can*) guàntou

tinfoil xīzhǐ

tin-opener guàntou qǐzɪ

tiny yìdiánr diǎnr

tip (*to waiter etc*) xiǎofèi; **are we expected to give a tip?** wǒmen yīnggai géi xiǎofèi ma?

tire (*for car*) lúntāi

tired lèi; **I'm tired** wǒ lèile

tiring lèirén

tissues zhǐjīn

to dào; **we are going to Beijing/the airport** wǒmen dào Běijīng/jīchǎng qu; **from here to there** cóng zhèr dào nàr; **from three o'clock to four o'clock** cóng sāndiǎn dào sìdiǎn; **here's to you!** (*toast*) zhù nǐ jiànkāng!; *see page 112*

toast (*bread*) kǎomiànbāo; (*drinking*) zhùjiǔ

tobacco yānsī

today jīntian; **today week** xià xīngqī de jīntian

toe jiǎozhítóu

toffee nǎiyóutáng

together yíkuàir; we're together wǒmen shì yíkuàir de; can we pay together? wǒmen kéyi yíkuàir fù ma?

toilet cèsuǒ; where's the toilet? cèsuǒ zai nǎr?; I have to go to the toilet wó děi qù fāngbian fāngbian; she's in the toilet tā zai cèsuǒli

toilet paper shóuzhǐ

toilet water huālùshuǐr

toll (for motorway) tōngxíngfèi; (for bridge) guòqiáofèi

tomato xīhóngshì, fānqié

tomato juice fānqié zhī

tomato ketchup fānqiéjiàng

tomorrow míngtian; tomorrow morning míngtian zǎoshang; tomorrow afternoon míngtian xiàwu; tomorrow evening míngtian wǎnshang; the day after tomorrow hòutian; see you tomorrow míngtian jiàn

ton dūn

toner (cosmetic) tiáosèjì

tongue shétou

tonic (water) tuōníkè

tonight jīntian wǎnshang; not tonight jīntian wǎnshang bù xíng

tonsillitis biǎntáoxiànyán

tonsils biǎntáoxiàn

too (excessively) tài; (also) yě; too much tài duō; I'm not feeling too good wǒ bú tài shūfu; they are going/coming too tāmen yě qù/lái; he's having tea – me too tā hē chá – wó yě hē chá

tooth yá

toothache yáténg

toothbrush yáshuā

toothpaste yágāo

top: on top of ... zai ... shàngtou; on top of the car zai chēdǐng; on the top floor zai dǐnglóu; at the top zai dǐngshang; at the top of the hill zai shāndǐng; top quality yōuzhì; bikini top bǐjīní shàngshēnr

torch (electric) shǒudiàntǒng; (in procession) huǒbǎ

total (noun) zǒngshù

touch (verb) dòng; don't touch it bié

dòng; let's keep in touch wǒmen yào cháng liánxì

tough (meat) lǎo; tough luck! zhēn dǎoméi!

tour (noun) lǚyóu; is there a tour to the North East/Tibet? yóu zǔzhī qù Dōngběi/Xīzàng de lǚyóu ma?; is there a guided tour to the museum/exhibition? zhèige bówùguǎn/zhánlǎnhuì yóu dǎoyóu kéyi lǐngzhe cānguān ma?

tour guide dǎoyóu

tourist yóukè

touristy yóu lǚyóu wūrǎn; let's go somewhere not so touristy wǒmen háishì qù ge méi yǒu zhème duō ren de dìfang ba

tow: can you give me a tow? qǐng nín bāng wo bǎ chē tuōhuiqu, xíng ma?

toward(s) cháozhe; toward(s) Beijing cháozhe Běijīng

towel máojīn

town chéng; in town zai chénglǐ; which bus goes into town? něiliàng chē jìn chéng?; we're staying out of town wǒmen zai chéng wài zhù

town hall shìzhèngfǔ dàlóu

tow rope tuōchē lǎnshéng

toy wánjù

tracksuit yùndòngfú

traditional chuántǒng; traditional Chinese food chuántǒng de Zhōngguó fàn

traffic jiāotōng

traffic circle huánxíng jiāochà

traffic cop jiāotōngjǐng

traffic jam jiāotōng dǔsāi

traffic light(s) hónglǜ dēng

trailer (for carrying tent etc) tuōchē; (caravan) lǚxíng sùyíngchē

train huǒchē; when's the next train to ...? xiàyìtàng qù ... de huǒchē shì jídiǎn?; by train zuò huǒchē

trainers (shoes) lǚyóuxié

train station huǒchēzhàn

tram yóuguǐ diànchē

tramp (person) wúyè yóumín

tranquillizers zhènjìngjì

transfer desk bànlǐ zhōngzhuǎn shǒuxù chù

transformer (electric) biànyāqì

ong	ou	q	u	un	ü	ʊ	ui	uo	x	yan	z	zh
ung	soul	ch	soon	open	huge	huge	way	wor	sh	yen	dz	j

transistor (radio) bàndáotǐ

transit lounge zhōngzhuán lǚkè hòujīshì

translate fānyì; **could you translate that?** qǐng nín fānyì yíxia, hǎo ma?

translation fānyì

translator fānyì

transmission (of car) chuándòng zhuāngzhì

travel lǚxíng; **we're travel(l)ing around** wǒmen zai lǚxíng

travel agency lǚxíngshè

travel(l)er lǚkè

traveller's cheque, traveler's check lǚxíng zhīpiào

tray chápán

tree shù

tremendous hǎojíle

trendy (person, clothes, restaurant) shímáo

tricky (difficult) nánbàn

trim: just a trim please (to hairdresser) qíng zhǐ xiūxiu biānr

trip: how was your trip? nǐ zhèicì lǚxíng zěnmeyàng?; **I'd like to go on a trip to ...** wó xiǎng qù ...; **have a good trip** yílù shùnfēng

tripod (for camera) sānjiǎojià

tropical (climate) rèdài; (heat) rèjíle

trouble (noun) máfan; **I'm having trouble with ...** wǒ ... yùdàole diǎnr máfan; **sorry to trouble you, but ...** duìbuqǐ, máfan nín ...

trousers kùzi

trout zūnyú

truck kǎchē

truck driver kǎchē sījī

true zhēnde; **it is/is not true** shì/bú shì zhēnde; **is it true?** shì zhēnde ma?; **that's not true** bú duì

trunk (of car) xínglixiāng; (big case) dàxiāngzi

trunks (swimming) yóuyǒngkù

truth shíhuà; **I'm telling you the truth** wǒ shuō de shì shíhuà; **is it the truth?** shì zhēnde ma?

try shì; **please try!** nǐ shìshi!; **will you try for me?** nǐ bāng wǒ shìshi, hǎo ma?; **I've never tried it** (food) wǒ cónglái méi chīguo; **can I have a try?** (food) wǒ kéyi chángchang ma?; (at doing something) wǒ kéyi shìshi ma?; **may I try it on?** (clothes) wǒ kéyi shìshi ma?

T-shirt yuánlǐng duǎnxiù hànshānr

tube (for tyre) nèitāi

Tuesday xīngqi'èr

tuition: I'd like tuition wó xiáng zhǎo ren jiāojiao wǒ

tulip yùjīnxiāng

tuna fish jīnqiāngyú

tune (noun) qǔzi

tunnel suídào

turkey huǒjī

turn: it's my turn now gāi wǒ le; **turn left/right** wǎng zuó/yòu guǎi; **where do we turn off?** wǒmen zài nar guǎiwānr?; **can you turn the air-conditioning on/off?** qǐng nín dǎkāi/guānshang kōngtiáo, hǎo ma?; **he didn't turn up** tā méi lái

turning (in road) zhuǎnwānr

TV diànshì

tweezers nièzi

twice liǎngcì; **twice a day/year** yìtiān/yìnián liǎngcì; **twice as much** duō yíbèi

twin beds liǎngge dānrenchuáng

twin room shuāngrenjiān

twins shuāngbāotāi

twist: I've twisted my ankle wǒde jiǎobózi niǔle

type (noun) zhǒng; **a different type of ...** lìng yìzhǒng ...

typewriter dǎzìjī

typhoid shānghán

typical (dish etc) diǎnxíng; **is this typical Chinese food?** zhè shì diǎnxíng de zhōngguo fàn ma?; **that's typical of him/her!** tā/tā lǎoshì zhèiyang!

typist dǎzìyuán

tyre lúntāi

U

ugly (*person, building*) nánkàn
ulcer kuìyáng
umbrella yúsǎn
uncle: my uncle (*my father's elder brother*) wǒ bóbo; (*my father's younger brother*) wǒ shūshu; (*my mother's brother's husband*) wǒ jiùjiu; (*my father's sister's husband*) wǒ gūfù; (*my mother's sister's husband*) wǒ yífù
uncomfortable (*chair etc*) bù shūfu
unconscious bù xǐng rénshì
under (*spatially*) zai ... dǐxia; (*less than*) ... yǐxià
underdone (*meat*) bàn shēng bù shú
underground (*rail*) dìtiě
underpants kùchǎ
undershirt bèixīnr
understand: I don't understand wǒ bù dǒng; **I understand** wó dǒng le; **do you understand?** ní dǒngle?
underwear nèiyī
undo (*clothes*) jiěkāi
uneatable: this is uneatable zhèige bù néng chī
unemployed shīyè
unfair: that's unfair bù gōngpíng
unfortunately kěxī
unfriendly bù yóuhǎo
unhappy bù gāoxìng
unhealthy (*person*) bú jiànkāng; (*food, climate*) duì shēntǐ bù hǎo
United States Měiguó; **in the United States** zài Měiguó
university dàxué
unlock kāi; **can you unlock ... for me?** qǐng bāng wo kāikai ..., hǎo ma?; **the door was unlocked** mén méi suǒ
unpack dǎkāi
unpleasant (*person, taste*) bù zěnmeyàng

untie jiěkāi
until: we'll wait/work until 5 o'clock wǒmen děng/gàn dao wúdiǎn; **we're not going until tomorrow/Saturday** wǒmen míngtian/xīngqiliù cái zǒu; **until we meet again** (*said as parting words*) zàijiàn
unusual bù chángjiàn
up shàng; **up a bit!** (*instruction*) wǎng shàng diǎnr!; **up there** zai nàr; **he's not up yet** (*not out of bed*) tā hái méi qǐlai; **what's up?** zěnme huí shìr?
upmarket (*restaurant, hotel, goods etc*) gāoji
upset stomach wèi bù shūfu
upside down dàoguolai
upstairs lóushang
urgent jí; **this is very urgent** zhèi hěn jí
urinary tract infection niàodào gánrǎn
us wǒmen; **with us** gēn wǒmen yìqǐ; **this is for us** zhè shì géi wǒmen de; **he will do it for us** tā bāng wǒmen zuò; *see page 97*
use (*verb*) yòng; **may I use ...?** wǒ kéyi yòng yíxia ... ma?
used: I used to swim a lot wǒ guòqu chángchang yóuyǒng; **I haven't got used to the climate here** wǒ hái méi xíguàn zhèr de qìhou
useful yǒuyòng
usual (*normal*) píngcháng; (*habitual*) yuánlái de; **I'm hungry/thirsty as usual!** wǒ yòu èle/kěle!; **let's meet at the entrance/in the bar as usual** wǒmen háishì zài ménkǒur/jiǔbā pèngtóu, zěnmeyàng?
usually píngcháng
U-turn U-xíng zhuǎnwān

ong	ou	q	u	un	ü	ʊ	ui	uo	x	yan	z	zh
ung	soul	ch	soon	open	huge	huge	way	wor	sh	yen	dz	j

V

vacancy: do you have any vacancies? (*hotel*) zhèr yǒu kòng fángjiān ma?
vacation jiàqī; **we're here on vacation** wǒmen lái zhèr dùjià
vaccination zhòngdòu
vacuum cleaner xīchénqì
vacuum flask rèshuǐpíng
vagina yīndào
valid (*ticket etc*) yǒuxiào; **how long is it valid for?** duō cháng shíjiān nei yǒuxiào?
valley shāngǔ
valuable (*adjective*) guìzhòng; **can I leave my valuables here?** wǒ kéyi bá wǒ guìzhòng de dōngxi fàng zai zhèr ma?
value (*noun*) jiàzhí
valve fáménr; (*on bike wheel*) qìménzuǐr
van xiǎo yùnhuòchē
vanilla xiāngcǎojīng
varicose veins jìngmài qūzhàng
variety show wényì yǎnchū
vary: it varies jīngcháng biàn
vase huāpíng
vaudeville wényì yǎnchū
VD xìngbìng
veal xiǎoniúròu
vegetables shūcài
vegetarian chīsù de; **I'm a vegetarian** wǒ chī sù
velvet sīróng
vending machine zìdòng shòuhuòjī
ventilator tōngfēng zhuāngzhì
very hěn; **it's very hot/cold today** jīntian hěn rè/lěng; **I like it very much** wǒ hén xǐhuān; **I speak very**

little Chinese wǒde Zhōngwén hěn liáoliǎo; **just a very little for me** yìdīngdiǎnr
vest (*under shirt*) bèixīn; (*waistcoat*) xīfú bèixīn
via jīngguò; **via Wuhan/Nanjing** jīngguò Wǔhàn/Nánjīng
video (*noun: film*) lùxiàng; (*recorder*) lùxiàngjī; (*tape*) lùxiàngdài
Vietnam Yuènán
Vietnamese (*adjective*) Yuènan; (*person*) Yuènanren; (*language*) Yuènanyǔ
view jǐngr; **what a superb view!** duó měi de jǐngr!
viewfinder (*of camera*) qǔjǐngqì
villa biéshù
village cūnzi
vinegar cù
vineyard pútaoyuán
visa qiānzhèng
visibility (*for driving etc*) néngjiàndù
visit (*verb*) (*person*) qu kàn; (*place*) cānguān; **we are going to visit them tomorrow** wǒmen míngtian qu kàn tāmen; **I'd like to visit a factory/museum** wó xiǎng cānguān gōngchǎng/bówùguǎn; **if you're free come and visit us** yǒu kòngr lái wánr
vital: it's vital that ... ... fēicháng zhòngyào
vitamins wéishēngsù
vodka édékè
voice shēngyīn
voltage diànyā
vomit tù

W

wafer (*with ice cream*) wēifū
waist yāo
waistcoat xīfú bèixīn
wait děng; **wait for me** děngdeng wǒ; **don't wait for me** búyòng déng wǒ; **it was worth waiting for** zhèi děngde zhí; **I'll wait until my wife comes** wó děng wo àiren lái; **I'll wait a little longer** wǒ zài děng yìhuǐr; **can you repair it while I wait?** wǒ zai zhèr děngzhe, nín bāng wǒ xiū yíxia, hǎo ma?
waiter fúwùyuán; **waiter!** (*on mainland*) tóngzhì!
waiting room (*station*) hòuchēshì; (*doctor's*) hòuzhěnshì
waitress fúwùyuán; **waitress!** (*on mainland*) tóngzhì!
wake: will you wake me up at 6.30? nǐ liùdiǎn bàn jiào wǒ yíxia, hǎo ma?
Wales Wēi'ěrshì
walk: let's walk there wǒmen zǒuzhe qù ba; **is it possible to walk there?** kéyi zǒuzhe qù ma?; **I'll walk back** wó zǒuhuiqu; **is it a long walk?** yào zǒu hén yuǎn ma?; **it's only a short walk** zhǐ shì liùdaliùda; **I'm going out for a walk** wǒ chūqu sànsan bù; **let's take a walk around town** wǒmen zai chéngli zhuànzhuan, zěnmeyàng?
walking: I want to do some walking wó xiǎng zuò diǎnr túbù lǚxíng
walking stick guǎizhàng
walkman (*tm*) xiùzhēn fàngyīnjī
wall qiáng; **the Great Wall of China** Chángchéng
wallet qiánbāo
wander: I like just wandering around wó zhǐ shì suíbiàn zǒuzou
want: I want a ... wǒ yào yíge ...; **I don't want any ...** wǒ bú yào ...; **what do you want?** nǐ yào shénme?;

I want to go back wó xiǎng huíqu; **I don't want to ...** wǒ bù xiǎng ...; **he wants to ...** tā xiǎng ...
war zhànzhēng
ward (*in hospital*) bìngfáng
warm nuǎnhuo; **it's so warm today** jīntian zhēn nuǎnhuo; **I'm so warm** zhēn rè
warning (*noun*) jǐnggào
was: it was ... shı ...; *see page 104*
wash (*verb*) xǐ; **I need a wash** wǒ yào xǐxi; **can you wash the car?** zhèr kéyi xǐ chē ma?; **can you wash these?** qǐng xǐxi zhèixie, hǎo ma?; **it'll wash off** kéyi xǐdiào
wash basin xíshǒupénr
washcloth xíliǎn máojīn
washer (*for bolt etc*) diànquānr
washing (*clothes that need washing*) yào xǐ de yīfu; (*clothes that have been washed*) xíhǎo de yīfu; **here's my washing** zhèi shı wǒ yào xǐ de yīfu; **is my washing back?** wǒde yīfu xíhǎole ma?; **where can I hang my washing?** nǎr kéyi liàng yīfu?
washing machine xǐyījī
washing powder xǐyīfěn
washing-up: I'll do the washing-up wǒ lái xǐ wǎn
washing-up liquid jiéjìngjì
wasp huángfēng
wasteful: that's wasteful tài làngfèile
wastepaper basket fèizhǐlǒu
watch (*wrist-*) shóubiǎo; **please will you watch my things for me?** qǐng ni bāng wo kān yíxia dōngxi, hǎo ma?; **I'll just watch** wǒ jiù kànkan; **watch out!** xiǎoxīn!
watch strap biǎodàir
water shuǐ; **may I have some water?** qǐng lái diánr shuǐ, hǎo ma?
watercolo(u)r (*paints*) shuícǎi yánliào; (*painting*) shuícǎihuà

---

ong	ou	q	u	un	ü	ʊ	ui	uo	x	yan	z	zh
ung	soul	ch	soon	open	huge	huge	way	wor	sh	yen	dz	j

water sports shuǐshang yùndòng
wave (in sea) làng
way: which way is it? shı̌ něitiáo lù?;
it's this way shı̌ zhèitiáo lù; it's that
way shı̌ nèitiáo lù; could you tell
me the way to ...? qǐng nín gàosu
wǒ, dào ... zěnme zǒu, hǎo ma?; is
... on the way to Wuhan? qù Wǔhàn
de lùshang jīngguo ... ma?; this way
please zhèibiānr zǒu; you're block-
ing the way ní bǎ lù dǎngzhùle; is it
a long way to ...? dào ... qu yuǎn
ma?; would you show me the way
to do it? nín bāng wǒ shìfàn yíxia,
hǎo ma?; do it this way zhèiyang
zuò; no way! bù kěnéng!
we wǒmen; see page 97
weak (person) ruò; (drink) dàn
wealthy fù
weather tiānqi; what foul weather!
zhè shı̌ shénme tiānr!; what beautiful weather! duō hǎo de tiānr!
weather forecast tiānqi yùbào
wedding hūnlǐ
wedding anniversary jiéhūn jìniànrì
wedding ring jiéhūn jièzhı̌
Wednesday xīngqisān
week xīngqi; a week (from) today
xiàge xīngqi de jīntian; a week
(from) tomorrow xiàge xīngqi de
míngtian; Monday week xià xiàge
xīngqiyī
weekend zhōumò; at/on the weekend
zhōumò
weight zhòngliang; I want to lose
weight wó xiáng jiǎnféi
weight limit zhòngliang xiànzhı̌
weird (person) gǔguài; (custom, thing to
happen) qíguài
welcome: welcome to ... huānyíng
dào ... lái; you're welcome (don't
mention it) búxiè
well: I don't feel well wǒ juéde bù
shūfu; I haven't been very well wǒ
zuìjìn bú tài shūfu; she's not well tā
bù shūfu; how are you? – very well,
thanks ní hǎo? – hén hǎo, xièxie;
you speak English very well nǐ
Yīngyǔ jiǎngde hén hǎo; he's having
tea – me as well tā hē chá – wó yě
hē chá; well done! tài hǎole; well
well! (surprise) āiyā!

well-done (meat) lǎoyidiǎnr
wellingtons gāoyào yǔxuē
Welsh Wēi'ěrshì
were see page 104
west xī; to the west of ... zai ... yǐxī
West Indian (adjective) Xī Yìndu
qúndǎo; (person) Xī Yìndu qúndǎoren
Western-style xīshì
Western-style food xīcān
West Indies Xī Yìndu qúndǎo
wet shī; it's all wet quán shīle; it's
been wet all week xiàle yíge xīngqi
de yǔ
wet suit (for diving etc) qiánshuǐfú
what? shénme?; what's that? nà shı̌
shénme?; what is he saying? tā shuō
shénme?; I don't know what to do
wǒ bù zhīdào gāi zěnme bàn; what a
view! kàn zhè jǐngr!
wheel lúnzi
wheelchair lúnyǐ
when? shénme shíhou?; when do we
get there? wǒmen shénme shíhou
dào?; we'll eat when we get there/
back wǒmen dàole/huílai zài chīfàn
where? nǎr?; where is ...? ... zai nǎr?;
I don't know where he is wǒ bù
zhīdào tā zai nǎr; that's where I left
it wǒ yuánlái jiù fàng zai zhèr
which: which bus? něilù chē?; which
one? něige?; which is yours? něige
shı̌ nǐde?; I forget which it was wǒ
wàngle shı̌ něige le; the one which
... ... de nèige
while: while I'm here wǒ zai zhèr de
shíhou
whisky wēishìjì
whisper (verb) xiǎoshēng de shuō; in
a whisper xiǎoshēng de
white bái
white wine bái pútaojiǔ
who? shéi?; who was that? nà shı̌
shéi?; the man who ... ... de nèige
ren
whole: the whole week zhěngzheng
yíge xīngqi; two whole days
zhěngzheng liǎngtiān; the whole lot
quánbù
whooping cough bǎirìké
whose: whose is this/that? zhèi/nèi
shı̌ shéide?
why? wèishenme?; why not?

ai	ao	c	e	ei	en	h	i	ı	ian	ie	iu	o
I	how	ts	her	ay	open	loch	ee	sir	yen	yeh	yoyo	or

wèishenme bù?; **that's the reason why ... is not working** zhèi jiù shı̀ wèishenme ... bù lı́ng de yuányīn
wide kuān
wide-angle lens guángjiǎo jìngtóu
widow guǎfù
widower guānfū
wife: my wife wǒ qīzı̀
wig jiǎfà
will: will you ask him/them? nǐ wènwen tā/tāmen, hǎo ma?; *see page 107*
win (*verb*) yíng; **who won?** shéi yíngle?
wind (*noun*) fēng
windmill fēngchē
window chuānghu; **near the window** kào chuānghu; **in the window** (*of shop*) zai chúchuāngli
window seat kào chuāng de zuòwei
windscreen, windshield dǎngfēng bōli
windscreen wipers, windshield wipers guāshuǐqı̀
windy yǒu fēng; **it's windy today** jīntian yǒu fēng
wine pútaojiǔ; **can we have some more wine?** qǐng zài lái diǎnr pútaojiǔ, hǎo ma?
wine glass jiǔbēi
wine list jiǔdān
wing (*of plane, bird*) chìbǎng; (*of car*) yìzı̀bǎn
wing mirror fǎnguāngjìng
winter dōngtian; **in the winter** dōngtian
winter holiday hánjià
wire tiěsī; (*electrical*) diànxiàn
wireless wúxiàndiàn
wiring xiànlù
wish: wishing you were here (*as written on postcards*) yàoshı̀ nǐ zài zhèr jiù hǎole; **please give ... my best wishes** qǐng xiàng ... wèn hǎo
with gēn; **I'm staying with ...** wǒ gēn ... zhù zai yìqǐ
without méiyǒu
witness zhèngren; **will you be a witness for me?** máfan nǐ bāng wo zuò zhèngren, hǎo ma?
witty yǒu fēngqù
wobble: the wheel is wobbling chēlúnzı̀ huànghuang
woman nǚde
women nǚde
wonderful hǎojíle
won't: it won't start (*car*) bù dáhuǒ; *see pages 104-105*
wood (*material*) mùtou
woods (*forest*) shùlín
wool yángmáo
word cír; **you have my word** wó bǎozhèng
work (*verb*) gōngzuò; (*noun*) gōngzuò; **where do you work?** nǐ zai nǎr gōngzuò?; **I work in an office** wǒ zai bàngōngshı̀ gōngzuò; **do you have any work for me?** yào wǒ gàn shénme ma?; **when do you finish work?** nǐ shénme shíhou xiàbān?; **how do you work it?** zhèi zěnme yòng?; **it's not working** bù líng le
world shìjiè; **all over the world** quán shìjiè
worn-out (*person*) lèisı̀le; (*shoes, clothes*) chuānpòle
worry: I'm worried about her wǒ tı̀ tā dānxīn; **don't worry** fàngxīn
worse: it's worse nà gèng huài; **it's getting worse** yuè lái yuè huài
worst zuì huài
worth: it's not worth 500 kuai bù zhí wúbǎi kuài; **it's worth more than that** bǐ nèi zhíqián duōle; **is ... worth a visit?** ... zhíde qù kànkan ma?
would: would you give this to ...? qǐng nín bǎ zhèi gěi ..., hǎo ma?; **what would you do?** nǐ huì zěnme bàn?
wrap: could you wrap it up? qǐng nín bāng wo bāo yíxia, hǎo ma?
wrapping paper bāozhuāngzhǐ
wrench (*tool*) huó bānshǒu
wrist shǒuwànr
write xiě; **could you write it down?** qǐng nín bāng wo xiěxialai, hǎo ma?; **how do you write it?** zěnme xiě?; **I'll write to you** wó yǐhou gěi ni xiěxìn; **I wrote to you last month** wǒ shànggeyuè géi ni xiěle yìfēng xìn
write-off: it's a write-off (*car etc*) zhèi bùxíngle

writer zuòjiā
writing xiězuò; **Chinese writing** Hànzì
wrong: you're wrong nǐ cuòle; **the bill's wrong** zhàngdānr cuòle; **sorry, wrong number** duìbuqǐ, dǎcuòle; **I'm on the wrong train** wǒ shàngcuò chē le; **I went to the wrong room** wó zǒucuò wū le; **that's the wrong key** zhèi yàoshı bú duì; **there's something wrong with ... ...** yǒu máobìng; **what's wrong?** zěnmele?; **what's wrong with ...?** ... zěnmele?

X Y Z

X-ray áikesiguāng

yacht fānchuán
Yangtze Gorges Chángjiāng sānxiá
Yangtze River Chángjiāng
yard: in the yard zai yuànzıli; *see page 117*
year nián
yellow huáng
Yellow River Huánghé
Yellow Sea Huánghǎi
yes shìde; *see page 113*
yesterday zuótian; **yesterday morning** zuótian zǎoshang; **yesterday afternoon** zuótian xiàwu; **the day before yesterday** qiántian

zero líng
zip, zipper lāliànr; **could you put a new zip on?** qǐng nín bāng wo huànge xīn lāliànr, hǎo ma?

yet: has ... arrived yet? ... dàole ma?; **not yet** hái méiyǒu
yobbo liúmáng
yog(h)urt suānnǎi
you (*familiar*) (*sing*) nǐ; (*pl*) nǐmen; (*polite*) (*sing*) nín; (*pl*) nínmen; **this is for you** zhèi shı géi nǐ de; **with you** gēn nǐ yìqǐ; *see page 97*
young niánqīng
young people niánqīngren
your (*sing*) nǐde; (*pl*) nǐmende; **your camera** nǐde zhàoxiàngjī; *see page 98*
youth hostel *these don't exist in China*
yuan yuán

zoo dòngwùyuán
zoom lens kěbiàn jiāojù jìngtóu

ai	ao	c	e	ei	en	h	i	ı	ian	ie	iu	o
I	how	ts	her	ay	open	loch	ee	sir	yen	yeh	yoyo	or

Chinese-English

LIST OF SUBJECT AREAS

Abbreviations
Airport and plane
Banks
Buses
Bus stations
Cinemas/Movie theaters
Clothing labels
Countries and nationalities
Cultural interest
Customs
Days of the week
Department store sections
Doctors
Do not ...
Drinks
Eating and drinking places
Elevators
Emergencies
Food
Food labels
Forms
Garages
Geographical
Hairdressers
Historical interest
Hospitals
Hotels
Lifts/Elevators
Medical

Medicine labels
Months
Movie theaters
Nightlife
Notices in restaurants and on menus
Notices in shops
Notices on doors
Place names
Post offices
Public buildings
Rentals
Replies
Rest rooms
Road signs
Schedules
Shop names
Stations
Streets
Subway
Swearwords and terms of abuse
Taxis
Telephones
Theatres/Theaters
Timetables/Schedules
Toilets/Rest rooms
Tourism
Trains
Underground/Subway

ABBREVIATIONS

CAAC *[Zhōngguo Mínháng]* Civil Aviation Administration of China

CCP *[Zhōngguo gòngchándǎng]* Chinese Communist Party

CCPIT *[Zhōngguo Duìwài màoyì cùjìn wěiyuánhuì]* China Council for the Promotion of International Trade

CECF *[chūkǒu shāngpǐn jiāoyìhuì]* Chinese Export Commodities Fair

CITIC *[Zhōngguo guójì xìntuō tóuzī gōngsī]* China International Trust and Investment Corporation

CITS *[Zhōngguo guójì lǚxíngshè]* China International Travel Service

CTS *[Zhōngguo lǚxíngshè]* China Travel Service

FEC *[wàihuìjoànr]* Foreign Exchange Certificates

MFERT *[duìwài jīngjì màoyì bù]* Ministry of Foreign Economic Relations and Trade

NPC *[quánguó rénmín dàibiǎo dàhuì]* National People's Congress

PLA *[Zhōngguo rénmín jiěfàngjūn]* People's Liberation Army

PRC *[Zhōnghuá rénmín gònghéguó]* People's Republic of China

RMB *[Rénmínbì]* Chinese currency

¥ *[yuán]* unit of currency

AIRPORT AND PLANE

变更时间 *[biàngēng shíjian]* actual (*time*)

机场 *[jīchǎng]* airport

机场班车 *[jīchǎng bānchē]* airport bus

来自 *[láizì]* arriving from

行李牌 *[xínglipáir]* baggage check

行李领取处 *[xíngli lǐngqǔchù]* baggage claim

中国银行 *[Zhōngguo yínháng]* Bank of China

登机牌 *[dēngjīpáir]* boarding pass

办理乘机手续·托运行李 *[bànlǐ chéngjī shǒuxù, tuōyòn xíngli]* check-in

中国海关 *[Zhōngguo hǎiguān]* Chinese Customs

日期 *[rìqī]* date

延误 *[yánwù]* delayed

前往 *[qiánwǎng]* departing to

候机室 *[hòujīshì]* departure lounge

起飞时间 *[qǐfēi shíjian]* departure time

终点站 *[zhōngdiǎnzhàn]* destination

国内航班进站 *[guónèi hángbān jìnzhàn]* domestic arrivals

国内航班出站 *[guónèi hángbān chūzhàn]* domestic departures

免税商店 *[miǎnshuì shāngdiàn]* duty free (shop)

太平门 *[tàipíngmén]* emergency exit

系好安全带 *[jìhǎo ānqoándài]* fasten safety belts

航班号 *[hángbānhào]* flight (number)

登机口 *[dēngjīkǒu]* gate

报关 *[bàoguān]* goods to declare

绿色通道 *[lǜse tōngdào]* green channel

免疫检查 *[miǎnyì jiǎnchá]* health inspection

问讯处 *[wènxùnchù]* information (desk)

国际航班进站 *[guójì hángbān jìnzhàn]* international arrivals

国际航班出站 *[guójì hángbān chūzhàn]* international departures

已降落 *[yǐ jiàngluò]* landed

救生衣 *[jiùshēngyī]* life jacket

救生艇 *[jiùshēngtǐng]* life raft

请勿吸烟 *[qǐng wù xīyān]* no smoking

不用报关 *[búyòng bàoguān]* nothing to declare

护照检查 *[hùzhào jiǎnchá]* passport control

飞机号 *[fēijīhào]* plane number

红色通道 *[hóngse tōngdào]* red channel

预计时间 *[yòjì shíjian]* scheduled time

座位号 *[zuòweihào]* seat number

安全检查 *[ānqoán jiǎnchá]* security control

出租汽车 *[chūzū qìchē]* taxis

盥洗室 *[guànxǐshì]* toilet, rest room

ai	ao	c	e	ei	en	h	i	ɪ	ian	ie	iu	o
I	how	ts	her	ay	open	loch	ee	sir	yen	yeh	yoyo	or

中转旅客 *[zhōngzhuǎn lǚkè]* transfer passengers

中转 *[zhōngzhuǎn]* transfers

过境旅客 *[guòjìng lǚkè]* transit passengers

经停站 *[jīngtíngzhàn]* via

BANKS

帐户 *[zhànghù]* account

帐号 *[zhànghào]* account no.

澳元 *[Àoyuán]* Australian dollar

银行 *[yínháng]* bank

中国银行 *[Zhōngguo yínháng]* Bank of China

分行 *[fēnháng]* branch bank

营业时间 *[yíngyè shíjiān]* business hours

买价 *[mǎijià]* buying rate

加拿大元 *[Jiānádà yuán]* Canadian dollar

支票 *[zhīpiào]* cheque, check

人民币 *[Rénmínbì]* Chinese currency

信用证 *[xìnyòng zhèng]* credit card

存款 *[cúnkuǎn]* deposits

西德马克 *[Xīdé mǎkè]* Deutsche mark

外币兑换 *[wàibì duìhuàn]* foreign exchange

外汇券 *[wàihuìjuànr]* Foreign Exchange Certificates

法郎 *[Fǎláng]* French franc

港币 *[Gǎngbì]* Hongkong dollar

利息 *[lìxi]* interest

日元 *[Rìyuán]* Japanese yen

中国人民银行 *[Zhōngguo rénmín yínháng]* People's Bank of China

英镑 *[Yīngbàng]* pound sterling

卖价 *[màijià]* selling rate

今日牌价 *[jīnrì páijià]* today's exchange rate

旅行支票 *[lǚxíng zhīpiào]* traveller's cheque, traveler's check

美元 *[Měiyuán]* US dollar

取款 *[qǔkuǎn]* withdrawals

BUSES

就近下车 *[jiùjìn xiàchē]* alight on request

先下后上 *[xiān xià hòu shàng]* allow passengers to alight before boarding

售票员 *[shòupiàoyuán]* conductress, conductor

快车 *[kuàichē]* express bus

加车 *[jiāchē]* extra service (*rush-hour*)

保持车内清洁 *[bǎochí zhēnèi qīngjié]* keep the bus tidy

请勿吸烟 *[qǐng wù xīyān]* no smoking

请勿随地吐痰 *[qǐng wù suídì tǔtán]* no spitting

请勿与司机谈话 *[qǐng wù yǔ sījī tánhuà]* please don't speak to the driver

老人、孕妇专座 *[lǎoren yùnfù zhuānzuò]* seats for the elderly and for pregnant women

区间车 *[qūjiānchē]* shuttle bus (*going only part of route*)

招手上车 *[zhāoshǒu shàngchē]* stop on request

BUS STATIONS

通宵车 *[tōngxiāo chē]* all-night bus

到站时间 *[dàozhàn shíjiān]* arrival time

售票口 *[shòupiàokǒu]* booking office

书报亭 *[shūbàotíng]* bookstall

长途汽车站 *[chángtú qìchē zhàn]* bus station (*long distance*)

离站时间 *[lízhàn shíjiān]* departure time

头班车 *[tóubān chē]* first bus

问讯处 *[wènxùnchù]* information office

小卖部 *[xiǎomàibù]* kiosk

末班车 *[mòbān chē]* last bus

小公共汽车 *[xiǎo gōnggòng qìchē]* minibus

月票 *[yuèpiào]* monthly ticket

103路无轨电车 *[yāolíngsān lù wúguǐ diànchē]* No. 103 trolley bus

104路公共汽车 *[yāolíngsì lù gōnggòng qìchē]* No. 104 bus

公用电话 *[gōngyòng diànhuà]* public telephone

ong	ou	q	u	un	ü	o	ui	uo	x	yan	z	zh
ung	s**ou**l	ch	s**oo**n	op**en**	h**u**ge	h**u**ge	way	w**or**	sh	yen	dz	j

坐队 *[zuòduì]* queue/line up for seats
站队 *[zhànduì]* queue/line up for standing
小吃店 *[xiǎochīdiàn]* snack bar
始发 *[shǐfā]* starting point
候车室 *[hòuchēshì]* waiting room

CINEMAS/MOVIE THEATERS

售票口 *[shòupiàokǒu]* box office
电影院 *[diànyǐngyoànr]* cinema, movie theater
入场券 *[rùchǎngjoànr]* cinema/movie theater ticket
日场 *[rìchǎng]* daytime performance
楼下 *[lóuxià]* downstairs, stalls etc
太平门 *[tàipíngmén]* emergency exit
入口 *[rùkǒu]* entrance
夜场 *[yèchǎng]* evening performance
双号 *[shuānghào]* even numbers
出口 *[chūkǒu]* exit
男厕 *[náncè]* gents, men's room
全满 *[qoánmǎn]* house full
女厕 *[nǔcè]* ladies, ladies' room
早场 *[zǎochǎng]* morning performance
单号 *[dānhào]* odd numbers
...排 *[...pái]* row ...
...号 *[...hào]* seat number ...
票已售完 *[piào yǐ shòu wán]* sold out
放映时间 *[fàngyìng shíjian]* times of performance
楼上 *[lóushàng]* upstairs, balcony etc

CLOTHING LABELS

全棉 *[qoánmián]* 100% cotton
全毛 *[qoánmáo]* 100% wool
腈纶 *[jīnglún]* acrylic
胸围 *[xiōngwéi]* bust
领大 *[lǐngdà]* collar
身长 *[shēncháng]* jacket length
真丝 *[zhēnsī]* pure silk
人造丝 *[rénzàosī]* rayon
规格 *[guīgé]* size
涤纶 *[dílún]* terylene

涤棉 *[dímián]* terylene and cotton
裤长 *[kùcháng]* trouser length
腰围 *[yāowéi]* waist
毛涤纶 *[máodílún]* wool and polyester blend

COUNTRIES AND NATIONALITIES

澳大利亚 *[Àodàlìyà]* Australia
加拿大 *[Jiānádà]* Canada
中国 *[Zhōngguó]* China
傣 *[Dǎi]* Dai, minority people from South West China
法国 *[Fǎguó]* France
香港 *[Xiānggǎng]* Hong Kong
回 *[Huí]* Hui, Moslem minority
日本 *[Rìběn]* Japan
朝鲜 *[Cháoxiǎn]* Korean
满 *[Mǎn]* Manchu
苗 *[Miáo]* Miao, minority people from South West China
蒙 *[Měng]* Mongol
中华人民共和国 *[Zhōnghuá rénmín gònghéguó]* People's Republic of China
苏联 *[Sūlián]* Soviet Union
台湾 *[Táiwān]* Taiwan
藏 *[Zàng]* Tibetan
英国 *[Yīngguó]* UK
美国 *[Měiguó]* USA
维吾尔 *[Wéiwúěr]* Uighur, minority people living mainly in North West China
西德 *[Xīdé]* West Germany
彝 *[Yí]* Yi, minority people from South West China
壮 *[Zhuàng]* Zhuang, minority people from South West China

CULTURAL INTEREST

寺 *[sì]* Buddhist temple
书法 *[shūfǎ]* calligraphy
汉 *[Hàn]* Han Dynasty (206 BC-AD 220)
康熙 *[Kāngxī]* Kangxi (Kang-Hsi) (AD 1662-1722)

明 [*Míng*] Ming Dynasty (AD 1368-1644)
年画 [*niánhuà*] New Year prints
塔 [*tǎ*] pagoda
京剧 [*jīngjù*] Peking opera
木偶戏 [*mùǒuxì*] puppet show
乾隆 [*Qiánlóng*] Qianlong (Chien-Lung) (AD 1736-1795)
清 [*Qīng*] Qing (Ching) Dynasty (AD 1644-1911)
皮影戏 [*píyǐngxì*] shadow plays
宋 [*Sòng*] Song (Sung) Dynasty (AD 960-1279)
唐 [*Táng*] Tang Dynasty (AD 618-907)
宫 [*gōng*] Taoist temple
庙 [*miào*] temple
长城 [*Chángchéng*] The Great Wall
兵马佣 [*bīngmáyǒng*] The Terracotta Army
元 [*Yuán*] Yuan Dynasty (AD 1279-1368)

CUSTOMS

海关 [*hǎiguān*] customs
免税物品 [*miǎnshuì wùpǐn*] duty-free goods
入境签证 [*rùjìng qiānzhèng*] entry visa
出境签证 [*chūjìng qiānzhèng*] exit visa
边防检查站 [*biānfáng jiǎncházhàn*] frontier checkpoint
绿色通道 [*lùsè tōngdào*] green channel
免疫检查 [*miǎnyì jiǎnchá*] health inspection
护照 [*hùzhào*] passport
护照检查 [*hùzhào jiǎnchá*] passport inspection
红色通道 [*hóngsè tōngdào*] red channel
过境签证 [*guòjìng qiānzhèng*] transit visa
旅行证 [*lǚxíngzhèng*] travel permit

DAYS OF THE WEEK

星期日 [*xīngqirì*] Sunday
星期一 [*xīngqiyī*] Monday
星期二 [*xīngqi'èr*] Tuesday
星期三 [*xīngqisān*] Wednesday
星期四 [*xīngqisì*] Thursday
星期五 [*xīngqiwǔ*] Friday
星期六 [*xīngqiliù*] Saturday

DEPARTMENT STORE SECTIONS

床上用品 [*chuángshang yòngpǐn*] bedding
交款处 [*jiāokuǎnchù*] cashier
烟酒糖茶 [*yān jiǔ táng chá*] cigarettes, wine, sweets/candy, tea
钟表手表 [*zhōngbiǎo shǒubiǎo*] clocks and watches
男女服装 [*nánnǚ fúzhuāng*] clothing
化妆用品 [*huàzhuāng yòngpǐn*] cosmetics
棉布化纤 [*miánbù huàxiān*] cotton and synthetic fabrics
百货公司 [*bǎihuò gōngsī*] department store
家用电器 [*jiāyòng diànqì*] domestic appliances
布匹衣料 [*bùpǐ yīliào*] drapery
日用杂品 [*rìyòng zápǐn*] everyday articles
食品糕点 [*shípǐn gāodiǎn*] food and confectionery
家具灯具 [*jiājù dēngjù*] furniture and lighting
缝纫用品 [*féngrèn yòngpǐn*] haberdashery, notions
五金交电 [*wǔjīn jiāodiàn*] hardware and electrical
袜子鞋帽 [*wàzɪxiémào*] hosiery, shoes, hats
钢精制品 [*gāngjīng zhìpǐn*] kitchenware
皮革制品 [*pígé zhìpǐn*] leather goods
乐器唱片 [*yuèqì chàngpiàn*] musical instruments and records
照相器材 [*zhàoxiàng qìcái*] photographic equipment
雨伞雨具 [*yǔsǎn yǔjù*] rainwear
缝纫机自行车 [*féngrènjī zìxíngchē*] sewing machines and bicycles
丝绸呢绒 [*sīchóu níróng*] silk and wool fabrics

ong	ou	q	u	un	ü	ʊ	ui	uo	x	yan	z	zh
ung	s**ou**l	ch	s**oo**n	op**en**	h**u**ge	h**u**ge	way	w**or**	sh	y**en**	dz	j

香皂洗衣粉 [xiāngzào xǐyīfěn] soap and washing powder

体育用品 [tǐyò yòngpǐn] sports goods

文具用品 [wénjò yòngpǐn] stationery

牙膏牙刷 [yágāo yáshuā] toothpaste and toothbrushes

毛巾手帕 [máojīn shǒupà] towels and handkerchiefs

儿童玩具 [értóng wánjò] toys

针织用品 [zhēnzhī yòngpǐn] underwear

妇女用品 [fùnǔ yòngpǐn] women's articles

毛衣毛线 [máoyī máoxiàn] wool and woollen goods

DOCTORS see MEDICAL

DO NOT ...

危险！ [wēixiǎn!] danger!

请勿乱踏草地 [qǐng wù luàntā cǎodì] keep off the grass

军事要地，请勿靠近！ [jūnshì yàodì, qǐng wù kàojìn!] military zone, keep out!

禁止入内 [jìnzhǐ rù nèi] no entry

外国人未经许可，禁止超越！ [wàiguoren wèi jīng xókě, jìnzhǐ chāoyoè!] no foreigners beyond this point without permission!

请勿随地乱扔纸屑 [qǐng wù suídì luànrēng zhǐxiāo] no litter

请勿大声喧哗 [qǐng wù dàshēng xoānhuá] no noise, please

禁止拍照 [jìnzhǐ pāizhào] no photographs

请勿吸烟 [qǐng wù xīyān] no smoking

请勿随地吐痰 [qǐng wù suídì tǔtán] no spitting

肃静 [sùjìng] quiet

闲人免进 [xiánren miǎn jìn] staff only

油漆未干 [yóuqī wèi gān] wet paint

DRINKS

杏仁霜 [xìngrénshuāng] almond drink

小香槟 [xiǎoxiāngbīn] Chinese equivalent of Babycham (tm)

竹叶青 [Zhúyèqīng] Bamboo-leaf Green spirit (tm)

啤酒 [píjiǔ] beer

净咖啡 [jìng kāfēi] black coffee

红茶 [hóngchá] black tea

白兰地 [báilándì] brandy

香槟酒 [xiāngbīnjiǔ] champagne

沉缸酒 [Chénggāngjiǔ] Chenggang rice wine (tm)

樱桃白兰地 [yīngtao báilándì] cherry brandy

菊花茶 [júhuāchá] chrysanthemum tea

苹果酒 [píngguojiǔ] cider

白酒 [báijiǔ] clear, strong, vodka-like spirit, distilled from sorghum grain etc

白干 [báigānr] clear, strong, vodka-like spirit, distilled from sorghum grain etc

大曲 [dàqū] clear, strong, vodka-like spirit, distilled from sorghum grain etc

可口可乐 [kěkou kělè] Coca-cola (tm)

鸡尾酒 [jūwěijiǔ] cocktail

咖啡 [kāfēi] coffee

法国白兰地 [fǎguó báilándì] cognac

炼乳 [liànrǔ] condensed milk

董酒 [Dóngjiǔ] Dongjiu spirit (tm)

龙井茶 [Lóngjǐngchá] Dragon Well tea, famous type of green tea (tm)

干红葡萄酒 [gān hóng pútaojiǔ] dry red wine

干白葡萄酒 [gān bái pútaojiǔ] dry white wine

汾酒 [Fénjiǔ] Fenjiu spirit (tm)

五星啤酒 [wǔxīng píjiǔ] Five-star beer, well-known Chinese beer (tm)

果子汁 [guǒzizhī] fruit juice

金酒 [jīnjiǔ] gin

金奖白兰地 [jīnjiǎng báilándì] Gold-medal brandy (tm)

绿茶 [lǜ chá] green tea

古井贡酒 [Gújǐngòngjiǔ] Gujing gongjiu spirit (tm)

山楂酒 [shānzhājiǔ] haw liqueur

冰镇啤酒 [bīngzhèn píjiǔ] iced beer

冰水 [bīngshuǐ] iced water

速溶咖啡 [sùróng kāfēi] instant coffee

茉莉花茶 [mòli huāchá] jasmine tea

剑南春 *[Jiànnánchūn]* Jiannanchun spirit (*tm*)

崂山可乐 *[Láoshān kělè]* Laoshan cola, Chinese variety of coca-cola made from Laoshan water (*tm*)

崂山矿泉水 *[láoshān kuàngquánshuǐr]* Laoshan mineral water, famous type from the mountains of Laoshan in Shandong (*tm*)

柠檬汽水 *[níngméng qìshuǐr]* lemonade

柠檬茶 *[níngméngchá]* lemon tea

果子酒 *[guǒzıjiǔ]* liqueur

泸州老窖特曲酒 *[Lúzhōu lǎojiào tèqūjiǔ]* Luzhou laojiao tequ spirit (*tm*)

麦乳精 *[màirǔjīng]* malted milk

茅台酒 *[Máotáijiǔ]* Maotai spirit (*tm*)

牛奶 *[niúnǎi]* milk

冰奶 *[bīngnǎi]* milkshake

矿泉水 *[kuàngquánshuǐr]* mineral water

巢牌咖啡 *[Cháopáir kāfēi]* Nescafe (*tm*)

桔子汽水 *[józı qìshuǐr]* orangeade

桔子汁 *[józızhī]* orange juice

乌龙茶 *[wūlóngchá]* Oulung tea, famous semi-fermented tea, half green, half black (*tm*)

菠萝汁 *[bōluozhī]* pineapple juice

青岛啤酒 *[Qīngdǎo píjiǔ]* Qingdao beer, most famous type of Chinese beer (*tm*)

红葡萄酒 *[hóng pútaojiǔ]* red wine

黄酒 *[huángjiǔ]* rice wine

老酒 *[láojiǔ]* rice wine

兰姆酒 *[lánmújiǔ]* rum

花茶 *[huāchá]* scented tea

苏格兰威士忌 *[Sūgélán wēishìjì]* Scotch whisky

绍兴加饭酒 *[Shàoxìng jiāfànjiǔ]* Shaoxing jiafan rice wine (*tm*)

绍兴黄酒 *[Shàoxìng huángjiǔ]* Shaoxing rice wine (*tm*)

雪利酒 *[xuělìjiǔ]* sherry

汽水 *[qìshuǐr]* soda water

汽酒 *[qìjiǔ]* sparkling wine

酸梅汤 *[suānméitāng]* sweet-sour plum juice

通化山葡萄酒 *[Tōnghuà shānpútaojiǔ]*

味美思 *[wèiměisī]* vermouth

俄得克酒 *[édékèjiǔ]* vodka

威士忌 *[wēishìjì]* whisky

牛奶咖啡 *[niúnǎi kāfēi]* white coffee, coffee with milk

白葡萄酒 *[bái pútaojiǔ]* white wine

葡萄酒 *[pútaojiǔ]* wine

五粮液 *[Wǔliángyè]* Wuliangye spirit (*tm*)

烟台红葡萄酒 *[Yāntái hóng pútaojiǔ]* Yāntái red wine (*tm*)

洋河大曲酒 *[Yánghé dàqūjiǔ]* Yanghe daqu spirit (*tm*)

烟台味美思 *[Yāntái wèiměisī]* Yantai vermouth (*tm*)

EATING AND DRINKING PLACES

饮食店 *[yǐnshídiàn]* cafe

点心店 *[diǎnxīndiàn]* cafe

咖啡店 *[kāfēidiàn]* cafe (coffee house)

茶楼 *[chálóu]* cafe (teahouse)

茶馆 *[cháguǎn]* cafe (teahouse)

茶室 *[cháshì]* cafe (teahouse)

收款台 *[shōukuǎntái]* cashier

冷饮店 *[lěngyǐndiàn]* cold drinks bar

菜单 *[càidānr]* menu

清真饭店 *[qīngzhēn fàndiàn]* Moslem restaurant

面馆 *[miànguǎn]* noodle shop

饭店 *[fàndiàn]* restaurant (large)

饭庄 *[fànzhuāng]* restaurant (large)

酒楼 *[jiǔlóu]* restaurant (large)

酒家 *[jiǔjiā]* restaurant (large)

菜馆 *[càiguǎn]* restaurant (large)

餐厅 *[cāntīng]* restaurant; dining room

快餐部 *[kuàicānbù]* snackbar (fast food)

小吃店 *[xiǎochīdiàn]* snackbar

仿膳 *[Fǎngshàn]* The Fangshan Restaurant (in Beijing Beihai Park, serves dishes from the Imperial Court)

丰泽园 *[Fēngzéyuán]* The Fengzeyuan Restaurant (in Beijing, Shandong-style cooking with plenty of fish dishes)

全聚德 *[Quánjùdé]* The Quanjude

ong	ou	q	u	un	ü	ʋ	ui	uo	x	yan	z	zh
ung	**soul**	ch	**soon**	op**en**	h**uge**	h**uge**	way	wor	sh	yen	dz	j

Restaurant (Peking Duck Restaurant in Beijing)

四川饭庄 [*Sìchuān fànzhuāng*] The Sichuan Restaurant (in Beijing, hot, peppery, Sichuan-style food)

素菜馆 [*sùcàiguǎn*] vegetarian restaurant

西菜馆 [*xīcàiguǎn*] Western restaurant

ELEVATORS see LIFTS

EMERGENCIES

救护车 [*jiùhùchē*] ambulance

太平门 [*tàipíngmén*] emergency exit

火警、盗警、匪警 [*huǒjǐng, dàojǐng, féijǐng*] emergency telephone number: fire, burglary, robbery

消防队 [*xiāofángduì*] fire brigade, fire department

灭火器 [*mièhuǒqì*] fire extinguisher

消火栓 [*xiāohuǒshuān*] fire hydrant

急诊室 [*jízhěnshì*] first-aid room

警察 [*jǐngchá*] police

派出所 [*pàichūsuǒ*] police station

公安局 [*gōng'ānjó*] Public Security Bureau

FOOD

Main Types of Food

肉 [*ròu*] meat (usually pork)

猪肉 [*zhūròu*] pork

牛肉 [*niúròu*] beef

羊肉 [*yángròu*] lamb

鸡 [*jī*] chicken

鸭 [*yā*] duck

鱼 [*yó*] fish

汤 [*tāng*] soup

米饭 [*mǐfàn*] rice

面条 [*miàntiáo*] noodles

Meat, Fowl or Fish Preparation

...丸（圆）[*...wán (or yuán)*] ...balls

...块 [*...kuàir*] ... chunks, ... pieces

...丁 [*...dīng*] diced ...

鸡丁 [*jīdīng*] diced chicken

鸭块 [*yākuàir*] duck pieces

鱼片 [*yópiànr*] fish slices

肉丸（肉圆）[*ròuwán (or ròuyuán)*] meatballs

...丝 [*...sī*] shredded ...

肉丝 [*ròusī*] shredded pork

...片 [*...piànr*] sliced ..., ... slices

Basic Cooking Methods

烧... [*shāo...*] braised ...

炸... [*zhá...*] deep-fried ...

烤... [*kǎo...*] roasted ...

蒸... [*zhēng...*] steamed ...

烩... [*huì...*] stewed ...

炒... [*chǎo...*] stir-fried ...

Particular Cooking Methods

叉烧... [*chāshāo...*] barbecued ...

红烧... [*hóngshāo...*] ... braised in brown (sweet and soya) sauce

干烧... [*gānshāo...*] ... braised with chilli and bean sauce

香酥... [*xiāngsū...*] crispy deep-fried ...

咖喱... [*gāli...*] curried ...

家常... [*jiācháng...*] home-style ... (refers to a number of simple dishes)

火锅... [*huǒguō...*] ... casserole

麻酱... [*májiàng...*] quick-fried in sesame paste

葱爆... [*cōngbào...*] ... quick-fried with Chinese onions

酱爆... [*jiàngbào...*] ... quick-fried with bean sauce

清蒸... [*qīngzhēng...*] steamed ...

鱼香... [*yóxiāng...*] stir-fried ... in hot spicy sauce (lit. 'fish fragrance' as the sauce originally used to cook fish)

笋炒... [*súnchǎo...*] stir-fried ... with bamboo shoots

宫保... [gōngbǎo...] stir-fried ... with peanuts and chilli

滑溜... [huáliū...] stir-fried ... with thick sauce added

糖醋... [tángcù...] sweet and sour ...

古老（咕噜）... [gúlǎo (or gulu) ...] sweet and sour ...

Supporting Ingredients

什锦... [shíjǐn...] assorted ...

三鲜... [sānxiān...] 'three-fresh' ... (i.e. with 3 particular ingredients varying from dish to dish)

冬笋... [dōngsǔn...] ... with bamboo shoots

辣子... [làzɪ...] ... with chilli

麻辣... [málà...] ... with chilli and wild pepper

蟹肉... [xièròu...] ... with crab

奶油... [nǎiyóu...] ... with cream

芙蓉... [fúróng...] ... with egg white

木须... [mùxō...] ... with eggs, tree-ear (an edible fungus) and day lily (a type of dried lily)

火腿（云腿）... [huótuǐ (or yóntuǐ) ...] ... with ham

冬菇（香菇）... [dōnggū (or xiānggū) ...] ... with mushrooms

蚝油... [háoyóu...] ... with oyster sauce

榨菜... [zhàcài...] ... with pickled mustard greens

时菜... [shícài...] ... with seasonal vegetables

虾仁... [xiārén...] ... with shrimps

茄汁（番茄）... [qiézhī (or fānqié) ...] ... with tomato sauce

Hors d'Oeuvres (cold platters)

什锦拼盘 [shíjǐn pīnpánr] assorted cold platter

什锦冷盘 [shíjǐn lěngpánr] assorted cold platter

现拼彩盘 [xiànpīn cǎipánr] assorted cold platter

五冷荤 [wú lěnghūn] cold platter of five varieties

拼四样 [pīn sìyàng] cold platter of four varieties

三式拼盘 [sānshì pīnpánr] cold platter of three varieties

龙飞凤舞 [lóngfēi fèngwǔ] 'dragon and phoenix dance' cold platter

孔雀开屏 [kǒngquè kāipíng] 'peacock plumage' cold platter

凤凰展翅 [fènghuang zhǎnchì] 'phoenix with spreading wings' cold platter

海杂拌 [hǎi zábànr] seafood cold platter

七彩冷拼盘 [qīcǎi lěng pīnpánr] 'seven colo(u)rs' cold platter

六宝大拼盘 [liùbǎo dà pīnpánr] 'six treasures' cold platter

Pork

叉烧肉 [chāshāo ròu] barbecued pork

咖喱肉丸 [gālí ròuwán] curried meatballs

狮子头 [shīzɪ tóu] 'lion head' (a large meatball stewed with cabbage)

麻酱腰花 [májiàng yāohuā] pig's kidney quick-fried in sesame paste

红烧蹄筋 [hóngshāo tíjīnr] pig's trotters braised in brown sauce

板栗烧肉 [bǎnlì shāoròu] pork braised with chestnuts

火锅猪排 [huǒguō zhūpái] pork chop in casserole

葱爆里脊 [cōngbào lǐjī] pork fillet quick-fried with Chinese onions

酱爆三样 [jiàngbào sānyàng] pork, pig's liver and kidney quick-fried with bean sauce

烤小猪 [kǎo xiǎozhū] roast sucking pig

米粉蒸肉 [mǐfěn zhēngròu] steamed pork with rice

辣子肉丁 [làzɪ ròudīng] stir-fried diced pork with chilli

冬笋肉丝 [dōngsǔn ròusī] stir-fried shredded pork with bamboo shoots

榨菜炒肉丝 [zhàcài chǎo ròusī] stir-fried

shredded pork with pickled mustard greens

笋炒肉片 *[súnchǎo ròupiànr]* stir-fried sliced pork with bamboo shoots

芙蓉肉片 *[fúróng ròupiànr]* stir-fried sliced pork with egg white

木须炒肉 *[mùxūchǎoròu]* stir-fried sliced pork with eggs, tree-ear (edible fungus) and day lily (type of dried lily)

青椒炒肉片 *[qīngjiāo chǎo ròupiànr]* stir-fried sliced pork with green pepper

时菜炒肉片 *[shícài chǎo ròupiànr]* stir-fried sliced pork with seasonal vegetables

滑溜肉片 *[huáliū ròupiànr]* stir-fried sliced pork with thick sauce added

宫保肉丁 *[gōngbǎo ròudīng]* stir-fried diced pork with peanuts and chilli

鱼香肉丝 *[yóxiāng ròusī]* stir-fried shredded pork in hot spicy sauce

古老肉（咕噜肉） *[gúlǎo ròu (or gūlu ròu)]* sweet and sour pork

糖醋排骨 *[tángcù páigǔ]* sweet and sour spareribs

回锅肉 *[huíguō ròu]* twice-cooked pork (boiled then stir-fried)

Beef, Mutton and Lamb

麻酱牛肉 *[májiàng niúròu]* beef quick-fried in sesame paste

红烧牛肉/羊肉 *[hóngshāo niúròu|yángròu]* beef/mutton braised in brown sauce

葱爆牛肉/羊肉 *[cōngbào niúròu|yángròu]* beef/mutton quick-fried with Chinese onions

酱爆牛肉/羊肉 *[jiàngbào niúròu|yángròu]* beef/mutton quick-fried with bean sauce

咖喱牛肉/羊肉 *[gāli niúròu|yángròu]* curried beef/mutton

家常焖牛舌 *[jiācháng mèn niúshé]* home-style braised ox tongue

烤羊肉串 *[kǎo yángròuchuànr]* kebabs

灯影牛肉 *[dēngyíng niúròu]* 'lamp shadow' beef (spicy hot beef, steamed then deep-fried)

涮羊肉 *[shuàn yángròu]* Mongolian fondue, Mongolian hotpot

火锅羊肉 *[huǒguō yángròu]* mutton casserole

时菜牛肉片/羊肉片 *[shícài niúròupiànr| yángròupiànr]* shredded beef/mutton with seasonal vegetables

鱼香牛肉 *[yóxiāng niúròu]* stir-fried beef in hot spicy sauce

笋炒牛肉 *[súnchǎo niúròu]* stir-fried beef with bamboo shoots

宫保牛肉 *[gōngbǎo niúròu]* stir-fried beef with peanuts and chilli

麻辣牛肉/羊肉 *[málà niúròu|yángròu]* stir-fried beef/mutton with chilli and wild pepper

蚝油牛肉/羊肉 *[háoyóu niúròu|yángròu]* stir-fried beef/mutton with oyster sauce

茄汁牛肉 *[qiézhī niúròu]* stir-fried sliced beef with tomato sauce

Fowl

棒棒鸡 *[bàngbangjī]* Bangbang chicken (cold tenderized chicken with chilli and wild pepper)

叫化鸡 *[jiàohuājī]* 'beggar's' chicken (charcoal-baked marinaded chicken)

时菜扒鸭 *[shícài páyā]* braised duck with seasonal vegetables

冬笋焖胗 *[dōngsǔn mènzhēn]* braised gizzard (duck's stomach) with bamboo shoots

佛跳墙 *[fó tiào qiáng]* 'Buddha leaps the wall' (chicken with duck, pig's trotters and seafood stewed in rice wine)

火腿菜远鸡 *[huótuǐ càiyuǎn jī]* chicken and green vegetables with ham

茄汁鸡脯 *[qiézhī jīpǔ]* chicken breast with tomato sauce

芙蓉鸡片 *[fúróng jīpiànr]* chicken slices with egg white

冬菇/冬笋鸡片 *[dōnggū|dōngsǔn jīpiànr]* chicken slices with mushrooms/bamboo shoots

奶油鸡王 [nǎiyóu jīwáng] chicken with cream

珊瑚玉树鸡 [shānhú yùshù jī] 'coral and jade tree' chicken (chicken with crab or ham on vegetables)

香酥鸭/鸡 [xiāngsū yā/jī] crispy deep-fried whole duck/chicken

咖喱鸡块 [gālí jīkuàir] curried chicken pieces

酱爆鸡丁 [jiàngbào jīdīng] diced chicken quick-fried with bean sauce

辣子/麻辣鸡丁 [làzi/málà jīdīng] diced chicken with chilli/with chilli and wild pepper

香菇鸭掌 [xiānggū yāzhǎng] duck's foot with mushroom

茄汁煎软鸭 [qiézhī jiān ruǎnyā] fried duck with tomato sauce

家常焖鸡 [jiācháng mènjī] home-style braised chicken

北京烤鸭 [Běijīng kǎoyā] Peking Duck

白斩鸡 [báizhǎnjī] sliced cold chicken

酱爆鸭片菜心 [jiàngbào yāpiànr càixīn] sliced duck and green vegetables quick-fried with bean sauce

葱爆烧鸭片 [cōngbào shāoyāpiànr] sliced duck quick-fried with Chinese onions

宫保鸡丁 [gōngbǎo jīdīng] stir-fried diced chicken with peanuts and chilli

怪味鸡 [guàiwèirjī] 'strange-tasting' chicken (whole chicken with peanuts and pepper)

汽锅蒸鸡 [qìguō zhēngjī] whole chicken steamed in a pot

樟茶鸭子 [zhāngchá yāzi] whole duck smoked with tea and camphor leaves

红烧全鸭/鸡 [hóngshāo quányā/quánjī] whole duck/chicken braised in brown sauce

Fish

红烧鲤鱼 [hóngshāo lǐyó] carp braised in brown sauce

干烧桂鱼 [gānshāo guìyó] Chinese perch braised with chilli and bean sauce

葱爆海螺/海参 [cōngbào hǎiluó/hǎishēn] conch/sea cucumber quick-fried with Chinese onions

咖喱鱿鱼 [gāli yōuyó] curried squid

茄汁石斑块 [qiézhī shíbānkuàir] deep-fried grouper with tomato sauce

火锅鱼虾 [huǒguō yóxiā] fish and prawn casserole

家常鱼块 [jiācháng yókuàir] home-style fish

干烧黄鳝 [gānshāo huángshàn] paddyfield eel braised with chilli and bean sauce

时菜虾球 [shícài xiāqiú] prawn balls with seasonal vegetables

虾仁干贝 [xiārén gānbèi] scallops with shrimps

蟹肉鱼翅 [xièròu yóchì] shark's fin with crab

三丝鱼翅 [sānsī yóchì] shark's fin with shredded sea cucumber, abalone and bamboo shoots

菠饺鱿鱼 [pōjiǎo yōuyó] squid with spinach-wrapped minced meat/ground beef

清蒸鲥鱼/加吉鱼/鲈鱼/平鱼/鲳鱼 [qīngzhēng shíyó/jiājiyó/lúyó/píngyó/chāngyó] steamed hilsa herring/red snapper/bass/plaice/pomfret

蚝油鲍鱼 [háoyóu bāoyó] stir-fried abalone with oyster sauce

滑溜鱼片 [huáliū yópiànr] stir-fried fish slices with thick sauce added

鱼香龙虾 [yóxiāng lóngxiā] stir-fried lobster in hot spicy sauce

冬笋炒海参 [dōngsǔn chǎo hǎishēn] stir-fried sea cucumber with bamboo shoots

芙蓉虾仁 [fúróng xiārénr] stir-fried shrimps with egg white

松鼠黄鱼 [sōngshǔ huángyó] sweet and sour crispy deep-fried croaker

糖醋鱼块 [tángcù yókuàir] sweet and sour fish

两吃大虾 [liǎngchī dàxiā] 'two-eat' king prawns (prawn heads deep-fried and bodies stir-fried)

Bean Curd (Tofu)

锅塌豆腐 [guōtā dòufu] bean curd fried in batter

沙锅豆腐 [shāguō dòufu] bean curd casserole

麻辣豆腐 [málà dòufu] bean curd with chilli and wild pepper

虾仁豆腐 [xiārén dòufu] bean curd with shrimps

家常豆腐 [jiācháng dòufu] home-style bean curd

麻婆豆腐 [mápó dòufu] 'pock-marked woman' bean curd (bean curd with minced/ground beef in hot spicy sauce)

三鲜豆腐 [sānxiān dòufu] 'three-fresh' bean curd (made with three ingredients – which vary)

Vegetables

烧茄子/胡萝卜 [shāo qiézɪ/ húluóbo] stewed eggplant/carrot

海米白菜 [hǎimǐ báicài] stir-fried Chinese cabbage with dried shrimps

炒白菜/卷心菜/玉兰片 [chǎo báicài/ juǎnxīncài/ yùlánpiànr] stir-fried Chinese cabbage/ cabbage/ bamboo shoots

奶油芦荀 [nǎiyóu lúsǔn] stir-fried asparagus with cream

素什锦 [sù shíjǐn] stir-fried assorted vegetables and meat

鱼香茄子 [yúxiāng qiézɪ] stir-fried eggplant in hot spicy sauce

冬笋扁豆 [dōngsǔn biǎndòu] stir-fried French beans with bamboo shoots

烧二冬 [shāo èr dōng] stir-fried mushrooms and bamboo shoots with vegetables

双菇炒笋 [shuānggū chǎosǔn] stir-fried mushrooms with bamboo shoots

冬菇菜心 [dōnggū càixīn] stir-fried oilseed rape with mushrooms

鲜蘑豌豆 [xiānmó wāndòu] stir-fried peas with mushrooms

炒萝卜丝/土豆丝/豆芽 [chǎo luóbosɪ/ tǔdòusɪ/ dòuyá] stir-fried shredded turnip/ shredded potato/ bean sprouts

青椒/芹菜/莴苣/菜花炒肉片 [qīngjiāo/ qíncài/ wōju/càihuā chǎo ròupiànr] stir-fried sliced pork with green pepper/ celery/ woju/ cauliflower (woju is lettuce-like vegetable with edible stalk)

时菜炒肉片 [shícài chǎo ròupiànr] stir-fried sliced pork with seasonal vegetables

西红柿/韭菜/黄瓜/菠菜炒鸡蛋 [xīhóngshɪ/ jiǔcài/ huánggguā/ bōcài chǎo jī dàn] stir-fried tomato/ Chinese chives/ cucumber/ spinach with eggs

火腿烖白 [huótuǐ jiāobái] stir-fried wild rice shoots with ham

烧三鲜 [shāo sānxiān] stewed 'three-fresh' (three vegetables)

Game etc

红烧熊掌 [hóngshāo xióngzhǎng] bear's paw braised in brown sauce

芙蓉燕窝 [fúróng yànwō] bird's nest with egg white

烧鸡腿并田鸡腿 [shāojīluǐ bìng tiánjīluǐ] braised frog's legs and chicken legs

炖穿山甲 [dùn chuānshānjiǎ] braised pangolin (type of anteater – please refuse this dish as pangolin is an endangered species!)

锅炒鹌鹑蛋 [guōchǎo ānchúndàn] quail's eggs on a vegetable base

鲜笋炒鸽片 [xiānsǔn chǎo gēpiànr] stir-fried pigeon slices with bamboo shoots

三鲜猴头 [sānxiān hóutóu] 'three-fresh monkey head' (giant mushroom with three other ingredients)

Soups

开水白菜 [kāishuǐ báicài] Chinese cabbage in clear soup

八宝冬瓜汤 [bābǎo dōngguā tāng] 'eight-treasure' winter marrow soup (eight ingredients)

酸辣汤 [*suān là tāng*] hot and sour soup

什锦冬瓜盅 [*shíjǐn dōnggua zhōng*] soup served in winter marrow

竹笋鲜蘑汤 [*zhúsǔn xiānmó tāng*] soup with bamboo shoots and mushrooms

西红柿鸡蛋汤 [*xīhóngshì jīdàn tāng*] soup with eggs and tomato

紫菜汤 [*zǐcài tāng*] soup with laver (edible seaweed), dried shrimps etc

榨菜肉丝汤 [*zhàcài ròusī tāng*] soup with shredded pork and pickled mustard greens

时菜肉片汤 [*shícài ròupiàn tāng*] soup with sliced pork and seasonal vegetables

木须汤 [*mùxu tāng*] soup with sliced pork, eggs, tree-ear (an edible fungus) and day lily (dried lily)

菠菜粉丝汤 [*bōcài fěnsī tāng*] soup with spinach and vermicelli

圆汤素烩 [*yuántāng sùhuì*] vegetable chowder

三鲜汤 [*sānxiān tāng*] 'three-fresh' soup (normally prawns, a meat and a seasonal vegetable)

Rice, Noodles, Bread etc

包子 [*bāozi*] baozi (steamed dumplings with various filling, normally including minced/ground pork)

面包 [*miànbāo*] bread (white)

黑面包 [*hēi miànbāo*] brown bread

叉烧包 [*chāshāobāo*] chashaobao (steamed dumplings with barbecued pork filling)

葱油饼 [*cōngyóubǐng*] Chinese onion pancake

水饺 [*shuǐjiǎo*] Chinese ravioli

锅贴 [*guōtiē*] fried Chinese ravioli

炒面 [*chǎomiàn*] fried noodles

炒饭 [*chǎofàn*] fried rice

炒米粉 [*chǎomǐfěn*] fried rice noodles

蛋炒饭 [*dàn chǎofàn*] fried rice with eggs

鸡丝炒饭/炒面 [*jīsī chǎofàn/ chǎomiàn*] fried rice/ noodles with shredded chicken

肉丝炒饭/炒面 [*ròusī chǎofàn/ chǎomiàn*] fried rice/ noodles with shredded pork

虾仁炒饭/炒面 [*xiārén chǎofàn/ chǎomiàn*] fried rice/ noodles with shrimps

面条 [*miàntiáo*] noodles

米饭 [*mǐfàn*] (boiled) rice

稀饭 [*xīfàn*] rice porridge, congee

烧卖 [*shāomài*] shaomai (steamed dumplings open at the top, containing various fillings)

馒头 [*mántou*] steamed bread

蒸饺 [*zhēnjiǎo*] steamed Chinese ravioli

花卷 [*huājuǎnr*] steamed rolls

开口馒头 [*kāikǒu mántou*] sweet steamed bread

三鲜水饺 [*sānxiān shuǐjiǎo*] 'three-fresh' Chinese ravioli ('three fresh' here usually means pork, shrimps and Chinese chives)

馄饨（云吞、抄手）[*húntun (or yóntún or chāoshǒu)*] wonton (smaller Chinese ravioli in soup)

小笼包 [*xiǎolóngbāo*] xiaolongbao (steamed dumplings with various fillings, served on the bamboo steamers in which they have been cooked)

Desserts

杏仁豆腐 [*xìngrén dòufu*] almond junket

拔丝苹果/山药/香蕉 [*básī píngguo/ shānyào/ xiāngjiāo*] apple/ yam/ banana fritters

西瓜盅 [*xīgua zhōng*] assorted fruit in water melon

八宝饭 [*bābǎo fàn*] 'eight-treasure' rice pudding (with eight varieties of fruit and nuts)

什锦水果羹 [*shíjǐn shuǐguo gēng*] fruit salad

莲子羹 [*liánzi gēng*] lotus-seed in syrup

菠萝捞糟 [*bōluo láozāo*] pineapple in fermented glutinous rice

冰糖银耳 [*bīngtáng yín'ěr*] silver tree-ear (edible fungus) in syrup

food 82 **food**

豌豆黄 [*wāndòuhuáng*] sweet pea cake
"三不沾" ['*sān bù zhān*'] 'three non-stick'
(sweets made from egg yolk, mung bean
powder etc – won't stick to your plate,
chopsticks or teeth)
酸奶 [*suānnǎi*] yoghurt

Fruit

苹果 [*píngguo*] apple
杏 [*xìng*] apricot
香蕉 [*xiāngjiāo*] banana
血橙 [*xuěchéng*] blood orange
樱桃 [*yīngtao*] cherry
椰子 [*yēzi*] coconut
海棠果 [*hǎitángguǒ*] crab apple
枣 [*zǎo*] date
无花果 [*wúhuāguǒ*] fig
蟠桃 [*pántáo*] flat peach
葡萄 [*pútao*] grape
广柑 [*guǎnggān*] Guangdong orange
(sweet orange)
山楂 [*shānzhā*] haw, hawthorn berry
(sour tasting)
哈密瓜 [*hāmìguā*] honeydew melon
金桔 [*jīnjó*] kumquat (kind of small
tangerine)
柠檬 [*níngméng*] lemon
龙眼 [*lóngyǎn*] longan (similar to lychee)
枇杷 [*pípa*] loquat (sweet yellow fruit)
荔枝 [*lìzhī*] lychee
柑子 [*gānzi*] orange
木瓜 [*mùguā*] papaya (large yellow-green
fruit)
桃子 [*táozi*] peach
梨 [*lí*] pear
柿子 [*shìzi*] persimmon (large soft yellow
fruit)
菠萝 [*bōluo*] pineapple
李子 [*lǐzi*] plum
石榴 [*shíliu*] pomegranate
沙田柚 [*shātiányòu*] shatian pomelo (very
sweet fruit)
草莓 [*cǎoméi*] strawberry
桔子（蜜桔） [*józi (or mìjó)*] tangerine
西瓜 [*xīgua*] water melon

Snacks

豆沙酥饼 [*dòushā sūbǐng*] baked flaky
cake with sweet bean paste filling
火烧 [*huǒshāo*] baked wheaten bun
糖火烧 [*táng huǒshāo*] baked wheaten
bun with sugar
油饼 [*yóubǐng*] deep-fried savo(u)ry
pancake
油炸糕 [*yóuzhágāo*] deep-fried sweet
pancake
馅饼 [*xiànrbǐng*] savo(u)ry fritter
烧饼 [*shāobǐng*] sesame pancake
豆浆（豆汁） [*dòujiāng (or dòuzhī)*] soya
bean milk
春卷 [*chūnjuǎnr*] spring rolls
豆沙包 [*dòushābāo*] steamed dumpling
with sweet bean paste filling
油条 [*yóutiáo*] unsweetened doughnut
sticks

Basics

大麦 [*dàmài*] barley
腐竹 [*fǔzhú*] bean curd 'bamboo' (dried
soya bean milk cream, in shape of
bamboo)
豆腐皮 [*dòufu pír*] bean curd skin
黑/白胡椒 [*hēi/bái hújiāo*] black/ white
pepper
红糖 [*hóng táng*] brown sugar
荞麦 [*qiáomài*] buckwheat
黄油 [*huángyóu*] butter
奶酪 [*nǎilào*] cheese
辣椒油 [*làjiāo yóu*] chilli oil
辣椒酱 [*làjiāo jiàng*] chilli paste
辣椒/辣椒面 [*làjiāo/làjiāo miànr*] chilli/
chilli powder
桂皮（肉桂） [*guìpí (or ròuguì)*] Chinese
cinnamon
丁香 [*dīngxiāng*] cloves
椰子油 [*yēzi yóu*] coconut oil
玉米油 [*yùmǐ yóu*] corn oil
奶油 [*nǎiyóu*] cream
冻粉 [*dòngfěn*] dried agar-agar (seaweed
jelly)

ai	ao	c	e	ei	en	h	i	ı	ian	ie	iu	o
ı	h**ow**	ts	h**er**	ay	op**en**	lo**ch**	ee	sir	yen	yeh	**yo**yo	or

豆腐干 *[dòufu gānr]* dried bean curd
茴香 *[huíxiāng]* fennel
豆腐乳 *[dòufu rǔ]* fermented bean curd
豆豉 *[dòuchǐ]* fermented soya beans
五香面 *[wǔxiāng miànr]* 'five fragrance' powder (mixed spice of fennel, wild pepper, star aniseed, Chinese cinnamon and cloves)
大蒜 *[dàsuàn]* garlic
生姜 *[shēngjiāng]* ginger
黄米 *[huángmǐ]* glutinous millet
糯米 *[nuòmǐ]* glutinous rice
砂糖 *[shā táng]* granulated sugar
豆瓣辣酱 *[dòubànr làjiàngr]* hot soya bean paste
海蜇 *[hǎizhé]* jellyfish
海带 *[hǎidài]* kelp
紫菜 *[zǐcài]* laver (an edible seaweed)
玉米 *[yòmǐ]* maize
人造奶油（麦淇淋）*[rénzào nǎiyóu (or màiqílín)]* margarine
小米 *[xiǎomǐ]* millet
味精（味素）*[wéijīng (or wèisù)]* MSG (monosodium glutamate)
芥末 *[jièmo]* mustard
燕麦 *[yànmài]* oats
橄榄油 *[gǎnlǎn yóu]* olive oil
蚝油 *[háoyóu]* oyster sauce
花生油 *[huāshēng yóu]* peanut oil
胡椒 *[hújiāo]* pepper
咸菜 *[xiáncài]* pickles
松花蛋 *[sōnghuādàn]* preserved eggs
菜籽油 *[càizi yóu]* rape oil
大米 *[dàmǐ]* rice
冰糖 *[bīng táng]* rock sugar
黑麦 *[hēimài]* rye
盐 *[yán]* salt
芝麻油 *[zhīma yóu]* sesame oil
高粱 *[gāoliáng]* sorghum (a cereal similar to corn)
酱油 *[jiàngyóu]* soy sauce
豆油 *[dòu yóu]* soya bean oil
八角（大料）*[bājiǎo (or dàliào)]* star aniseed (seed casing is star-shaped)
发菜 *[fàcài]* star jelly (a water-plant)
糖 *[táng]* sugar

方糖 *[fāng táng]* sugar lumps
精盐 *[jīngyán]* table salt
蕃茄酱 *[fānqié jiàng]* tomato paste
素鸡 *[sùjī]* 'vegetarian chicken' (rolled bean curd skin)
醋 *[cù]* vinegar
小麦 *[xiǎomài]* wheat
面粉 *[miànfěn]* wheat flour
白糖 *[bái táng]* white sugar
白醋 *[bái cù]* white vinegar
花椒 *[huājiāo]* wild pepper

FOOD LABELS

成份 *[chéngfèn]* ingredients
净重 *[jìngzhòng]* net weight
重量 *[zhòngliàng]* weight

FORMS

从何处来 *[cóng héchù lái]* arriving from
出生年月 *[chūshēng niányuè]* date of birth
到何处去 *[dào héchù qu]* destination
籍贯 *[jíguàn]* father's place of birth
拟住天数 *[nǐzhù tiānshù]* length of stay
姓名 *[xìngmíng]* name (full name)
国籍 *[guójí]* nationality
护照号码 *[hùzhào hàomǎ]* passport number
永久地址 *[yóngjiǔ dìzhǐ]* permanent address
旅客登记表 *[lǚkè dēngjìbiǎo]* registration form
性别（男/女）*[xìngbié (nán/nǚ)]* sex (male/female)
签名 *[qiānmíng]* signature

GARAGES

柴油 *[cháiyóu]* diesel
严禁烟火 *[yánjìn yānhuǒ]* no smoking or naked flames
加油站 *[jiāyóuzhàn]* petrol station, gas

ong	ou	q	u	un	ü	ʊ	ui	uo	x	yan	z	zh
ung	soul	ch	soon	open	huge	huge	way	wor	sh	yen	dz	j

station
汽油 [qìyóu] petrol, gas

GEOGRAPHICAL

自治区 [zìzhìqū] autonomous region
盆地 [péndì] basin
运河 [yùnhé] canal
市 [shì] city
洲 [zhōu] continent
国家 [guójiā] country
县 [xiàn] county
森林 [sēnlín] forest
岛 [dǎo] island
湖 [hú] lake
纬度 [wěidù] latitude
经度 [jīngdù] longitude
地图 [dìtú] map
山 [shān] mountain, hill
山脉 [shānmài] mountains
海洋 [hǎiyáng] ocean
半岛 [bàndǎo] peninsula
平原 [píngyoán] plain
高原 [gāoyoán] plateau
省 [shěng] province
河 [hé] river
江 [jiāng] river (big)
海 [hǎi] sea
镇 [zhèn] town
山谷 [shāngǔ] valley
村 [cūn] village
树林 [shùlín] woods

HAIRDRESSERS

女部 [nǚbù] (ladies') hairdresser
男部 [nánbù] barber
美容厅 [měiróngtīng] beauty salon
吹风 [chuīfēng] blow dry
冷烫 [lěnglàng] cold perm
理发店 [lǐfàdiàn] hairdresser
理发厅 [lǐfàtīng] hairdresser
染发 [rǎnfà] hair dyeing
修指甲 [xiūzhǐjiā] manicure
电烫 [diàntàng] perm

整发 [zhěngfà] setting
洗发 [xǐfà] shampoo
修面 [xiūmiàn] shave

HISTORICAL INTEREST

"反右"斗争 ['fǎnyòu' dòuzhēng] 'anti-rightist' campaign
义和团运动 [yìhétuán yòndòng] Boxer Movement (1900)
文化大革命 [wénhuà dàgémìng] Cultural Revolution (1966-1976)
大跃进 [dàyoèjìn] Great Leap Forward (1958)
太平天国 [tàipíng tiānguó] Kingdom of Heavenly Peace (Taiping)
五四运动 [wǔsì yòndòng] May 4th Movement (1919)
鸦片战争 [yāpiàn zhànzhēng] Opium War
人民公社 [rénmín gōngshè] People's Commune
辛亥革命 [xīnhài gémìng] Xinhai Revolution (1911)

HOSPITALS see MEDICAL

HOTELS

工艺美术服务部 [gōngyì měishù fúwùbù] arts and crafts shop
银行 [yínháng] bank
酒吧 [jiǔbā] bar
中国国际旅行社 [Zhōngguo guójì lǚxíngshè] China International Travel Service
中国旅行社 [Zhōngguo lǚxíngshè] China Travel Service
中餐厅 [Zhōng cāntīng] Chinese dining room
餐厅 [cāntīng] dining room, restaurant
外币兑换 [wàibì duìhuàn] foreign exchange
宾馆 [bīnguǎn] guest house
饭店 [fàndiàn] hotel
小卖部 [xiǎomàibù] kiosk

ai	ao	c	e	ei	en	h	i	ɪ	ian	ie	iu	o
I	how	ts	her	ay	open	loch	ee	sir	yen	yeh	yoyo	or

新华书店 *[xīnhuá shūdiàn]* New China
  (xinhua) bookshop/ bookstore
邮局 *[yóujú]* post office
总服务台 *[zǒng fúwùtái]* reception
游艺室 *[yóuyìshì]* recreation room
快餐 *[kuàicān]* snackbar
出租汽车 *[chūzū qìchē]* taxis
电传室 *[diànchuánshì]* telex office
西餐厅 *[xī cāntīng]* Western dining room

LIFTS/ELEVATORS

上 *[shàng]* up
下 *[xià]* down
开 *[kāi]* open
关 *[guān]* close
电梯 *[diàntī]* lifts, elevators

MEDICAL

阑尾炎 *[lánwěiyán]* appendicitis
支气管炎 *[zhīqìguǎnyán]* bronchitis
中医科 *[zhōngyīkē]* Chinese medicine
  (department)
中药房 *[zhōngyàofáng]* Chinese medicine
  dispensary
牙科（口腔科） *[yákē (or kǒuqiāngkē)]*
  dental (department)
皮肤科 *[pífūkē]* dermatology
耳鼻喉科 *[ěrbíhóukē]* ear, nose and throat
  (department)
急诊室 *[jízhěnshì]* emergency
眼科 *[yǎnkē]* eye department
初诊 *[chūzhěn]* first treatment
食物中毒 *[shíwù zhòngdú]* food poisoning
外宾门诊部 *[wàibīn ménzhěnbù]* foreign
  out-patients
骨折 *[gǔzhé]* fracture
胃炎 *[wèiyán]* gastritis
妇产科 *[fùchǎnkē]* gyn(a)ecology and
  obstetrics
肝炎 *[gānyán]* hepatitis
医院 *[yīyuàn]* hospital
住院处 *[zhùyuànchù]* hospital admissions

office
内科 *[nèikē]* medical (department)
门诊部 *[ménzhěnbù]* out-patients
小儿科 *[xiǎoérkē]* p(a)ediatrics
肺炎 *[fèiyán]* pneumonia
挂号 *[guàhào]* registration
挂号费 *[guàhàofèi]* registration fee
复诊 *[fùzhěn]* subsequent treatment
外科 *[wàikē]* surgical (department)
病房 *[bìngfáng]* ward
取药 *[xīyàofáng]* Western medicine
  dispensary
放射科 *[fàngshèkē]* X-ray (department)

MEDICINE LABELS

抗菌素 *[kàngjūnsù]* antibiotics
阿斯匹林 *[āsīpǐlín]* aspirin (tm)
棕色合剂 *[zōngsè héjì]* cough mixture
止咳糖浆 *[zhǐké tángjiāng]* cough syrup
咳必清 *[kébìqīng]* cough tablet
剂量 *[jìliàng]* dosage
每四/六小时服一次 *[měi sì/ liù xiǎoshí fú
  yícì]* every four/ six hours
失效期 *[shīxiàoqī]* expiry date
外用 *[wàiyòng]* for external use
每次一片/丸/格 *[měi cì yí piànr/ wán/ gé]*
  one tablet/ pill/ measure at a time
止痛片 *[zhǐténgpiànr]* pain-killer
青霉素 *[qīngméisù]* penicillin
一日三/四次 *[yírì sān/sì cì]* three/four
  times a day
含碘片 *[hándiǎnpiànr]* throat pastille
内服 *[nèifú]* to be taken orally
饭前/后温开水送服 *[fàn qián/hòu
  wēnkāishuǐ sòngfú]* to be taken with
  water before/after food
必要时服 *[bìyào shí fú]* when necessary

MONTHS

一月 *[yīyue]* January
二月 *[èryue]* February
三月 *[sānyue]* March

ong	ou	q	u	un	ü	o	ui	uo	x	yan	z	zh
ung	s**ou**l	ch	s**oo**n	op**en**	h**u**ge	h**u**ge	way	wor	sh	yen	dz	j

四月 [sìyuè] April
五月 [wǔyuè] May
六月 [liùyuè] June
七月 [qīyuè] July
八月 [bāyuè] August
九月 [jiǔyuè] September
十月 [shíyuè] October
十一月 [shíyīyuè] November
十二月 [shí'èryuè] December

MOVIE THEATERS see CINEMAS

NIGHTLIFE

迪斯科 [dísīkè] disco
夜市 [yèshì] night market
音乐茶座 [yīnyuè cházuò] teatime concert

NOTICES IN RESTAURANTS AND ON MENUS

酒水在外 [jiǔshuǐ zai wài] drinks not included
今日供应 [jīnrì gòngying] today's menu

NOTICES IN SHOPS

收款台 [shōukuǎntái] cashier
展品概不出售 [zhánpǐn gài bù chūshòu] display only
出口转内销 [chūkǒu zhuǎn nèixiāo] export rejects
不退不换 [bú tuì bú huàn] no exchange or refunds
钱票当面点清，过后概不负责 [qián piào dāngmiàn diǎnqīng, guòhòu gài bù fùzé] please check your change before leaving as mistakes cannot be rectified afterwards
大减价 [dàjiǎnjià] sale
处理品 [chúlipǐn] seconds
试销产品 [shìxiāo chánpǐn] trial samples

NOTICES ON DOORS

顾客止步 [gùkè zhǐ bù] no entry for customers
未经许可，禁止入内！ [wèi jīng xókě, jínzhǐ rù nèi!] no entry without permission, authorized personnel only
拉 [lā] pull
推 [tuī] push
闲人免进 [xiánren miǎn jìn] staff only

PLACE NAMES

Northeast China

长白山 [Chángbáishān] Changbai Mountains
长春 [Chángchūn] Changchun
大连 [Dàlián] Dalian
哈尔滨 [Hā'ěrbīn] Harbin
沈阳 [Shěnyáng] Shenyang (Mukden)

North China

八达岭 [Bādálǐng] Badaling (pass at Great Wall)
白云观 [Báiyúnguàn] Baiyunguan (Taoist Temple in Beijing)
北海公园 [Běihǎi gōngyóan] Beihai Park (in Beijing)
北京 [Běijīng] Beijing (Peking)
长陵 [Chánglíng] Changling (one of the Ming Tombs)
承德 [Chéngdé] Chengde
景山公园 [Jǐngshān gōngyóan] Coal Hill Park (in Beijing)
大同 [Dàtóng] Datong
定陵 [Dìnglíng] Dingling (one of the Ming Tombs)
长城 [Chángchéng] Great Wall
呼和浩特 [Hūhéhàotè] Hohhot
十三陵 [Shísānlíng] Ming Tombs (near Beijing)
圆明园 [Yóanmíngyóan] original Summer Palace (ruin near Beijing)
故宫博物院 [Gùgōng bówùyòan] Palace Museum (in Beijing)
前门 [Qiánmén] Qianmen (Front Gate,

ai	ao	c	e	ei	en	h	i	ı	ian	ie	iu	o
I	how	ts	her	ay	open	loch	ee	sir	yen	yeh	yoyo	or

in Beijing)
石家庄 [*Shíjiāzhuāng*] Shijiazhuang
颐和园 [*Yíhéyuán*] Summer Palace (near
　Beijing)
太原 [*Tàiyuán*] Taiyuan
天坛 [*Tiāntán*] Temple of Heaven
　(Beijing)
天安门 [*Tiān'ānmén*] Tian'anmen
　(Gate of Heavenly Peace, in Bejing)
天津 [*Tiānjīn*] Tianjin (Tientsin)
锡林浩特 [*Xīlínhàotè*] Xilinhot
雍和宫 [*Yōnghégōng*] Yonghegong (Lama
　Temple, in Beijing)
云冈石窟 [*Yúngāng shíkū*] Yungang
　Caves (Datong)

East China

常州 [*Chángzhōu*] Changzhou
福州 [*Fúzhōu*] Fuzhou
杭州 [*Hángzhōu*] Hangzhou (Hangchow)
合肥 [*Héféi*] Hefei
黄山 [*Huángshān*] Huangshan
　Mountains
济南 [*Jǐnán*] Jinan (Tsinan)
景德镇 [*Jǐngdézhèn*] Jingdezhen (noted
　for porcelain)
井冈山 [*Jǐnggāngshān*] Jinggang
　Mountains
庐山 [*Lúshān*] Lushan Mountains
南昌 [*Nánchāng*] Nanchang
南京 [*Nánjīng*] Nanjing (Nanking)
青岛 [*Qīngdǎo*] Qingdao (Tsingtao)
绍兴 [*Shàoxìng*] Shaoxing
苏州 [*Sūzhōu*] Suzhou (Soochow)
泰山 [*Tàishān*] Taishan Mountains
温州 [*Wēnzhōu*] Wenzhou
西湖 [*Xīhú*] West Lake (Hangzhou)
无锡 [*Wúxī*] Wuxi
厦门 [*Xiàmén*] Xiamen
扬州 [*Yángzhōu*] Yangzhou
烟台 [*Yāntái*] Yantai

South China

长沙 [*Chángshā*] Changsha

佛山 [*Fóshān*] Foshan
广州 [*Guǎngzhōu*] Guangzhou (Canton)
桂林 [*Guìlín*] Guilin
漓江 [*Líjiāng*] Lijiang River (Guilin)
龙门石窟 [*Lóngmén shíkū*] Longmen
　Caves (Luoyang)
洛阳 [*Luòyáng*] Luoyang
南宁 [*Nánníng*] Nanning
曲阜 [*Qūfù*] Qufu (home of Confucius)
深圳 [*Shēnzhèn*] Shenzhen
武汉 [*Wǔhàn*] Wuhan
阳朔 [*Yángsuò*] Yangsuo (Guilin)
长江三峡 [*Chángjiāng sānxiá*] Yangtze
　Gorges
肇庆 [*Zhàoqìng*] Zhaoqing (Guangzhou)
郑州 [*Zhèngzhōu*] Zhengzhou

Southwest China

成都 [*Chéngdū*] Chengdu
重庆 [*Chóngqìng*] Chongqing
　(Chungking)
大理 [*Dàlǐ*] Dali
峨嵋山 [*Éméishān*] Emei Mountains
九寨沟 [*Jiǔzhàigōu*] Jiuzhaigou (nature
　reserve in Songpan)
昆明 [*Kūnmíng*] Kunming
拉萨 [*Lāsā*] Lhasa
松潘 [*Sōngpān*] Songpan
路南石林 [*Lùnán shílín*] Stone Forest
　(area of interesting rock formations in
　Kunming)
卧龙沟 [*Wòlónggōu*] Wolonggou (in
　Songpan, noted for pandas)

Northwest China

敦煌 [*Dūnhuáng*] Dunhuang
兰州 [*Lánzhōu*] Lanzhou
秦佣坑 [*Qínyǒngkēng*] Terracotta Army
　Exhibition (Xi'an)
吐鲁番 [*Túlǔfān*] Turpan
　(Turfan)
乌鲁木齐 [*Wūlǔmùqí*] Urumqi
　(Urumchi)
西安 [*Xī'ān*] Xi'an (Sian)

ong	ou	q	u	un	ü	ʋ	ui	uo	x	yan	z	zh
ung	so**u**l	ch	soon	op**en**	huge	huge	way	wor	sh	yen	dz	j

POST OFFICES

开箱时间 [kāixiāng shíjian] collection times

信封 [xìnfēng] envelope

信箱 [xìnxiāng] letterbox

信函 [xìnhān] letters

长途电话 [chángtú diànhuà] long-distance telephones

杂志报刊 [zázhì bàokān] magazines and newspapers

汇款单 [huìkuǎndānr] money order form

汇款 [huìkuǎn] money orders

包裹单 [bāoguǒdānr] parcel form

包裹、印刷品 [bāoguǒ, yìnshuāpǐn] parcels, printed matter

信筒 [yóutǒng] pillar box, mailbox

邮电局 [yóudiànjó] post and telecommunications office

邮局 [yóujó] post office

邮票、挂号 [yóupiào – guàhào] stamps, registered mail

电报纸 [diànbàozhǐ] telegram form

电报 [diànbào] telegrams

PUBLIC BUILDINGS

浴池 [yòchí] bath house

电影院 [diànyǐngyoàn] cinema, movie theater

影剧院 [yǐngjòyoàn] cinema, movie theater

民政局 [mínzhèngjó] Civil Affairs Bureau

学院 [xóyoàn] college

领事馆 [lǐngshìguǎn] consulate

大使馆 [dàshíguǎn] embassy

工厂 [gōngchǎng] factory

医院 [yīyoàn] hospital

幼儿园 [yòuéryoàn] kindergarten

图书馆 [túshūguǎn] library

长途汽车站 [chángtú qìchēzhàn] long-distance bus station

中学 [zhōngxó] middle school, secondary school

博物馆 [bówùguǎn] museum

公证处 [gōngzhèngchù] notary's office

托儿所 [tuōérsuǒ] nursery

人民法院 [rénmín fǎyoàn] People's Court

...人民政府 [...rénmín zhèngfǔ] ... People's Government (local government)

派出所 [pàichūsuǒ] police station

邮局 [yóujó] post office

小学 [xiǎoxó] primary school

公安局 [gōng'ānjó] Public Security Bureau

体育馆 [tǐyòguǎn] sports hall, indoor stadium

体育场 [tǐyòchǎng] stadium

游泳馆 [yóuyóngguǎn] swimming pool (indoor)

电报大楼 [diànbào dàlóu] telegraph building

剧院 [jòyoàn] theatre, theater

剧场 [jòchǎng] theatre, theater

大学 [dàxoé] university

RENTALS

出租自行车 [chūzu zìxíngchē] bikes for hire, bikes to rent

租船 [zū chuán] boat hire, boats to rent

出租照相机 [chūzū zhàoxiàngjī] camera rentals

出租 [chūzū] for hire, to rent

REPLIES

xièxie thanks

bú kèqi not at all

zhè shì yīnggāi de it's a pleasure

duìbuqí sorry

méi guānxi it doesn't matter

zàijiàn goodbye

REST ROOMS see TOILETS

ROAD SIGNS

注意行人 [zhùyì xíngren] beware

ai	ao	c	e	ei	en	h	i	ɪ	ian	ie	iu	o
I	how	ts	her	ay	open	loch	ee	sir	yen	yeh	yoyo	or

pedestrians

危险！ *[wēixiǎn!]* danger!

中速行，驶，安全礼让！ *[zhōngsù xíngshǐ, ānquán lǐràng!]* drive steadily, carefully and courteously

让路 *[rànglù]* give way, yield

禁止驶入 *[jìnzhǐ shǐrù]* no entry

禁止超车 *[jìnzhǐ chāochē]* no overtaking, no passing

禁止停车 *[jìnzhǐ tíngchē]* no parking

此路不通 *[cǐlù bù tōng]* no through road, dead end

单行线 *[dānxíngxiàn]* one-way traffic

人行横道 *[rénxíng héngdào]* pedestrian crossing

铁路道口 *[tiělù dàokǒu]* railway/railroad crossing

禁区 *[jìnqū]* restricted area, no-go area

禁止通行 *[jìnzhǐ tōngxíng]* road closed

前面施工 *[qiánmian shīgōng]* roadworks ahead

慢驶 *[mànshǐ]* slow

一慢，二看，三通过 *[yī màn, èr kàn, sān tōngguò!]* slow down, look and then cross (notice to pedestrians)

陡坡 *[dǒupō]* steep hill

停车 *[tíngchē]* stop

小心路滑 *[xiǎoxīn lù huá]* take care, road slippery

SCHEDULES see TIMETABLES

SHOP NAMES

文物商店 *[wénwù shāngdiàn]* antique shop/store

工艺美术商店 *[gōngyì měishù shāngdiàn]* arts and crafts shop

钟表店 *[zhōngbiǎodiàn]* clocks and watches

服装店 *[fúzhuāngdiàn]* clothes shop/store

百货公司 *[bǎihuò gōngsī]* department store

百货商店 *[bǎihuò shāngdiàn]* department store

百货大楼 *[bǎihuò dàlóu]* department store

商场 *[shāngchǎng]* department store

食品商店 *[shípǐn shāngdiàn]* food store

友谊商店 *[yǒuyì shāngdiàn]* Friendship Store

菜市场 *[càishìchǎng]* greengrocer

菜店 *[càidiàn]* greengrocer

副食品商店 *[fùshípǐn shāngdiàn]* grocery

理发店 *[lǐfàdiàn]* hairdresser

日用杂品店 *[rìyòng zápǐndiàn]* household goods shop/store

土产店 *[túchǎndiàn]* ironmonger, hardware store

洗衣店 *[xǐyīdiàn]* laundry (sometimes including dry-cleaning)

市场 *[shìchǎng]* market

新华书店 *[xīnhuá shūdiàn]* New China (Xinhua) bookshop/bookstore

眼镜店 *[yǎnjìngdiàn]* optician

复印 *[fùyìn]* photocopying

照相馆 *[zhàoxiàngguǎn]* photographer

古旧书店 *[gǔjiù shūdiàn]* secondhand bookshop/bookstore

信托商店 *[xìntuō shāngdiàn]* secondhand shop/store

文具商店 *[wénjù shāngdiàn]* stationery

五金店 *[wǔjīndiàn]* tools and ironmongery/hardware

STATIONS

列车到站时刻表 *[lièchē dàozhàn shíkèbiǎo]* arrival times

检票口 *[jiǎnpiàokǒu]* barrier

列车离站时刻表 *[lièchē lízhàn shíkèbiǎo]* departure times

入口 *[rùkǒu]* entrance

出口 *[chūkǒu]* exit

问讯处 *[wènxònchù]* information desk

行李寄存处 *[xínglǐ jìcúnchù]* left luggage, baggage checkroom

"旅客留言" *['lǚkè liúyán']* messages (for passengers)

站台票 *[zhàntáipiào]* platform ticket

站台 *[zhàntái]* platform, track

火车站 *[huǒchēzhàn]* railway/railroad station

ong	ou	q	u	un	ü	ʋ	ui	uo	x	yan	z	zh
ung	**soul**	ch	**soon**	op**en**	huge	h**u**ge	way	wor	sh	yen	dz	j

售票口 *[shòupiàokǒu]* ticket office
车次 *[chēcì]* train number
候车室 *[hòuchēshì]* waiting room

STREETS

大街 *[dàjiē]* avenue
胡同 *[hútòng]* lane
巷 *[xiàng]* lane
里弄 *[lǐnòng]* lane (in South China)
路 *[lù]* road
广场 *[guǎngchǎng]* square
街 *[jiē]* street

SUBWAY see UNDERGROUND

SWEARWORDS AND TERMS OF ABUSE

bèndàn! idiot!
chǔnhuò! idiot!
dàbízı! big nose! (Westerner)
ěxīn! disgusting!
fèihuà! nonsense!
gǔn! get lost!
hēiguǐ! black devil!
húndàn! bastard!
lǎowài! bloody foreigner!
Měiguólao! Yank!
shénjīngbìng! crazy!
tāmāde! hell!, damn!
yángguizı! foreign devil!

TAXIS

出租汽车 *[chūzū qìchē]* taxis

TELEPHONES

长途区号 *[chángtú qūhào]* area code, STD code
查号台 *[cháhàotái]* directory inquiries, information
分机 *[fēnjī]* extension

一次四分 *[yícì sìfēn]* four fen per call
国际长途 *[guójì chángtú]* international call
长途电话 *[chángtú diànhuà]* long-distance call
公用电话 *[gōngyòng diànhuà]* public telephone
总机 *[zǒngjī]* switchboard
电话簿 *[diànhuàbù]* telephone directory

THEATRES/THEATERS see also CINEMAS

休息 *[xiūxi]* interval
京剧 *[jīngjù]* Peking Opera
节目单 *[jiémùdānr]* program(me)
剧场 *[juchǎng]* theatre, theater
剧院 *[juyuàn]* theatre, theater
戏院 *[xìyuàn]* theatre, theater

TIMETABLES/SCHEDULES

特快 *[tèkuài]* express
直快 *[zhíkuài]* fast through train
快客 *[kuàikè]* fast train
硬席 *[yìngxí]* hard seat
硬卧 *[yìngwò]* hard sleeper
客 *[kè]* ordinary passenger train
软席 *[ruǎnxí]* soft seat
软卧 *[ruǎnwò]* soft sleeper
站名 *[zhànmíng]* station
市郊 *[shìjiāo]* suburban train
直客 *[zhíkè]* through train
时刻表 *[shíkèbiǎo]* timetable, schedule
开往... *[kāiwǎng...]* to ...
旅游 *[lǚyóu]* tourist train
车次 *[chēcì]* train number

TOILETS/REST ROOMS

有人 *[yǒurén]* engaged, occupied
男厕所 *[náncèsuǒ]* gents, men's rest room
男厕 *[náncè]* gents, men's room

ai	ao	c	e	ei	en	h	i	ı	ian	ie	iu	o
I	h**ow**	ts	h**er**	**ay**	op**en**	lo**ch**	**ee**	s**ir**	**yen**	**yeh**	**yo**yo	**or**

女厕所 [nǚcèsuǒ] ladies, ladies' rest room
女厕 [nǚcè] ladies, ladies' room
公厕 [gōngcè] public toilets, comfort station
无人 [wúrén] vacant, free

TOURISM

城市交通图 [chéngshì jiāotōngtú] city transport map
票价 [piàojià] fare
导游 [dǎoyóu] guide (person)
旅游指南 [lǚyóu zhǐnán] guidebook
一/三日游 [yī/sān rì yóu] one/three day tour
游览车 [yóulǎnchē] tourist bus
游览图 [yóulǎntú] tourist map

TRAINS

紧急制动闸 [jǐnjí zhìdòngzhá] communication cord, emergency brake

餐车 [cānchē] dining car
列车员 [lièchēyuán] guard, conductor
"YZ"硬席车 [yìngxíchē] hard seat carriage
"YW"硬卧车 [yìngwòchē] hard sleeper carriage
列车长 [lièchēzhǎng] head guard/conductor
乘警 [chéngjǐng] railway/railroad police
"RZ"软席车 [ruǎnxíchē] soft seat carriage
"RW"软卧车 [ruǎnwòchē] soft sleeper carriage
乘务员 [chéngwùyuán] train attendant

UNDERGROUND/SUBWAY see also STATIONS

开往...方向 [kāiwǎng...fāngxiàng] to ...
地铁 [dìtiě] underground, subway

Reference Grammar

SOME GENERAL CHARACTERISTICS OF THE LANGUAGE

Chinese has no inflections for case, number or gender. Verbs do not decline for past, present or future, which are identified by time references such as **míngtian** 'tomorrow', **jīntian** 'today', or **zuótian** 'yesterday'. There is also a tendency to keep statements to a minimum and to leave out what is clearly understood at any given point. This means that pronouns (especially the impersonal 'it') and conjunctions are often omitted.

NOUNS

Nouns are the same whether singular or plural. **Fángjiān** for instance is either 'room' or 'rooms' depending on context:

wǒ yào yíge fángjiān	I want one room
wǒ yào liǎngge fángjiān	I want two rooms

The only exception is the possible addition of the suffix **men** to a small number of nouns which refer to human beings:

péngyoumen	friends
háizımen	children

men is never used when numbers are involved:

sānge háizı	three children

ARTICLES

There is no definite article 'the' or indefinite article 'a', 'an' in Chinese. Definiteness is conveyed by context and/or word order.

If something (e.g. **shū** 'a book' or 'books') has already been referred to then further reference to it/them is automatically definite:

    wǒ qù mǎi shū   I am going to buy the book(s)

If there has been no previous mention of books or buying them, then **shū** would be indefinite:

    wǒ qù mǎi shū   I am going to buy a book/some books

A noun object brought forward before the verb for emphasis has almost certainly been referred to previously in the conversation and is therefore likely to be definite:

    shū wó mǎile   I've bought the book(s)

If there is any doubt about specifying the noun the demonstrative adjective **nèi** 'that' or **zhèi** 'this' with the appropriate measure (see page 99) is added:

    wǒ qù mǎi nèiběn shū   I'm going to buy the/that book

The numeral **yi** 'one' with measure can also be used to express 'a', 'an'. In these circumstances the **yi** is usually not stressed and is often omitted leaving the measure alone:

    wǒ qù mǎi yiběn/běn shū   I am going to buy a book

ADJECTIVES

Adjectives precede the noun, usually with **de** inserted between the adjective and the noun:

fùzá de wènti	complicated question(s)
hěn guì de dōngxi	very expensive thing(s)

If the adjective is monosyllabic the **de** is often omitted:

lǎo péngyou	old friends
hǎo jīhuì	a good opportunity

A noun may also be used like an adjective to qualify another noun:

kēxué wènti	scientific question(s) (*lit.* science)
Hànyǔ cídiǎn	Chinese dictionary (*lit.* Chinese language)

ADJECTIVAL VERBS

Adjectives also function as adjectival verbs:

wènti hěn fùzá	the question is complicated
dōngxi dōu hěn guì	the things are all expensive

Notice that there is no verb 'to be'. **Fùzá** itself means 'to be complicated' and **guì** 'to be expensive'.

Adjectival verbs normally do not stand alone but are qualified in some way. The most common and minimal qualification is the adverb **hěn**. **Hěn** with the adjectival verb carries little meaning, unless it is stressed, when it means 'very'.

COMPARATIVES (BIGGER, BETTER etc)

An adjectival verb (see page 95), which stands alone, usually conveys a comparative meaning:

zhèige hǎo	this (one) is better
nèige piányi	that (one) is cheaper

Degrees of comparatives are conveyed by linking **(yi)diǎnr/xiē**, **de duō**, **duōle**, or **gèng** with the adjectival verb:

zhèige hǎo (yi)diǎnr/xiē	this (one) is (a bit) better
zhèige hǎo de duō	this (one) is much better
zhèige hǎo duōle	this (one) is far better
zhèige gèng hǎo	this (one) is even better

To express a comparison **bǐ** followed by the object of comparison is placed before the adjectival verb:

Shànghǎi bǐ Běijīng dà	Shanghai is bigger than Beijing
jīntian bǐ zuótian lěng	today is colder than yesterday
zhèige bǐ nèige hǎo duōle	this one is far better than that one

SUPERLATIVES (BIGGEST, BEST etc)

For the superlative, **zuì** is placed before the adjective or adjectival verb:

zuì piányi de fángjiān	the cheapest room
zhèige fángjiān zuì piányi	this room is cheapest

PRONOUNS
PERSONAL PRONOUNS

wǒ	I/me
nǐ	you (*singular*)
tā	he/him, she/her, it
wǒmen	we/us
nǐmen	you (*plural*)
tāmen	they/them

Nín is a polite alternative for **nǐ** 'you'.

Chinese does not have different forms for subject and object:

wǒ kànjian tā le	I saw him/her
tā kànjian wǒ le	he/she saw me

Tā is used rarely as 'it'. Occasionally it occurs in the object position, but almost never as a subject:

bié dòng tā	don't touch it

Most of the time, context makes any reference to 'it' unnecessary:

huàr hén měi – wó hén xǐhuān	the painting is beautiful – I like it
wó xǐhuān nèizhang huàr – hén měi	I like the/that painting – it's beautiful

Similarly **tāmen** rarely occurs as 'they' or 'them' when referring to things.

DEMONSTRATIVE PRONOUNS

zhè	this
nà	that

For example:

zhè shɪ wǒde	this is mine
nà hén hǎo	that's good

The demonstrative pronouns are never found in the object position. For 'this' or 'that' as object the demonstrative adjective and measure, **zhèige** or **nèige**, is used:

wǒ yào zhèige/nèige	I want this/that (one)

POSSESSIVE ADJECTIVES AND POSSESSIVE PRONOUNS

To form possessive adjectives and pronouns, simply add **-de** to the personal pronouns:

wǒde	my/mine
nǐde	your/yours (*singular*)
tāde	his, her/hers, its/its
wǒmende	our/ours
nǐmende	your/yours (*plural*)
tāmende	their/theirs

For example:

wǒde shū	my book
zhè shɪ wǒde	this is mine

Nínde is a polite alternative for **nǐde**.

De is, in fact, used generally to express possession, comparable to 'of' or '-'s' in English. All **de** phrases **precede** the noun:

Běijīng de rénkǒu	the population of Beijing
jīntian de tiānqi	today's weather
wǒ érzɪ de péngyou	my son's friend

In the case of personal relationships or close identity the **de** may be omitted, with the personal pronoun acting as possessive adjective:

wǒ érzɪ	my son
tā jiā	his/her home
wǒ guó	my country

The possessive adjective can be omitted if possession is made clear by the context:

wǒ chīle zǎofàn le	I've had (my) breakfast
wǒ míngtian bǎ yúsǎn huán gei nǐ	I'll give you back (your) umbrella tomorrow

DEPENDENT CLAUSES AND 'DE'

Dependent clauses are placed **before** the noun they modify and **de** is inserted between the clause and the noun:

wó mǎi de piaò	the ticket(s) **(which/that) I bought**
zuótian lái de nèige rén	the person **who came yesterday**
tāmen zhù de dìfang	the place **where they live**

DEMONSTRATIVE ADJECTIVES AND MEASURES

The demonstrative pronouns **zhè** 'this' and **na** 'that', usually in the alternative forms of **zhèi** and **nèi**, can themselves function as demonstrative adjectives. This occurs when the tone of what is said is somewhat emphatic or vehement:

zhèi fàndiàn hěn guì	this hotel is very expensive
nèi rén bú kèqi	that person is not polite

However, the demonstrative adjective is normally formed with the demonstrative **nèi** or **zhèi** together with a **measure** or **classifier**. Measures are a distinctive feature of the Chinese language and are used with demonstratives and numerals. They are placed between the demonstrative (or numeral – see page 102) and the noun. There are many measures in Chinese, some of which are similar to the ordinary measures of weight, length, capacity etc, e.g. **gōngjīn** 'kilogram', **mǐ** (or **gōngchǐ**) 'metre', **bēi** 'cup' etc:

yìgōngjīn píngguo	a kilo of apples
sānmǐ chóuzı	three metres of silk
zhèibēi chá	this cup of tea

By far the most common measure is **gè**, which can be used with a large number of nouns:

zhèige háizı	this child
nèige diànyǐng	that film

Other measures are associated with specific nouns or groups of nouns, e.g.:

běn	with books, magazines etc
jiàn	with things, affairs etc
liàng	with vehicles
kē	with trees, flowers
suǒ	with houses
wèi	in polite language with gentlemen, ladies, guests etc

For example:

zhèibĕn záizhì	this magazine
nèijiàn dōngxi	that thing
zhèiliàng qìchē	this car
nèikē shù	that tree
zhèisuǒ fángzı	this house
nèiwei xiānsheng	that gentleman

If in doubt about which measure to use, you can always use **gè**.

If the context is clear, as is the case with 'this one' or 'that one' in English, then the noun may be omitted:

wǒ yào nèige	I want that (one)
zhèibĕn hén yǒu yìsı	this (one – *implying a book, magazine etc*) is interesting
zhèiwei shı ...	this is ... (*in polite introductions*)

NUMBERS (see also page 120)

CARDINAL NUMBERS

1–10

yī	one
èr (or **liǎng**)	two
sān	three
sì	four
wǔ	five
liù	six
qī	seven
bā	eight
jiǔ	nine
shí	ten

Yī in counting is first tone (**yī, èr, sān**). Otherwise it is fourth tone (**yìběn shū** 'a book', **yìbēi chá** 'a cup of tea') unless followed by a fourth tone, when it changes to second tone (**yíliàng qìchē**).

11–19 consist of **shí** 'ten' followed by the numbers **yī** 'one' to **jiǔ** 'nine':

shíyī	eleven
shí'èr	twelve
shísān etc	thirteen etc

20, 30 etc to **90** are formed by placing **èr** 'two' to **jiǔ** 'nine' before **shí** 'ten':

èrshí	twenty
sānshí	thirty
sìshí etc	forty etc

For the other numbers from **21–99**, **yī** 'one' to **jiǔ** 'nine' are added to the multiples **shí** 'ten' – **èrshí, sānshí** etc:

èrshíyī	twenty-one
sānshíwǔ	thirty-five
jiǔshíjiǔ	ninety-nine

The sequence then continues in the same pattern with **bǎi** 'hundred', **qiān** 'thousand' and **wàn** 'ten thousand':

sānbǎi	three hundred
sānbǎi wǔshí	three hundred and fifty
sānbǎi wǔshí liù	three hundred and fifty-six
wǔqiān sānbǎi	five thousand three hundred
liùwàn wǔqiān sānbǎi	sixty-five thousand three hundred

After **wàn** the sequence restarts with **shí, bǎi, qiān** and **wàn** being placed in succession before **wàn**:

shíwàn	hundred thousand
bǎiwàn	million
qiānwàn	ten million
wànwàn	hundred million

For 'hundred million' **yì** can also be used (this is different from **yì** meaning 'one'!).

Líng 'nought' or 'zero' is used when there are noughts in the middle of a number sequence.

yìbǎi líng wǔ	a hundred and five
yìqiān líng wǔ	a thousand and five
yìqiān líng wǔshí	a thousand and fifty

NUMBERS AND MEASURES (see also Demonstrative Adjectives page 99)

As with demonstrative adjectives, numerals are normally used with **measures** when they are linked with nouns:

sānběn shū	three books
èrshíjiàn dōngxi	twenty things
yìbǎi wǔshíge rén	a hundred and fifty people

Èr and **liǎng** both mean 'two'.

Èr is used for 'two' in counting or in telephone, room, bus numbers etc:

yī, èr, sān ...	one, two, three ...
èr hào	no. two (room, house etc)
èr lù chē	no. two bus
sān – èr – liù – liù – yāo – sì	326614 (telephone number)

(Notice that in number sequences **yāo** is used for 'one' instead of **yī**.)
Èr, of course, also occurs in compound numbers **shí'èr** 'twelve', **èrshíge rén** 'twenty people' etc.

Liǎng is normally used with measures:

liǎngge rén	two people
liǎngjiàn shì	two matters

DEMONSTRATIVES AND NUMBERS
When a demonstrative and a number occur together the order is demonstrative –
number – measures – (noun).

nèi liángběn cídiǎn	those two dictionaries
zhèi sānwei kèren	these three guests
nèi sìge	those four

ORDINAL NUMBERS
Ordinal numbers are formed by adding the prefix **dì** to the number:

dìyī	(the) first
dìsān	(the) third
dìliùshíqī	(the) sixty-seventh
dìyìbǎi	(the) hundredth

Where ordinal numbers are linked with a noun a measure must be used:

dìsìge rén	the fourth person
dì'èrliàng qìchē	the second car
dìwǔshíběn	the fiftieth (book, volume)

VERBS

Chinese verbs do **not** change to take account of first, second, or third person subjects, singular or plural:

wǒ qù	I go *or* am going
tā qù	he/she goes *or* is going
tāmen qù	they go *or* are going

Chinese verbs have **no tenses**:

wǒ míngtian qù	I **will go** tomorrow
wǒ zuótian qù de shíhou, tā bú zài jiā	when I **went** yesterday, he was not at home

In these two examples the future and the past are established by the time words **míngtian** 'tomorrow' and **zuótian** 'yesterday'. The form of the verb remains the same: qù.

A number of verb suffixes and sentence particles influence the meaning of verbs. (See Verb Suffixes page 106 and Sentence Particles pages 107).

A verb standing alone without any suffixes or associated sentence particles tends to imply either something done by habit:

Zhōngguoren yòng kuàizi   Chinese people use chopsticks

or that the action is about to take place:

ní mǎi shénme?   what are you going to buy?

TO BE

The verb 'to be', when followed by a noun, is **shì**:

wǒ shì tāde tóngshì	I am his/her colleague
zhè shì shénme?	what is this?
tāmen bú shì Zhōngguoren	they aren't Chinese (people)

Remember that **shì** does not normally occur with adjectival verbs (see page 95).

If you want to say that something is in or at a particular place then you use **zài** (see page 109).

Remember also that **shì**, when it is used, corresponds to all the English forms of 'to be' – the one word is used for 'am, are, is, was, were' etc.

NEGATIVES

The usual negative is **bù** (or **bú** if it precedes a word in the fourth tone):

wǒ bù mǎi zhèige	I'm not going to buy this one
tā bú qù	he's not going
nà wǒ bù zhīdào	I didn't know that

Bù is also used with adjectives/adjectival verbs:

bù hǎo de tiānqi	bad (not good) weather
tiānqi bù hǎo	the weather isn't good

The verb **yǒu** 'to have' differs from other verbs in that its negative is **méi** not **bù**:

tā yǒu shíjiān	he/she has time
wǒ méi yǒu shíjiān	I don't have time

Méi by itself can be used to mean 'have not':

wǒ méi shíjiān	I don't have time

Yǒu also means 'there is/are':

jīntian wǎnshang yǒu diànyǐng	there's a film tonight
fángjianli méi yǒu rén	there's no-one in the room
méi yǒu bànfa	there is no way, there is nothing to be done
yǒu rén	there is someone there; (*on a toilet door*) occupied

VERB SUFFIXES

i) **Le** indicates that the action of the verb has been completed:

wó mǎile liángběn shū	I bought two books
tā yǐjing zǒule	he/she has already gone
wǒ hēwánle chá jiù qu kàn tā	I'll go and see him when I finish (my) tea

The last example above is evidence that the completed action is not necessarily in the past.

The negative of completed action **le** is formed by placing **méi** or **méi yǒu** before the verb **without le**:

wǒ méi (yǒu) kànjian tāmen	I didn't see them
tā méi (yǒu) zǒu	he hasn't gone

ii) **Zhe** as a verb suffix indicates that the action is continuing or has some duration:

tā názhe yiběn shū	he/she is holding a book
tā dàizhe hēi màozɪ	he/she is wearing a black hat

Zhe is often used to convey the idea of doing one thing while doing another:

tā xiàozhe duì wǒ shuō ...	he said to me smiling ...
wǒmen zǒuzhe tán ba	let's chat as we walk

For the negative, **méi** is placed before the verb with **zhe**:

tā méi dàizhe màozɪ	he/she isn't wearing a hat

(Remember that **zhe** has no connection with tense. In all these cases if the context had been in the past the translations would have been 'he/she wasn't holding a book', 'he/she wasn't wearing a hat' etc)

An alternative construction which expresses continuous action is the placing of **zài** before the verb:

tā zai kàn shū	he is reading
nǐ zai zuò shénme?	what are you doing?

iii) **Guò** conveys the idea that something has been experienced or happened (once) in the past:

wǒ qùguo Shànghǎi	I have been to Shanghai
wǒ kànguo nèige diànyǐng	I have seen that film

For the negative, **méi** is placed before the verb with **guò**:

wǒ méi qùguo Rìběn	I have never been to Japan
tā méi chīguo Zhōngguo fàn	he/she's never eaten Chinese food

SENTENCE PARTICLES

i) **Le** at the end of a sentence has in general two functions:

1) It indicates that something happened in the past which has some relevance, however slight, to the present situation:

tāmen mǎi dōngxi qù le	they've gone shopping
wǒ zuótian kànjian tā le	I saw him yesterday
wǒmen zai nàr zhùle wǔnián le	we have been living there for five years

Contrast this last example with the following, which includes the verb suffix **le** only:

wǒmen zai nàr zhùle wǔnián	we lived there for five years

2) It implies a change of circumstances:

xiàyǔ le	it's raining (now)
tā xiànzai hǎo le	he/she is better now
tāmen bù lái le	they aren't coming any more

The new circumstances can be in the future:

wǒmen zǒu le	we are off (going now)
huǒchē kuài kāi le	the train will be leaving soon

ii) **Ne** adds emphasis to what is said, drawing attention to something or contradicting something:

tāmen hái méi lái ne	they still haven't come
zuò fēijī kě guì ne	(but) it's too expensive to go by plane

Similarly **ne** can add emphasis to a question:

zěnme bàn ne?	what's to be done then?
nǐ hē shénme ne?	well what are you going to have to drink?

Ne can itself convey the idea 'and what about ...?':

wǒ hén hǎo – nǐ ne?	I'm fine – what about you?
zhèige tài zhòng – nèige ne?	this one's too heavy – what about that one?

iii) **Ma** at the end of a sentence makes it into a question:

tāmen shı Zhōngguoren ma?	are they Chinese (people)?
nǐ lèi ma?	are you tired?
nǐ bù mǎi zhèige ma?	aren't you buying this one?
tā qùguo Yīngguó ma?	has he/she been to England?
ní yǒu háizı ma?	do you have (any) children?

iv) **Ba** indicates a suggestion. The suggestion can be an exhortation or a piece of advice:

zǒu ba!	let's go!
wǒmen míngtian zài tán ba	let's talk about it again tomorrow
duō chī yidiǎnr ba	have a bit more to eat
ní kǎolù yíxià ba	think about it

It can also imply 'I suggest' or 'I suppose':

tāmen shı Rìbenren ba?	they are Japanese, aren't they?
ní hěn máng ba?	you are very busy, aren't you?

LOCATION AND PLACE WORD SUFFIXES

Zài functions either as a verb meaning 'to be in/at' a place or as the preposition 'in', 'at':

tāmen zai nǎr?	where are they?
tāmen zai Běijīng	they are in Beijing
shū zai lǐbiānr	the book is inside
tā zai dàxué xuéxi Yīngwén	he/she is studying English at the University
wǒ zai zhèr méi yǒu péngyou	I don't have any friends here

The main place word suffixes are **lǐ** 'inside', **wài** 'outside', **shàng** 'above', **xià** 'below' and **zhōng** 'in the middle', 'between'. These suffixes are added to nouns to indicate location:

yàoshī bú zai kǒudàili ma?	isn't (your) key in (your) pocket?
chéngwài yóu tǐyùchǎng	there's a stadium outside the town
nǐde hùzhào zai zhuōzishang	your passport is on the table

ADVERBS

Adverbs which describe the manner of an action are placed with **de** before the verb. These adverbs usually have the same form as adjectives. Some of them can be reduplicated:

qíng *zìxì* de kàn yíxià   please read it **carefully**
wǒmen *mànmānr* de zǒuhuíqù ba   let's walk back **slowly**
tāmen *gāogāoxìngxìng* de tánzhe   they were chatting **happily**

Adverbs which indicate the degree or result of an action come after the verb and the linking word **de**:

tāmen qǐde *hén hǎo*   they got up **early**
wǒ shuìde *hén hǎo*   I slept **well**
tā Hànyǔ shuōde *fēicháng liúlì*   he/she speaks Chinese
                                          extremely fluently

QUESTIONS

One way of forming questions in Chinese is to add the particle **ma** to the end of a sentence (see also page 107):

tā huì shuō Hànyǔ	he can speak Chinese
nǐ huì shuō Hànyǔ ma?	can you speak Chinese?

Another way of asking a question is to repeat the verb with the negative **bù** or **méi** (**yǒu**) as appropriate:

tāmen shì bu shì Zhōngguoren?	are they Chinese (people)?
nǐ lèi bu lei?	are you tired?
ní mǎi bu mai zhèige?	are you buying this one?
tā qùguo Yīngguó méi yǒu?	has he/she been to England?
ní yǒu mei you háizı?	do you have (any) children?

The main interrogative pronouns are **shéi** 'who?' and **shénme** 'what?'. Sentence word order in an interrogative sentence is not changed and the interrogative pronoun occupies a position in the sentence where the noun it is intended to identify would come:

tā shı shéi?	who is he?
(tā shı wǒ gēge)	(he's my elder brother)
shéi jiāo ni Zhōngwén?	who is teaching you Chinese?
(tā jiāo wo Zhōngwén)	(he is teaching me Chinese)
ní mǎi shénme?	what are you going to buy?
(wó mǎi yiben shū)	(I'm going to buy a book)

Other interrogatives are:

nǎr/nǎli	where?
duōshao	how many?, how much?
nèi with measure	which? (compare **zhèi** and **nèi** with measure page 102)
shéide	whose?
zěnme	how?
wèishenme	why?

For example:

fàndiàn zai nǎr?	whère is the hotel?
yǒu duōshao rén?	how many people are there?
něige fángjiān zuì piányi?	which room is cheapest?
ní mái něige?	which (one) are you buying?
zhè shı shéide?	whose is this?
ní zěnme zhīdao ...?	how do you know ...?
tāmen wèishenme bú qù?	why aren't they going?

Háishı '... or ...?' is used in questions posing alternatives:

ní xǐhuān zhèige háishı nèige?	do you like this one or that one?
tāmen jīntian zǒu háishı míngtian zǒu?	are they going today or tomorrow?

PREPOSITIONS

Chinese prepositions, which are also referred to as 'co-verbs' since they can often stand independently as verbs (see **zài** page 109), normally come before the verb. Apart from **zài**, the most common are:

dào	to
cóng	from
duì	towards, with regard to
lí	from/to (in expressions of distance)
yòng	with, by means of,
zuò	by (referring to forms of transport)
gěi	for
gēn	with

For example:

wǒ míngtian dào Běijīng qừ	I'm going to Beijing tomorrow
nǐmen jīntian cóng nǎr lái?	where have you come from today?
cóng sāndiǎn dào sìdiǎn	from three o'clock to four o'clock
tā duì lìshǐ hén gǎn xìngqừ	he/she is interested in history
Běijīng lí Shànghǎi hén yuǎn	Beijing is a long way from Shanghai
Zhōngguoren yòng kuàzɪ chīfàn	Chinese people eat with chopsticks
wǒmen zuò gōnggòng qìchē qừ ba	let's go by bus
wǒ géi nǐ zuò	I'll do (it) for you
qǐng gēn wǒ lái	please come with me

Some prepositions e.g. **zài, dào** and **gěi** can be placed after certain verbs of directed movement or position:

qǐng fàng zai zhèr	please put (it) here
zhèifēng xìn wǒ yào jì dao Yīngguó qừ	I want to send this letter to England

YES AND NO

There are no standard words for 'yes' and 'no' although **shì(de)** 'yes (it is the case)', **duìle** 'yes (that's right)' and **bú shì** 'no (it is not the case)' are quite common.

Chinese speakers are more likely to repeat the verb of the question with or without **bù** (or **méi**) as appropriate:

ní yǒu gōngfu ma?	do you have time?
yǒu (méi yǒu)	yes (no)
tā shì Zhōngguoren ma?	is he Chinese?
shì (bú shì)	yes (no)
nǐ qùguo Yīngguó méi yǒu?	have you been to England?
qùguo (méi yǒu *or* **méi qùguo)**	yes (no)

IMPERATIVES

For an imperative in Chinese you simply pronounce the verb in an emphatic way usually without any subject:

zhànzhù!	halt! (stop!, stand still!)
gǔnchūqù!	get out!

Imperatives in Chinese are quite rare because of their curt tone and the verb is more likely to be preceded by **qǐng** 'please' or followed by **ba** (see page 108):

qǐng lái ba	come along

A negative imperative is expressed by **bié** (or **bú yào**) 'don't':

bié wàngle	don't forget
bú yào dòng	don't move

TELLING THE TIME

In telling the time **diǎn** is used for the hours, **bàn** for the half hour, **yíkè** and **sānkè** for quarter past and quarter to, and **fēn** for minutes. **Zhōng**, meaning 'clock', may come at the end of most time expressions:

liángdiǎn (zhōng)	two o'clock
shídiǎn bàn	half past ten
sāndiǎn yíkè	a quarter past three
sāndiǎn sānkè	a quarter to four
liùdiǎn shífēn	ten (minutes) past six, six ten
liùdiǎn sìshífēn	six forty

Chà can be used for minutes to the hour:

chà shífen qīdiǎn	ten minutes to seven
chà èrshífēn jiúdiǎn	twenty minutes to nine

A.m. and p.m. are split up into **zǎoshang** (early morning up to about 9 o'clock), **shàngwǔ** (the rest of the morning up to noon), **xiàwǔ** (afternoon), **wanshang** (evening) and **yèli** (in the night):

zǎoshang qīdiǎn	seven a.m.
xiàwǔ sìdiǎn	four p.m.

CONVERSION TABLES

1. LENGTH

centimetres, centimeters
1 cm = 0.39 inches

metres, meters
1 m = 100 cm = 1000 mm
1 m = 39.37 inches = 1.09 yards

kilometres, kilometers
1 km = 1000 m
1 km = 0.62 miles = 5/8 mile

km	1	2	3	4	5	10	20	30	40	50	100
miles	0.6	1.2	1.9	2.5	3.1	6.2	12.4	18.6	24.9	31.1	62.1

inches
1 inch = 2.54 cm

feet
1 foot = 30.48 cm

yards
1 yard = 0.91 m

miles
1 mile = 1.61 km = 8/5 km

miles	1	2	3	4	5	10	20	30	40	50	100
km	1.6	3.2	4.8	6.4	8.0	16.1	32.2	48.3	64.4	80.5	161

2. WEIGHT

gram(me)s
1 g = 0.035 oz

g	100	250	500	
oz	3.5	8.75	17.5	= 1.1 lb

kilos
1 kg = 1000 g
1 kg = 2.20 lb = 11/5 lb

kg	0.5	1	1.5	2	3	4	5	6	7	8	9	10
lb	1.1	2.2	3.3	4.4	6.6	8.8	11.0	13.2	15.4	17.6	19.8	22

kg	20	30	40	50	60	70	80	90	100
lb	44	66	88	110	132	154	176	198	220

tons
1 UK ton = 1018 kg
1 US ton = 909 kg

tonnes
1 tonne = 1000 kg
1 tonne = 0.98 UK tons = 1.10 US tons

ounces
1 oz = 28.35 g

pounds
1 pound = 0.45 kg = 5/11 kg

lb	1	1.5	2	3	4	5	6	7	8	9	10	20
kg	0.5	0.7	0.9	1.4	1.8	2.3	2.7	3.2	3.6	4.1	4.5	9.1

stones
1 stone = 6.35 kg

stones	1	2	3	7	8	9	10	11	12	13	14	15
kg	6.3	12.7	19	44	51	57	63	70	76	83	89	95

hundredweights
1 UK hundredweight = 50.8 kg
1 US hundredweight = 45.36 kg

3. CAPACITY

litres, liters
1 l = 1.76 UK pints = 2.13 US pints
$\frac{1}{2}$ l = 500 cl
$\frac{1}{4}$ l = 250 cl

pints
1 UK pint = 0.57 l
1 US pint = 0.47 l

quarts
1 UK quart = 1.14 l
1 US quart = 0.95 l

gallons
1 UK gallon = 4.55 l
1 US gallon = 3.79 l

4. TEMPERATURE

centigrade/Celsius
$C = (F - 32) \times 5/9$

C	−5	0	5	10	15	18	20	25	30	37	38
F	23	32	41	50	59	64	68	77	86	98.4	100.4

Fahrenheit
$F = (C \times 9/5) + 32$

F	23	32	40	50	60	65	70	80	85	98.4	101
C	−5	0	4	10	16	20	21	27	30	37	38.3

NUMBERS

零 *[líng]* 0
一 *[yī]* 1
二 *[èr or liǎng]* 2
三 *[sān]* 3
四 *[sì]* 4
五 *[wǔ]* 5
六 *[liù]* 6
七 *[qī]* 7
八 *[bā]* 8
九 *[jiǔ]* 9
十 *[shí]* 10
十一 *[shíyī]* 11
十二 *[shí'ér]* 12
十三 *[shísān]* 13 etc
二十 *[èrshì]* 20
三十 *[sānshí]* 30
四十 *[sìshí]* 40 etc
二十一 *[èrshíyī]* 21
三十五 *[sānshíwǔ]* 35
九十九 *[jiǔshíjiǔ]* 99
百 *[bǎi]* 100
一百零五 *[yìbǎi líng wǔ]* 105
三百 *[sānbǎi]* 300
三百五十 *[sānbǎi wǔshí]* 350
三百五十六 *[sānbǎi wǔshí liù]* 356
千 *[qiān]* 1,000
一千零五 *[yìqiān líng wǔ]* 1,005
一千零五十 *[yìqiān líng wǔshí]* 1,050
五千三百 *[wǔqiān sānbǎi]* 5,300
万 *[wàn]* 10,000
六万五千三百 *[liùwàn wǔqiān sānbǎi]* 65,300
十万 *[shíwàn]* 100,000
百万 *[bǎiwàn]* 1,000,000
千万 *[qiānwàn]* 10,000,000
万万 *[wànwàn]* 100,000,000
亿 *[yì]* 100,000,000

The following alternative complex characters are used on bills, accounts etc to avoid confusion or possible illicit changes:

零 *[líng]* 0
壹 *[yī]* 1
貳 *[èr]* 2
叁 *[sān]* 3
肆 *[sì]* 4
伍 *[wǔ]* 5
陆 *[liù]* 6
柒 *[qī]* 7
捌 *[bā]* 8
玖 *[jiǔ]* 9
拾 *[shí]* 10
佰 *[bǎi]* 100
仟 *[qiān]* 1,000